Developing Preschool Language Programs

A Resource Guide for the Speech-Language Pathologist

Paul E. Quin, M.S., CCC-SLP, Program Coordinator
Judith L. Bergman, M.A., CCC-SLP, Speech-Language Pathologist
Mary Ann Gianni, B.S.E., Early Childhood Educator
Barbara Zellan, M.S.W., A.C.S.W., Clinical Social Worker

Communication Skill Builders®
a division of
The Psychological Corporation
3830 E. Bellevue / P.O. Box 42050
Tucson, Arizona 85733
1-800-866-4446

Dedication

This publication is dedicated to the memory of William D. Mullins, co-founder of Children's Language Institute. Through his work as a parent of a child who was language impaired, an educator, an officer of CLI's Board of Directors, and a legislator in the Commonwealth of Massachusetts, Bill always sought the highest quality of education for all students. His support of the staff and this project will be remembered by his frequent reminder that "No one said it was going to be easy."

Reproducing Pages from This Book

Many of the pages in this book can be reproduced for instructional or administrative use (not for resale). To protect your book, make a photocopy of each reproducible page. Then use that copy as a master for photocopying or other types of reproduction.

© 1990 by

Communication Skill Builders®
a division of
The Psychological Corporation

3830 E. Bellevue / P.O. Box 42050
Tucson, Arizona 85733
1-800-866-4446

All rights reserved. Permission is granted for the user to photocopy and to make duplicating masters of those pages so indicated in any form for instructional or administrative use only. No other parts of this book may be reproduced or transmitted in any form or by any means, electronic or mechanical, including photocopying and recording, or by any information storage and retrieval system, without written permission from the Publisher.

ISBN 0-88450-338-0   Catalog No. 7613

10 9 8 7 6 5 4
Printed in the United States of America

For information about our audio and/or video products, write us at: Communication Skill Builders, a division of The Psychological Corporation, P.O. Box 42050, Tucson, AZ 85733.

Contents

Acknowledgments vi

Preface vii

Part I

Introduction
Paul E. Quin

    Meeting the Needs of the Mildly Language-Impaired
        Preschool Child 1

    The Need for Early Intervention 2

    Models of Intervention in Speech and Language 2

    Use of the Classroom Model 3

    Purpose of this Manual 3

    References 4

Literature Review:
A Pragmatic Approach to the Classroom
Judith L. Bergman

    Rationale 5
        Pragmatic-based language intervention 5
        Classrooms: The ideal context 6

    Promoting Language in the Classroom 7
        Language training as children act on the environment 7
        Language training within the curriculum 9
        The timing of language intervention 11
        Intervention strategies 11

    Conclusion 13

    Appendix A: Pragmatic Skills: Basic Definitions 14

    Appendix B: A Pragmatic Skill Taxonomy for
        Assessment and Intervention 16

    Appendix C: Research Overview: Normal Development
        of Pragmatic Skills 17

    References 22

    Additional Readings: Annotated Early Childhood Bibliography 27

Preparing the Classroom: Use of Space, Furniture, and Learning Materials
Mary Ann Gianni

- Creating the Optimal Physical Environment ... 31
  - Modifying the environment ... 32
  - Storage space for children's personal items ... 32
  - Room layout ... 33
- Specific Interest Areas ... 35
  - Block area ... 35
  - Home area ... 35
  - Art area ... 36
  - Music area ... 36
  - Sand-and-water area ... 37
  - Circle area ... 37
  - Concept and manipulation areas ... 37
- Conclusion ... 39
- Appendix: Checklist for Arranging and Equipping a Classroom ... 41
- References ... 44

Staffing and Training in the Preschool Language Classroom
Paul E. Quin, Judith L. Bergman, Barbara Zellan

- Staffing Recommendations ... 45
  - Speech-language pathologist ... 45
  - Early childhood educator ... 46
  - Classroom aides ... 46
  - Parents ... 46
  - Ancillary staff ... 46
  - Peer models ... 46
- Training Classroom Adults to Facilitate Language ... 47
  - Role releasing ... 47
  - Staff training ... 48
- Involving Parents in the Treatment Process and in Classroom Dynamics ... 55
  - Important attitudes in working with parents ... 56
  - Degree of parental involvement ... 57
  - School-home communication ... 57
  - Home visits ... 58
  - Parent training ... 61
- Appendix A: Samples of School Newsletters and Communications ... 65
- Appendix B: Sample Forms for Training and Home Visits ... 67-77
- References ... 78

Planning and Scheduling Language Intervention
Judith L. Bergman

    Scheduling to Guide Energy Flow 80

    Components of the Daily Schedule 82

    Planning for Language Intervention 85

    Conclusion 88

    References 89

Classroom Management: Guidelines for Understanding and Managing Behavior
Mary Ann Gianni

    Facilitating Young Children's Total Growth in a Preschool Setting 90

    Techniques for Guiding Young Children 92

    Creating a Healthy and Positive Social/Emotional Environment 94

    Respecting the Value of Play 96

        Establishing rules and guidelines 96

        Play areas 97

        Free play 97

    Appendix: Social and Emotional Development of the
       Preschool Child *(Barbara Zellan)* 98

    References 102

Data Collection
Judith L. Bergman

    Classroom Contexts for Data Collection 103

    Additional Testing 104

    Appendix: Forms 105-122

    References 123

Part II

Sample Lesson Plans
Mary Ann Gianni, Judith L. Bergman, Paul E. Quin

    Structured Language Therapy 127

    Arts and Crafts 147

    Circle Time 186

    Cooking 201

    Music 218

    Science 228

    Story Time 244

    Theme Areas 263

    Theme Days and Weeks 275

Acknowledgments

Funding for this three-year demonstration project has been provided by the United States Department of Education, Handicapped Children's Early Education Program, grant number G008401387. The staff, as well as the children and families served by this project, appreciate the financial support and philosophical commitment to providing services to children "at risk" for future language/learning problems.

The time, knowledge, and guidance of the Advisory Committee of this grant have been invaluable to the completion of the grant activities. The following committee members are to be commended for their donation of time and talents, as well as the direction they provided to this project:

- Albert Bail, Special Education Director, Ludlow Public Schools, Ludlow, Massachusetts

- Dr. Arthur Bertrand, Grant Specialist, Professor of Psychology, American International College, Springfield, Massachusetts

- Diana Gagnon, Parent

- Dr. Patricia Mercaitis, Clinic Coordinator, Communication Disorders Program, University of Massachusetts, Amherst, Massachusetts

- Linda Pollak, School Psychologist, Longmeadow, Massachusetts

- Dr. Linda Rosen, Speech-Language Pathologist, Palo Alto Veterans' Administration Hospital, Palo Alto, California

- Janis Santos, Executive Director, Holyoke/Chicopee Head Start, Holyoke, Massachusetts

- Joy Staples, Early Childhood Specialist, Greater Springfield Regional Education Center, Massachusetts Department of Education, West Springfield, Massachusetts

- Betsy Talbot, Parent

The format and design of this publication were conceptualized by Judith Bergman. Her ideas and outlines have provided a guide for the organization of this book.

The staff, administration, and Board of Directors of the Children's Language Institute have provided knowledge for the development of this project, as well as support for the continued activities required to meet the goals of the project. Their expertise in the areas of language remediation—specifically in a classroom setting—and grant management have greatly augmented the product provided herein, as well as the service delivery to the "at risk" children and their families.

Paul E. Quin, Program Coordinator

Preface

In 1984, the Children's Language Institute was awarded a three-year demonstration grant to service mildly language-impaired preschool children. The major goals of this Handicapped Children's Early Education Program grant were:

1. to identify a population of children whose language deficit can be described as mild or mild-to-moderately impaired as measured by a speech-language pathologist using standardized tests;

2. to standardize and norm the developed screening instrument;

3. to plan and implement a remedial program for such children;

4. to provide consultation to public school personnel and follow-up services for this population as they are mainstreamed into public schools; and

5. to develop and disseminate a model program that can easily be replicated in a public setting to substantiate the need and cost effectiveness of early intervention for language impaired children.

The *Children's Language Institute Preschool Placement Test* (published elsewhere) was developed and standardized to identify children appropriate for the classroom-home program described herein.

The information presented in this text is designed to assist a speech-language pathologist, an early childhood educator, and a social worker to replicate a successful classroom-home language intervention program for mildly to mild-to-moderately language-impaired preschool children. Elements of the program may be applicable to a variety of disorders or different degrees of severity, but this staff's success and results are based on the specified target population.

The first portion of the manual discusses the rationale and operation of the program. The sample lesson plans in the second part provide specific examples of the integration of language remediation targets into preschool activities.

Throughout the text, the terms "at risk" and "high risk" are used interchangeably to describe the target population for this program. These children are not medically "at risk" in the usual sense of the term, but have a high probability for developing more severe language/learning problems in the elementary school years.

It is hoped that the publication of this information will expand interest in and services to this previously underserved population.

Paul E. Quin, Program Coordinator

Part I

Introduction

Paul E. Quin, M.S., CCC/SLP

Meeting the Needs of the Mildly Language-Impaired Preschool Child

When children who have demonstrated language/learning difficulties at the preschool level enter elementary school, they often encounter difficulties. Each year, many of these children, described as immature or making slow progress, complete kindergarten or first grade. By second grade, it becomes obvious that these same children are in need of intensive support and/or remedial services in order to progress. They *must* master language concepts for academic success. Without a firm language foundation, they often fail in many areas, and the feelings of failure and frustration can lead to emotional difficulties or poor self-esteem.

Children who are recognized and classified as having moderate to severe speech-language deficits generally begin therapy before entering regular public schools. The child with mild or mild-to-moderate deficits, however, is often undiagnosed and therefore untreated. These children frequently are not identified and do not receive services until they experience failure in the elementary grades.

Parents, teachers, and other professionals often refer to these mildly language-impaired children as immature, inattentive, or distractible. Many of these children have difficulties with the following areas:

Auditory memory. Given a two- or three-step command, the child may complete only one part because of not remembering all of what was said.

Word finding. Given a question requiring a one- or two-word response, the child cannot respond appropriately, despite knowing the answer.

Word association. Given a question requiring the response "table," the child may say "chair."

Vocabulary. A language-impaired child may have problems not only acquiring basic specific vocabulary, but may also experience difficulty with multiple-meaning words; this affects prereading and premath skill development.

Language concepts. The language-disordered child often has difficulty learning basic concepts (such as size, shape, and quantity in comparative relationships) needed for premath development.

Abstractions. The child may have difficulty learning about concepts that are not concrete or tangible. This will affect future reading and/or listening skills by hindering the child's ability to abstract the meaning of written and/or verbal material. This also can have an impact on the child's ability to do math computations when tangible objects are removed and mental computations are required.

Sequencing abilities. Many language-impaired students cannot properly order a sequence of events. This leads to confusion in communication style, and produces difficulties with reading and math story problems.

Grammatical, syntactical errors. Limited sentence types, restricted verb forms, and lack of qualifiers in expressive communication often lead to confusion or misinterpretation by the listener.

When children displaying these problems enter a public school classroom, teachers are frequently at a loss to understand why they are not learning, since their articulation and some spontaneous language may be excellent.

The Need for Early Intervention

During the past decade, many early intervention programs and therapeutic models have been established. Head Start centers and other early education programs have provided facilities which service many children from various backgrounds and economic levels, as well as children with identified handicaps. The programs generally provide good language stimulation and are excellent for children with language delays who have lacked the appropriate stimulation and exposure for normal language development. For the child with a *specific language impairment,* however, these programs are inadequate. These children are not language deficient due to lack of stimulation but have specific language deficits requiring structured and direct intervention.

Most research and clinical judgment in the field of speech-language pathology agree that early intervention is beneficial. Programs providing early educational and therapeutic programming to meet the needs of young children and their families are reducing the number of children who need intensive or long-term help (Jordan et al. 1977). When children have minimal problems, early remediation may avoid or reduce the development of more severe problems (Mecham and Willbrand 1979). In a study of over 700 language-impaired youth, it was found that the younger the child began language treatment, the more rapid was the progress seen over a two- to three-year period (Schery 1985). It is extremely important that difficulties in language learning be detected in the preschools, since a foundation in language skills is a prerequisite for academic success and is a palliative factor in reducing the severity of problems in later years.

Models of Intervention in Speech and Language

Not only have schools and agencies changed to an emphasis on early intervention with children exhibiting communication disorders, but there has been a notable shift in the context and style in which treatment occurs. One model frequently utilized during the last 10 to 15 years for preschoolers has been individual or small-group therapy in a clinical setting. For school-age children, the itinerant or pull-out model has been the predominant treatment format. Many professionals recognize that this has not been the most efficient or beneficial format for the delivery of services. Consequently, a growing trend in speech-language pathology is to use the speech-language clinician as a consultant to the classroom teacher (Frassinelli et al. 1983; Fujiki and Brinton 1984), or to combine consulting with one-to-one intervention (ASHA 1986). Another model uses the speech-language specialist as the classroom teacher for children with language disorders.

Use of the Classroom Model

Utilizing the classroom model for preschool intervention leads to a greater chance of the student succeeding in the public school setting. The classroom affords the opportunity for social interaction during language remediation, as well as providing the foundation for success in later academic routines that may present problems to this population. Early compensations can be taught, as appropriate, in realistic settings. This remediation model, supported by numerous authors (Creaghead 1984; Gold 1985; Wilkinson 1982), fosters the social activities that have been shown to produce greater language gains in children (Schery 1985).

Purpose of this Manual

Despite this emergence of classroom language programming, the prospect of managing an entire class of language-disordered children is a double-edged sword for many speech-language pathologists. On the one hand, intervention on an all-day, everyday basis is an ideal opportunity to impact positively on a child's cognitive-linguistic-social system. At the same time, the specialist may approach this task with some uncertainty because the requirements of classroom intervention are not consistent with previous training or experience. Although some graduate programs include special preparation for intervention in naturalistic settings such as the classroom, there are still a number of graduate programs that do not offer academic or clinical experiences which adequately prepare the graduate to do language therapy in a classroom setting. Young professionals entering the field are not alone in their limited exposure to this model of language therapy. As school districts extend services to preschool children, many experienced speech-language clinicians will be asked to shift from an itinerant model of treating school-age children to that of managing preschoolers in self-contained classrooms. For these skilled individuals, there is sparse information available to help in making this transition.

There is a need, then, for resource materials which could be used by both the entering-level professional and the skilled specialist as they assume responsibilities for classroom-based language intervention. This manual supplies information that helps bridge the gap between one-to-one intervention and the classroom setting. The first section of the manual includes a literature review that outlines the theoretical basis and research support for moving therapy from the clinic cubicle to the classroom. Additional chapters include suggestions for the physical preparation of the classroom, staffing recommendations, guidelines for involving and training parents and other classroom adults in the intervention process, implementing language therapy in a preschool classroom, managing groups of preschool children at different levels of social and emotional development, and methods for data collection and record keeping in a classroom context. The second section of the manual provides sample lesson plans that demonstrate how language therapy can be incorporated into the different activities that make up the preschool day. For the most part, assessment and evaluation tools are not included in this manual; it is assumed that the speech-language pathologist has available the knowledge and tools necessary for assessing language-impaired children, selecting objectives, and choosing individual treatment strategies.

References

American Speech-Language-Hearing Association (ASHA). 1986. From preschool to high school: A class act. *Asha* 28(5):18-21.

Creaghead, N. A. 1984. Strategies for evaluating and targeting pragmatic behaviors in young children. *Seminars in Speech and Language* 5(3):241-251.

Frassinelli, L., K. Superior, and J. Myers. 1983. A consultation model for speech and language intervention. *Asha* 25(11):25-30.

Fujiki, M., and B. Brinton. 1984. Supplementing language therapy: Working with the classroom teacher. *Language, Speech and Hearing Services in Schools* 15:98-109.

Gold, J. P. 1985. Pragmatics—Teaching the social use of language in the classroom. *Churchill Forum* 7(4):2.

Johnston, J. R., and A. B. Heller. 1987. Effectiveness of a curriculum for preschool language intervention specialists. *Asha* 29:34-43.

Jordan, J., A. Hayden, M. Karnes, and P. Wood. 1977. *Early childhood education for exceptional children.* Reston, VA: Council for Exceptional Children.

Mecham, M. J., and M. L. Willbrand. 1979. *Language disorders in children: A resource book for speech/language pathologists.* Springfield, IL: Charles C. Thomas.

Schery, T. K. 1985. Correlates of language development in language-disordered children. *Journal of Speech and Hearing Disorders* 50:73-83.

Wilkinson, L., ed. 1982. *Communicating in the classroom.* New York, NY: Academic Press.

Literature Review: A Pragmatic Approach to the Classroom

Judith L. Bergman, M.S., CCC/SLP

Pragmatics refers to a component of language competence as well as to a style of intervention. The pragmatic intervention model for preschool children ideally is group- or classroom-based. In this chapter, the rationale for classroom group language intervention is reviewed, along with the research that supports specific language intervention strategies to use in the classroom.

Appendices to this chapter discuss pragmatics as a skill area and include definitions for basic pragmatic skills, a classification system that may assist in planning assessment and intervention in this area, and a research overview of normal development of pragmatic skills. Additionally, an annotated bibliography is included with the list of references, covering a broad range of books and journals dealing with early childhood education, social and emotional development, and activities for preschoolers.

Rationale

Three premises shape the rationale for implementing language therapy in the classroom: (1) pragmatic principles should be the foundation for all language training; (2) classrooms are ideal situations for implementing pragmatic-based approaches; and (3) classrooms offer ideal opportunities for generalization of newly learned communication skills.

Pragmatic-based language intervention

Many authors see the primary goal of all intervention as pragmatic, regardless of the type of language problem that exists, arguing that intervention should "ultimately lead to improved communication at home and at school, in speaking, listening, reading, and writing. Intervention should assist the child in developing a desire to communicate and provide him with the means to do so" (Carrow-Woolfolk and Lynch 1982, p. 275).

Approaches which have a pragmatic bias do not overlook the need to modify language form or expand semantic knowledge and expression of meaning. Rather, components of form and content can be emphasized within a pragmatic context. Deficits in specific pragmatic skills, such as underlying intentions, discourse features, and relevance/clarity of message to speaker, can be targeted concurrently in order to enhance communicative competence. The interdependence of pragmatic and linguistic skills has been borne out by research on the normal development of pragmatic skills as well as investigations of the pragmatic skills of children with specific language impairment.

Although children with specific language impairment (SLI) may demonstrate a typical *range* of communicative intentions, normal awareness of how to keep a conversation going and appropriate judgments of listeners' prior knowledge and linguistic status may be lacking. Consequently, the SLI child tends to use compensatory nonverbal means or strategies typical of younger children to maintain conversational interactions or to express intentions. On the other hand, even if basic pragmatic functions and discourse rules are intact, children with deficits in form and content may not possess the linguistic means necessary to express pragmatic functions. Linguistic impairments place constraints on pragmatics. Deficits that are primarily pragmatic, and not linguistic, could affect overall communicative competence. Given this interdependence, it seems logical to couch linguistic training in a pragmatic framework.

Classrooms: The ideal context

The motivation to learn language skills, and to refine them, comes from the need to *use* language (Craig 1983). Research demonstrates that, in response to being unsuccessful communicators, children may adapt by using nondesired linguistic alternatives or react by withdrawing conversationally. Either behavior will tend not to lead to improvements in communicative competence without specific remedial efforts.

The classroom is the ideal setting for such remedial efforts because, in the social context of the classroom, linguistic training can be integrated with a variety of intentions and conversational acts. With a speech-language pathologist in charge of a preschool classroom, there is a marriage between opportunity and operationally teaching linguistic skill as an aspect of broader communicative competence. "Language growth should be facilitated via experiences with functional communication.... The natural consequences of the communicative exchanges serve to reinforce and shape appropriate communication" (Friel-Patti and Lougeay-Mottinger 1985, p. 47). Where better to engage children in "natural" communicative exchanges than in a preschool setting where materials and activities are of high interest and where ongoing peer interaction occurs?

The potency of classroom-based intervention is obvious when compared to the traditional model of speech and language therapy which is usually characterized by one-to-one, table top interactions. Clinicians who use such techniques as elicited imitation, reinforcement, and drill may be omitting the very features that facilitate language learning. Such intervention does not demonstrate the functional benefit of communication to the child, and evidence exists that "highly constrained therapy situations focusing on questions and commands tend to inhibit rather than encourage talking" (Hubbell 1977, in Carrow-Woolfolk and Lynch, 1982, p. 306). The traditional stimulus-response format may even contribute to persistent language-learning disabilities in later years (Steckol 1983, cited in Friel-Patti and Lougeay-Mottinger 1985).

In contrast, the classroom setting promotes the use of a wide range of language functions. These include requesting information, requesting clarification, relating socially to others, directing the action of others, giving information, participating in play, hypothesizing, answering, giving reasons, pretending and entertaining, offering help, and conveying past or future behavior (referent present or not present) (Creaghead 1984, Hart 1984, Kwiatkowski 1984, Staab 1983).

The environment provided by the preschool classroom, with its variety of settings and play centers, does not preclude a systematic approach to language training. "With some experience and concentration on the part of the language teacher, such environments can be developed so that the communicative functions and context can become highly controlled and predictable. In this way, training can become rather systematic in its targets and procedures" (McLean and Snyder-McLean 1978, p. 211).

Finally, the classroom setting promotes generalization of language skills. "Children generalize language skills by trying out how language works in many different places with many different people" (Hart 1982). In a classroom setting, a child has opportunities to talk about a variety of topics with the therapist, the teacher, aides, and other adults who have been trained to model and otherwise cue correct use of targeted forms, functions, and conversational skills.

The above discussion applies to generalization of the social use of language form. Language generalization, or the lack thereof, may not be the result of variables typically assumed to be operating when considering generalization of speech behavior. It may well be, as Johnston (1988) and Connell (1987) suggest, that language generalization is not necessarily fostered by extension of stimulus control. Even if it is determined that the promotion of generalization relates to intrasubject variables and the salience of input the child receives during initial learning trials, the fact that language and communication are pervasive throughout the day still bodes well for the classroom environment. If nothing else, the self-contained classroom affords the clinician and rewards the child with the maximum number of opportunities to foster induction and deduction of language rules.

Promoting Language in the Classroom

Most therapists have been trained to intervene in a fairly structured environment and are used to exerting control over the stimuli presented to the child, the nature of the verbal interaction, and the manner in which responses are recorded and evaluated. Managing a number of language-impaired children in a classroom environment, then, offers a unique opportunity and a distinct challenge. It is, as Feinberg (1981) has stated, a matter of maintaining a balance between structured training and functional use of selected linguistic targets. The teacher or therapist in a classroom environment needs to become adept at choreographing language therapy.

It is not the intent of this chapter to detail numerous specifics about language intervention strategies. Clearly there are a number of time-honored methods available, and the choice of methodology will be influenced by educational philosophy, biases in training, and clinical background experiences. The nature and severity of language disorders among the children in the classroom will also influence the choice. Still, procedures that have evolved from incidental language teaching (Warren and Kaiser 1986) seem well suited to the dynamics of the classroom. Despite the variety of methods one could choose, certain classroom dynamics provide logical opportunities to implement language change. These features of classroom dynamics, described below, are universally adaptable to any of a variety of methods.

Language training as children act on the environment

There are several commonly occurring events during the preschool day in which children will spontaneously act upon their environment. And, with slight modification in routines, the therapist can increase the number of occasions during which language training can take place (Halle 1984). The material below gives several suggestions for promoting spontaneous verbalization.

Make desired materials inaccessible. From the time children enter the room, there will be several instances when they need to acquire materials or when they spontaneously wish to choose materials. Generally, by keeping such materials visible but not readily accessible, the clinician can evoke comments or requests from the children. Children will feel the need to request assistance from therapist, teacher, aide, or classmate. One of the keys to this strategy is to be sure the materials are desirable (Halle 1984; Hart and Rogers-Warren 1978). A balance must be struck between creating a need to communicate and preventing frustration.

Group activities provide ideal settings that allow clinicians to use a number of intervention techniques that honor the child's communicative intent and that avoid direct correction or reinforcing incorrect responses. For example, in an arts and crafts activity conducted by the clinician, scissors are deliberately omitted from the array of necessary tools.

Dialogue	*Intervention technique/targets*
Child #1: Me no cut.	
Clinician: *I* can't cut out my picture either. *I* can't cut it.	Model's pronoun "I," negative "can't"
Child #2: I can't cut out mine either. I need scissors.	Child uses "I" and "can't"
Child #1: Need scissors.	
Clinician: I need scissors too.	Models "I" and plural noun

Evoke language within daily routines. In a classroom setting, a variety of activities may be planned to cue and model use of targeted language forms and functions.

> Such routine activities (snack, free play, arrival and dismissal, transitions between activities, toileting) are settings in which self-help skills or a variety of loosely specified objectives from different developmental domains are typically targeted. Unfortunately, language/communication skills are often neglected as objectives in these settings, even though such situations offer optimal and plentiful opportunities for targeted language/communication skills in natural contexts. (Kaczmarek 1985, p. 187)

It seems clear that a particular activity will greatly influence the speaker's language choices. Nursery school children engaged in sand play and constructing villages were found to use language to plan, to discuss materials, and to ask for help (Fox and Zidonis 1975). Miles (1978, cited in Staab 1983) found that drawing and painting elicit many ego-enhancing utterances from preschool children. Constable (1983) proposes that intervention strategies use familiar social routines such as birthday parties, food preparation, and washing dishes for facilitating progressively more specific language use, with conversational support provided by clinicians.

The daily schedule will include a number of activities (free play, snack, motor skill training, recess, craft time) that become, over time, identifiable routines that children can anticipate and know what to expect in terms of the participants and their roles (Snyder-McLean et al. 1984). As children become familiar with daily routines, particularly potent exchanges can be planned at the beginning and end of expected routines. Halle (1984) suggests that if the clinician introduces an unexpected delay at the critical moment of opening or closing an activity, children will be stimulated to respond.

Conveying and reviewing information. Another language intervention strategy useful in the classroom is to place the child in the role of conveyor of real information (Culatta 1984). The child may be asked to tell latecomers how to proceed with a crafts project. In a weekly "Home News" activity, children might bring in notebooks with parents' notes of interesting experiences they had the prior weekend. Using the notebooks, staff help each child share news with a small group, using appropriate prompting levels for each child. Children who have helped to "cook" the snack for the day may tell the other children how they prepared the food, using a picture "recipe" poster to guide them.

Such a strategy places the emphasis on communicating messages—*real* informational exchange—as opposed to drill on isolated sentences. Conveying and reviewing information is easily engineered throughout the course of the day. Opening activities including traditional "show and tell" and "calendar time" make for meaningful exchanges. Reviewing events of a field trip, a television show, or personal experiences can serve as a powerful stimulus for language programming (Feinberg 1981).

Language training within the curriculum

Along with the social-play and activity routines within the classroom, the presentation of day-to-day curriculum offers a context for language intervention. Language training can be interwoven into curricular activities in at least three ways: (1) linguistic content of the curriculum, (2) instructional language of the curriculum, and (3) language interaction during curricular activities.

Language content of the curriculum. Almost all preacademic or academic content has associated with it a host of linguistic content that is necessary for the acquisition of concepts or skills. As academic content is being presented, these key linguistic concepts can be trained receptively or their expressive use encouraged. For instance, a premath lesson might feature size relations (long/short, big/little), labels for quantity and number concepts (more/less, some/none, one, two, three, etc.), and notions of similarity (same/different). Likewise, any prereading activity can form the basis for teaching key metalinguistic concepts (concepts of words, sentences, language on paper). Rather than being avoided in language-impaired populations, the exposure to such preliteracy experiences has been advocated as part of a reading/language program (Kahmi and Koenig 1985).

Tasks involving fine and gross motor development offer excellent opportunities for real-life exposure to location concepts, action, locative action, and recurrence. Curricula that center on prescience concepts and social science have, historically, lent themselves to vocabulary expansion through categorization and semantic fields constructs. Descriptive language is introduced whenever physical attributes are reviewed in science.

The very content of the curriculum has an associated core vocabulary which should increase the child's receptive knowledge and productive use of vocabulary. An excellent example of weaving language training into curricular content has been outlined by Page and Culatta (1986). In their project, relational vocabulary (such as big/little, fast/slow, few/many) was taught in a classroom setting using a six-step teaching sequence. The first three steps center on receptive language and are designed to increase the child's awareness of the defining characteristics of target words. Gradually, recognition of words is stressed without situational support, and the final three steps, dealing with expressive language, lead to the use of the word with distractions added and in natural contexts.

Instructional language of the curriculum. Not only does curricular content have a language core, but the learning exchange between clinician/teacher/aide and child serves as a language training tool. The language of instruction refers to the dynamics of the verbal exchange between participants. The beginnings of school discourse occur in the preschool or early academic classroom. It is important to attend to the nature of this exchange, particularly for children evidencing receptive language deficits. Skills in receptive language, auditory attention, and knowledge of school "rules" can be shaped during the instructional interaction.

Blank et al. (1978) have developed a model of classroom discourse based on what they term perceptual-language distance, "perceptual" representing the material available to the child, and "language" representing the verbal formulations of the teacher. They propose four levels of increasing abstraction that capture the match between teacher language and the degree of contextual support available to the child: matching perception, selective analysis of perception, reordering perception, and reasoning about perception. The nature of verbal exchanges should be considered within the context of this framework when presenting instructional directions or requiring responses within lessons. Presumably, breakdowns occurring in the clinician-child dialogue may be related to a mismatch between the level of abstraction required in the teacher's input and the ability of the child to deal with abstraction. The value of this construct is that the classroom clinician can structure questions, requests, and comments to "fit" the child's capability at a given stage of development.

Specific strategies for altering language input during instructional exchanges are reviewed by Lasky (1985). Although this material addresses school-age children, many of the principles for altering the language signal or the listening environment are applicable to the preschool population.

Language through curricular engagement. Unlike the regular classroom, children in self-contained classes should be seen *and* heard! Engagement in curricular activities in and of itself may provoke a wide range of spontaneous questions, comments, or directives. Be sensitive to this fact and seize these moments as opportune times to model, expand, and shape this language of engagement. Almost all focused activity promotes children's expression, with science experiments and arts/crafts activities being particularly effective.

Creaghead suggests that clinicians and teachers view art projects and science experiments as naturally creating communicative demands:

> Allow children to work in groups and decide what to make and what they will need to make it. This strategy will encourage predicting and hypothesizing as well as many other behaviors required in conversations. It will probably also produce requests for information and will necessitate requests for objects. (1984, pp. 249-50)

Creative drama and language experiences may be integrated with structured language intervention strategies for elementary school-age children (Bush 1978). McCune-Nicholich and Carroll (1981) also point to sociodramatic play, which demands integration of linguistic skill, as an intervention technique to promote both linguistic and social competence. Dramatic play is readily adaptable to specific language intervention goals and particularly dynamic when involving groups of children.

The timing of language intervention

One of the greatest advantages of a classroom environment for language training compared to one-to-one itinerant services is the fact that language "intervention" need not be restricted to one point during the day. The classroom setting offers intervention opportunities of extended duration. Kaczmarek (1985) reviews literature which indicates that intervention which occurs throughout the day, rather than during time specifically set aside for it, is more effective. For preschool language-impaired children, opportunities to use new skills in varied contexts throughout the school day are critical for mastery to occur.

Most clinicians who manage self-contained classrooms will continue to schedule individual treatment times or small-group treatment interactions, because the needs of the population go beyond language (for example, phonological or fluency disorders accompanying the language problem) and individualized treatment is required. Additionally, clinicians may wish to intervene in specific language areas on a one-to-one basis and then use naturally occurring interactions within the classroom as opportunities for generalization. "Children generalize language skills by trying out how language works in many different places with many different people" (Hart 1982, p. 177).

Thus, timing of intervention can be viewed from two perspectives. One is that particular linguistic targets can be addressed at different times throughout the day. The other perspective of day-long opportunity is that you can plan to promote generalized use of a target in selected speaking situations.

Intervention strategies

While it is not the intent of this manual to review generic language therapy strategies, some attention to the unique adaptations of modeling seems relevant. Almost all clinicians are familiar with modeling and expansion strategies, especially as they differ from rote, imitation-based techniques. Various adaptations of modeling are suited to classroom intervention.

Third-person modeling. A variation of the clinician-child modeling and expansion strategy is to employ the use of a third person who models exemplars of responses containing a given linguistic rule. In this approach, which has been detailed by Courtright and Courtright (1979) and Leonard (1973), the child observes responses by the model which contain instances of the target linguistic behavior as well as responses that violate the rule being targeted. The child is not asked to replicate responses immediately but is encouraged to observe carefully the behavior of the model. Through the clinician's differential reaction to desired and undesired responses, it is believed that the child has information from which to induce the particular linguistic rule.

Third-person modeling strategies work well in structured or semistructured learning contexts, rather than spontaneous, naturalistic interactions. For instance, in individual therapy, the clinician may choose to use the paraprofessional aide as a third-person model. The aide can be instructed in advance or follow a script designed to highlight the inclusion or exclusion of key linguistic targets. The child or small group will delight in observing the "teacher" (the aide) being selectively reinforced through continuation or breakdown of communication depending on the adequacy of the response. If parent volunteers are available, they also can assume the role of third-person model. Semistructured situations include craft, snack, and table top play periods. Here, the model's responses can precede those of the language-impaired children. Requests, comments, or questions can be initiated by the model. After a few exemplars, the children can be asked to replicate the behavior.

Peer modeling. The classroom setting readily permits the use of peer models. Peer modeling is defined as "the use of the behavior of a peer as a model to induce positive change in the behavior of a target child" (Muma 1983, p. 208). It is possible that the language-impaired child may be more receptive to cuing from peers than from the "teacher" (Feinberg 1981).

Integration of normal-language peer models also may play an important part in facilitating the pragmatic component of language. Children may have certain interactions among themselves that do not tend to occur with adults, such as issuing demands, engaging in arguments, making accommodations, and inviting another child to participate in joint activity (Cole 1982). Creaghead (1984) states that using adult models exclusively may make development of pragmatic skills somewhat difficult, as adult pragmatics varies from that of children, a point often overlooked in language programs.

Ideally, peer modeling should be accomplished by integrating normal-language peers into the self-contained classroom. This often is possible when the self-contained classroom is located in proximity to other regular education classes. Peer modeling also could be arranged by inviting parents to bring their children's siblings to class for special events or on a given day when they are available. If normal-language peer models are not available, the clinician may want to rely on children with relatively advanced language to model for their peers, calling first on the child who is most apt to provide the desired response.

Responding without correcting. A clinician's behavior following undesired linguistic responses is critical in classroom intervention. As a general rule and consistent with techniques advocated in incidental language teaching (Hart 1984), direct correction cues should be avoided. This point was originally championed by Muma (1978) and is now a fundamental principle for those engaged in language intervention.

The technique of expansion is perhaps relied upon most frequently by clinicians who are comfortable with providing a corrected and expanded version of what the child said. Expansions produce a slight delay in the child's experience of "payoff," providing the achievement of communicative intent without the negative impact of being perceived as correction.

Another method of introducing this slight delay is *negotiation of meaning,* which may consist of a clarification question ("Huh? You want the water?"), an expansion, attempts at rephrasing, or simply repetition of the utterance (Snow et al. 1984). This type of negotiation continues the same topic, preserving semantic contingency, a principle that has been shown to facilitate language acquisition (Nelson 1973; Friel-Patti and Lougeay-Mottinger 1985).

Whatever specific strategy is employed, the goal should be to continue communication and not discourage the child from subsequent attempts. If the context permits the adult to guess at the content and intention of a completely unintelligible utterance, a direct model or even acceptance of a partially correct production that includes a nonverbal component would then be appropriate.

Basically, the child is never directly told to repeat, but the adult stalls "in confusion" (feigned or real), inviting the child to revise using the forms modeled by the adult. Subsequent incorrect revisions are always accepted.

Parent training and support. Home programming is of vital importance in ensuring continued skill gain after a child leaves an early education program (Hodges and Sheenan 1978), and many authors have discussed strategies for incorporating parents into intervention programs (Hastings and Hayes 1981; Kemper 1980; Newhoff and Browning 1983). The chapter on staffing and training details several methods to achieve parental involvement in the program objectives.

Follow-up consultation. White and Casto's (1985) study of the effects of numerous early intervention programs suggests that long-term gains may be lacking because of insufficient follow-up activities after a child leaves the program and enters public school. Hodges and Sheenan (1978) also indicate that immediate gains from structured programs often erode after children leave a program.

It is important that the speech-language pathologist or teacher visit a former student's new educational placement, perhaps two times during the first year after departure and once during the second year. When possible, this professional should observe the class, meet with the teacher and any specialist serving the child, and make oral and written suggestions. This will help the receiving staff gain a better understanding of the child as well as helping them modify their methods of presentation for specific children.

Conclusion

Children with specific language impairments need specific language interventions. "Language intervention programs must address the semantic and syntactic as well as the pragmatic aspects of language" (Cole 1982, p. 146). This language intervention will be greatly empowered, especially in preschool but also significantly with school-age children, by the use of indirect teaching techniques such as modeling, expansion, and incidental teaching in a naturalistic, experiential setting which may include the use of peer models and other adult staff.

Pragmatic skills develop from early infancy and the expression of social and pragmatic awareness is closely linked to developing linguistic skill. Preschool children with specific language impairments attempt to compensate by using nonverbal or less linguistically demanding communicative strategies to achieve their intent and conduct conversations. However, this effort may decrease as they grow older and become more aware of their language limitations and, by elementary-school age, they may have become conversationally withdrawn. They then choose to avoid situations which will create linguistic stress and may gradually become unassertive conversationally and relatively withdrawn socially. Both classroom performance and social acceptance by peers may suffer.

The speech-language pathologist as well as all professionals who work with language-impaired children should therefore be aware of pragmatics both as an intervention model and as a foundation skill area for successful communication, social interaction, and academic success.

Appendix A
Pragmatic Skills: Basic Definitions

An operational definition of *language learning* (Kemp 1983) includes five patterns of organization: phonology, morphology, syntax, semantics, and pragmatics. Pragmatics, "the use of language in context by real speakers and hearers in real situations" (Bates 1974, p. 277), may also be viewed as the "overall framework from which to study syntax and semantics" (Prutting 1982, p. 125). Pragmatists assert that language form is determined by function.

> The basic principle in talking is contextual control; individuals must say the right thing in the right way at the right time and place in accordance with the norms of society . . . What is said must change with each change in the topic, material, or activity talked about, with each change in hearer, and with each utterance and hearer response. Everything a person says changes the situation in some way—adds information, asks for an answer, directs to action—so that both hearer and speaker have to adjust subsequent talk in terms of that change. (Hart 1982, pp. 175-176)

Language use is defined as "the reason individuals communicate through language and why context determines which forms are chosen among alternatives" (Schirmer 1984, p. 81).

Children are considered to be *normally acquiring language* if they are uniformly acquiring age-appropriate skills across the five patterns of linguistic organization. A child is considered *language delayed* (and may also be developmentally delayed with respect to motor and social-emotional development) if language skills are uniformly below chronological age, usually 12 months or more. A child is *language disordered, language deviant,* or *specifically language impaired* if there is uneven development within the five patterns of organization with at least one of them at or close to age level and a relative absence of impairment in other areas of development (Kemp 1983). Children are considered "high risk" and mild to moderately language impaired if they fit the description for specific language impairment or deviance but the most impaired area is not more than 6 to 12 months below chronological age.

A number of terms are frequently found in the research literature on pragmatic skill development and include the following:

Code switching is the "regulation and modification of speech according to the situation and the listener" (Donahue 1983, p. 17). In other words, code switching is one reflection of the speaker's presuppositions relating to the listener.

Contingent queries are three-part sequences consisting of (1) an occasion message which is the preceding utterance, (2) the query, and (3) the response. For example: (1) "I'm going outside." (2) "Where?" (3) "Outside." There are two types of contingent queries, solicited and unsolicited. Solicited queries are used to gain attention in discourse, whereas unsolicited queries are used for requesting clarification and correcting misunderstandings (Corsaro 1981; Garvey 1977).

Conversational postulates or rules of discourse relate to a higher level of organization than the speech act. This is dialogue, discourse, or successive utterances joined by a common topic (Carrow-Woolfolk and Lynch 1982). Certain conventions or "unstated rules" govern the quality, relevance, and quantity of information and shared assumptions. These rules are (1) tell the truth, (2) offer new and relevant information, and (3) request only the information you want. These also involve rules for taking turns and such conventions as presupposition, indirect speech acts, and deixis.

Deixis is the term for linguistic devices that anchor the utterance to the communicative setting in which it occurs (Rees 1978). These include *deixis of person* (personal pronouns), of *place* (this, here, there, come, go, bring, take), *deixis of time* through tense markers and words such as *yesterday* and *later*. To learn deixis requires the ability to gain the perspective of another or to exchange roles (Cole 1982).

Indirectives are usually polite forms of requests, that is, asking rather than telling ("Do you have the time?" "Will you please open the window?") Indirectives may also be hints ("My mommy always lets me have a cookie before lunch," or "It's hot in here").

Metapragmatics refers to "explicit awareness of pragmatic knowledge or talking about talking" (Bates 1976, p. 135).

Presupposition is "information that is not contained in an utterance but must be known if the sentence is to be understood" (Carrow-Woolfolk and Lynch 1982, p. 188). Presuppositions represent knowledge that the speaker presumes the listener shares. They "include judgments that speakers and listeners must make about the spoken and unspoken context, about the other person, and about prior shared experiences in order to comprehend messages and to produce comprehensible messages" (Creaghead 1984, p. 241). Presuppositions take into account such things as the listener's age and linguistic competence, background, functioning level, and other things such as context, emotional issues, and the topic. The appropriateness of the utterance is determined by the correctness of the presuppositions (Savich 1983). Presuppositions modify how and what the speaker says (Johnson et al. 1984).

Requests for clarification are the signals a cooperative listener is expected to give a speaker when a remark is not comprehended.

Revision behaviors are the manner in which a speaker alters a preceding utterance to make it more comprehensible to the listener in order to keep the conversation going. Revision behaviors may also be called *conversational repairs*.

Speech acts are the functions that utterances are intended to serve (Leonard 1983). These "include such things as directing actions, commenting on objects and actions, and expressing feelings" (Creaghead 1984, p. 241). Speech acts are "characterized by intended interactive efforts between speaker and listener ... They are communicative in nature, they occur in conversation, they perform acts as well as contain words and meanings (performatives), and they are intentional and goal-directed" (Wollner 1983, p. 2).

Appendix B
A Pragmatic Skill Taxonomy for Assessment and Intervention

There are a number of orderly classification systems or taxonomies of pragmatic skills in the literature, none of which are identical, although all include the categories of communicative intentions and of conversational postulates (Carrow-Woolfolk and Lynch 1982; Cole 1982; Creaghead 1984; Donahue 1983; Johnson et al. 1984; Prutting 1982; Roth and Spekman 1984; Schirmer 1984). For the purposes of guiding an examination of the research literature and for suggesting assessment and curriculum areas, the following classification system has been adopted.

Communicative intentions or speech acts

Range of intentions (Dore 1975; Dore et al. 1978)

Form of intentions (Roth and Spekman 1984)
- Gestural, paralinguistic, or linguistic
- Linguistic structures used to convey an intention
- Degree of explicitness (use of indirectives and polite forms)
  - Direct imperative ("Give me some ice cream.")
  - Embedded imperative ("Can you give me some ice cream?")
  - Permission directive ("May I have some ice cream?")
  - Personal need or desire statement ("I need/want some ice cream.")
  - Question directive ("Is there any more ice cream?")
  - Hint ("Gee, that ice cream looks good.")
    (from Ervin-Tripp and Mitchell-Kernan 1977)

Conversational skills

Maintaining the flow of conversation or dialogue between and among partners (Cole 1982)
- Turn taking
- Topic initiation and maintenance, coherency, sequential organization
- Repair of conversation: revision behaviors and requests for clarification
  - Repair strategies (Roth and Spekman 1984, p. 9)
    - Change in linguistic structure: phonologic, morphologic, lexical, syntactic
    - Change in linguistic content: repetition, confirmation, specification, elaboration
    - Extralinguistic: changes in pitch, stress, or volume, or a gestural demonstration
- Linguistic contingency
- Pronominalization
- Grammatical ellipsis

Presuppositions and code switching
- Old versus new information
- Social role and interpersonal relationship
- Setting

Speaker's intentions
Cultural expectations
Listener's linguistic facility

Deixis of person and object, place and time; indirect versus direct reference
Personal pronouns
Demonstrative pronouns
Adverbs of location (*here, there*)
Adverbs of time (*before, after, then, now*), tense markers and lexical items (*tomorrow, later*)
Certain verbs (*come, go, bring, take*)

Metapragmatic awareness

Ability to judge the politeness of requests

Ability to judge the adequacy of information in a description

Ability to match request forms to speakers

Awareness of metalinguistic features (intonational patterns, tone and quality of voice) and their appropriateness

Appendix C
Research Overview: Normal Development of Pragmatic Skills

Communicative intentions or speech acts

Although Roth and Spekman (1984) caution that formal pragmatic assessments are still experimental and a complete knowledge of normal developmental sequences has not been gained, there is considerable data on the normal developmental stages of expressing communicative intentions. Cole (1982) summarizes the research regarding early milestones, and Carrow-Woolfolk and Lynch (1982) present a detailed discussion of the regulatory function of preverbal communication. Some early milestones are listed below.

Preverbal

Between 2 and 10 months
- Regulates joint attention on an activity through eye contact and gaze exchange (Carrow-Woolfolk and Lynch 1982)

Between 10 and 16 months
- Regulatory function consisting of sound plus gesture in three stages:
  — Attends to objects. Holds up object and vocalizes (showing).
  — Requests objects. Looks at object, points, vocalizes (pointing).
  — Requests transfer of object. Holds out and gives object and reaches for another object (giving).
- Nonverbal turn taking in play (Bates 1976; Bates et al. 1975; Bruner 1975, 1978; Carrow-Woolfolk and Lynch 1982; Pylyshyn 1977)

Early words

- Performatives rather than symbols (*bye-bye, no-no*) (Greenfield and Smith 1976)
- Requesting may be 27% of all utterances. Requests for attention, objects, assistance (Dore 1977)
- Intents are to satisfy needs, control, interact, express self, explore, imagine (Halliday 1977)
- Labels, answers, requests action or answers, calls, greets (Dore 1975)
- Comments on obvious items, actions (Carrow-Woolfolk and Lynch 1982)

18 to 24 months

- Begins to ask for names of objects ("What's that?")
- Acts for functions, locations of objects
- Uses language to act on environment, learn about environment, provide others with new information (Halliday 1975, 1977)
- Conveys content, regulates conversation, expresses attitudes (Dore et al. 1978)

2 to 5 years

- By 2½, begins to express feelings verbally (Carrow-Woolfolk and Lynch 1982)
- Imaginative use of language in imaginative social play with peers ("Let's pretend...") (Garvey 1977)
- Speech acts classified into requestives, assertives, performatives, responsives, regulatives, and expressives (Dore et al. 1978)
- In 4-year-olds' conversation with peers, children spent much time describing and requesting, responded to requests less often. Four conversational patterns identified: *typical, organizer, requester, describer.* (Schober and Johnson 1985)
- Begins to develop ability to judge from context the different intentions that can underlie a single utterance. Children 2 and 3 years old judged correctly significantly more than incorrectly; 3-year-olds better at judging requests. Early conceptual skills permit inferences. (Reeder 1980)
- The major function of normal 2- to 3-year-olds' spontaneously produced questions was information seeking; 4- to 5-year-olds evenly distributed among *information seeking, conversational* and *directive.* (Information seeking: "What's this for?" Conversational: "You know what?" Directive: "Can I do it now?") Five-year-olds used 10% to 35% more directive questions than 4-year-olds. (James and Seebach 1982)

Communicative intentions: Indirectives

2 to 5 years

- Under 3 years of age, children respond to adults' indirect requests using nonverbal context, rather than recognizing linguistic structures. (Garvey 1975; Shatz and Gelman 1978)
- Says "please" and "thank you" by age 24 to 30 months but these are not understood as social forms. (Carrow-Woolfolk and Lynch 1982)

- Uses indirectives or hints to request, ages 3 years and up. Culture influences this practice. (Ervin-Tripp and Mitchell-Kernan 1977)
- Demonstrates sensitivity to context by age 3½ to 4. Changes form to conform to social convention. (Bates 1976)
- Children 5 years old use twice as many indirect request forms as 3-year-olds but the two groups use same number of direct request forms. (Garvey 1975)

Conversational skills

Although early preverbal exchanges such as vocal play, eye-gaze coupling, and joint activities with caregivers form the developmental foundation for conversation, basically a social activity (Carrow-Woolfolk and Lynch 1982; Cole 1982), children are not considered fairly adept at communication in a conversation until age six (Savich 1983).

Conversational skills: Turn taking

Single-word stage
- Takes turns speaking
- Uses verbal and nonverbal gestures, including calling person being addressed by name, to get attention (Bloom and Lahey 1978)
- Pauses to wait for listener's response or acknowledgment by 24 months (Keenan 1974, cited in Cole 1982)

2 to 5 years
- Among six 4-year-old girls in two- and three-party conversations, the current speaker selects the next speaker by the nonverbal turn-taking behaviors of gaze and proximity, and the listener self-selects the next turn option by proximity. By age four, white middle-class children are able to manage three-party conversations as well as two-party. (Craig and Gallagher 1982)

Conversational skills: Topic maintenance across turns

2 to 5 years
- Preschool children do not engage exclusively in egocentric monologues but do contribute to conversations both with adults and peers. (Bates 1976; Camioni 1977; Garvey 1977; Keenan 1974; Keenan and Schieffelin 1976; Mueller 1972; Sachs 1977; Shatz and Gelman 1978)
- Number of turns over which young children (2 and 3 years old) can maintain a topic is extremely variable. Larger number of turns maintained (1) when conversing with an adult, (2) when child initiates topic, and (3) when conversational focus is an object present in the environment. (Bloom et al. 1976; Keenan and Schieffelin 1976)
- Discourse participation and topic performance was studied in 30 mother-child dyads with children from 2:10 to 6:3. Although mothers facilitated the structure and cohesiveness of discourse, children exhibited greater topic maintenance, use of shading, and a more sophisticated conversational strategy with increasing age. (Wanska and Bedrosian 1985)

5 years to adult
- Manipulation of discourse topic in spontaneous conversation was examined in six peer dyads ages 5:0 to 5:11, 9:0 to 9:11, and adults. Patterns of topic introduction, reintroduction, maintenance, and shading were studied. Children 5 years old typically discussed 50 topics in a 15-minute period. Topic shading occurred frequently among adults too. Authors advise great caution in identifying disordered patterns. (Brinton and Fujiki 1984)

Conversational skills: Presuppositions and code switching

Single-word stage
- Use of presupposition to decide what *not* to say and to select the most informative word. Rudimentary awareness of given versus new information. Encodes changing or unusual element instead of constants in the nonverbal context. Examples: "cookie" instead of "want" ("want cookie"), and "running" instead of "Daddy" ("Daddy running"). (Greenfield and Smith 1976; Halliday 1975)

3 to 8 years
- Forty children ages 3 to 6 years judged whether utterances produced by speakers in various social situations were contextually appropriate. Accuracy increased with age but as a function of speech act—3-year-olds accurate on "thank," 4- and 5-year-olds accurately judged "thank" and "congratulate," and 6-year-olds accurate for all speech acts except "argue." Judgments based on appropriateness of various linguistic and nonlinguistic context features. Findings indicate that between ages 4 and 6, children have enough awareness about the relationship of context to utterance to be able to judge appropriateness and are aware to some extent of presupposed information shared by speaker and listener. (Leonard and Reid 1979)

- By 3 years of age, children changed linguistic form according to their understanding of the social relationship. (Bloom and Lahey 1978)

- Children 3 to 4 years old provided more detailed information to persons they considered to be blind than to those considered to have normal vision, assuming their listeners' access to topic-related information. (Maratsos 1973)

- Preschoolers spoke differently to younger or less advanced children (higher pitch, exaggerated intonation, syntactic simplification, greater proportion of questions and directives, greater degree of redundancy). (Camioni 1977; Gleason 1973; Guralnick and Paul-Brown 1977, 1980; Masur 1978; Roth and Spekman 1984)

- Children 4 years old used more direct, simpler, less ambiguous content, and fewer, shorter, and less complex sentences when talking to 2-year-olds. (Sachs and Devlin 1976; Shatz and Gelman 1978)

- Stylistic adaptations were noted in 4- to 8-year-olds who seemed to be responding to some type of feedback. (Gleason 1973)

- Children 4 years old have more awareness of listener's prior knowledge and encode new information more clearly. By age 5 years, children can make even greater changes in content and form to respond to the abilities and needs of listeners. (de Villiers and de Villiers 1978)

- Haynes et al. (1979) studied "egocentrism" versus taking the listener's perspective in 4- to 6-year-olds. Results showed that they are capable of changing their communicative behavior and taking the listener's perspective.

- Tourdot and Retherford-Stickler (1985) studied 6-year-olds' revision of the experimenter's directives to 3-year-old normal siblings and to a 3-year-old language-delayed child. Fourteen directives of two difficulty levels were relayed; children's responses were coded for revision types. There were statistically significant differences for directive levels and for revision types with specific techniques used to help the language-delayed child comprehend. Revision types were: (1) repetition, (2) length adjustments, (3) syntactic adjustments, (4) semantic clarification, (5) nonverbal clues, (6) performance of action, (7) monitoring of extraneous behavior, and (8) commenting about performance abilities of younger child.

Conversational skills: Deixis and indirect versus direct reference

Definitive developmental milestones cannot be given for all aspects of deixis and indirect/direct reference. Correct use of both improves over elementary school years. Even adults may use these terms incorrectly. (Roth and Spekman 1984)

Preverbal
- Basis for spatial, interpersonal deixis in infant-caregiver interactions in which infants learn to follow line of regard and play "give and take" games. (Bruner 1975, 1978, in Cole 1982)

2 to 5 years
- *Deixis of person/object: use of pronouns* to appear at MLU of 2.0. By MLU of 2.5, children should be able to use both pronouns and nouns. Still use gestures for pronouns and have poor understanding of rules for their use. (Bloom and Lahey 1978; Carrow-Woolfolk and Lynch 1982)

- Order of acquisition of personal pronouns (*I* before *you* before *he/she*) reflects relative frequency of change of referents. (Clark and Sengul 1978)

- *Deixis of place* not always understood when *here, there, this, that* are used to select objects, indicate task completion, or name places. Not used as true deictic contrasts until late four. Deictic shift between *here* and *there* observed when MLU approached 4.0. By age 5 years, children master the contrast fully. (Bloom and Lahey 1978; Clark 1977; Cole 1982)

- No true use of *come/go* and *bring/take* as deictic contrasts until after age 7 years. (Clark and Garnica 1974)

- *Deixis of time* through tense markers begins to appear around Stage III, third birthday. Also marked by words like *yesterday, tomorrow,* and adjectives like *long/short, far/near* to describe space and time, but there are more speculations than data available. (Brown 1973; Carrow-Woolfolk and Lynch 1982)

- Spontaneous narratives of 3- to 5-year-olds studied with respect to linguistic devices to orient events in time. All narratives of 3-year-olds pertained to immediate events. Half the narratives of 4- and 5-year-olds pertained to prior events, and linguistic devices to orient events in time were used. (Umiker-Sebeok 1979)

Metapragmatic Awareness

Sixty children between ages 3 and 7 years were studied with respect to awareness of politeness: ability to request in an "even nicer way" and to make judgments of relative politeness increased with age. Conclusion: ability to reason actively about pragmatic choices develops separately and later than passive pragmatic competence. (Bates 1976)

Preschool children judge utterances according to whether they agree/disagree with the utterance, or whether they feel the utterance is true; they do not use criteria of grammatic correctness or acceptability. (Brown and Bellugi 1964; Carrow-Woolfolk and Lynch 1982)

References

Bates, E. 1974. Acquisition of pragmatic competence. *Journal of Child Language* 3:277-281.

———. 1976. *Language and context: The acquisition of pragmatics.* New York: Academic Press.

Bates, E., L. Camioni, and V. Volterra. 1975. The acquisition of performatives prior to speech. *Merrill-Palmer Quarterly* 21:205-226.

Blank, M., S. A. Rose, and L. J. Berlin. 1978. *The language of learning: The preschool years.* Orlando, FL: Grune and Stratton, Inc.

Bloom, L., and M. Lahey. 1978. *Language development and language disorders.* New York: John Wiley.

Bloom, L., L. Rocissano, and L. Hood. 1976. Adult-child discourse: Developmental interaction between information processing and linguistic knowledge. *Cognitive Psychology* 8:521-552.

Brinton, B., and M. Fujiki. 1984. Development of topic manipulation skills in discourse. *Journal of Speech and Hearing Research* 27:350-358.

Brown, R. 1973. *A first language: The early stages.* Cambridge, MA: Harvard University Press.

Brown, R., and U. Bellugi. 1964. Three processes in the child's acquisition of syntax. *Harvard Educational Review* 34:133-151.

Bruner, J. 1975. The ontogenesis of speech acts. *Journal of Child Language* 2:1-19.

———. 1978. From communication to language: A psychological perspective. In *The social context of language,* edited by I. Markova, 17-48. New York: John Wiley.

Bush, C. S. 1978. Creative drama and language experiences: Effective clinical techniques. *Language, Speech and Hearing Services in Schools* 9:254-258.

Camioni, L. 1977. Child-adult and child-child conversations: An interactional approach. In *Developmental pragmatics,* edited by E. Ochs and B. B. Schieffelin. New York: Academic Press.

Carrow-Woolfolk, E., and J. I. Lynch. 1982. *An integrative approach to language disorders in children.* New York: Grune and Stratton.

Clark, E. 1977. Strategies and the mapping problem in first language acquisition. In *Language learning and thought,* edited by J. MacNamara, 147-168. New York: Academic Press.

Clark, E., and O. Garnica. 1974. Is he coming or going? On the acquisition of deictic verbs. *Journal of Verbal Learning and Verbal Behavior* 13:559-572.

Clark, E. V., and C. J. Sengul. 1978. Strategies in the acquisition of deixis. *Journal of Child Language* 5:457-475.

Cole, P. R. 1982. *Language disorders in preschool children.* Englewood Cliffs, NJ: Prentice Hall.

Connell, P. J. 1987. An effect of modeling and imitation teaching procedures on children with and without specific language impairment. *Journal of Speech and Hearing Research* 30:105-113.

Constable, C. 1983. Creating communicative context. In *Treating language disorders,* edited by H. Winitz. Baltimore, MD: University Park Press.

Corsaro, W. 1981. The development of social cognition in preschool children: Implications for language learning. *Topics in Language Disorders* 1:77-95.

Courtright, J., and I. Courtright. 1979. Imitative modeling as a language intervention strategy: The effects of two mediating variables. *Journal of Speech and Hearing Research* 22:389-402.

Craig, H. 1983. Applications of pragmatic language models for intervention. In *Pragmatic assessment and intervention issues in language,* edited by T. M. Gallagher and C. A. Prutting. San Diego, CA: College Hill Press.

Craig, H. K., and T. M. Gallagher. 1982. Gaze and proximity as turn regulators within three-party and two-party child conversations. *Journal of Speech and Hearing Research* 25:65-75.

Creaghead, N. A. 1984. Strategies for evaluating and targeting pragmatic behaviors in young children. *Seminars in Speech and Language* 5:241-251.

Culatta, B. 1984. A discourse-based approach to training grammatical rules. *Seminars in Speech and Language* 5:253-262.

de Villiers, J., and P. de Villiers. 1978. *Language acquisition.* Cambridge, MA: Harvard University Press.

Donahue, M. 1983. Learning-disabled children as conversational partners. *Topics in Language Disorders* 4(Dec.):15-27.

Dore, J. 1975. Holophrases, speech acts and language universals. *Journal of Child Language* 2:21-40.

_____. 1977. Children's illocutionary acts. *Discourse production and comprehension,* Vol. I, edited by R. Freedle, 227-244. Norwood, NJ: Ablex Publishing Corp.

Dore, J., M. Gearhart, and D. Newman. 1978. The structure of nursery school conversation. *Children's language,* Vol. I, edited by K. Nelson, 337-398. New York: Gardner Press.

Ervin-Tripp, S., and C. Mitchell-Kernan, eds. 1977. *Child discourse.* New York: Academic Press.

Feinberg, C. L. 1981. The pre-academic language classroom. *Language and Learning Disabilities* 8:249-268.

Fox, S. E., and F. Zidonis. 1975. Protocols of children's language. *Theory into Practice* 14:312-317.

Friel-Patti, S., and J. Lougeay-Mottinger. 1985. Preschool language intervention: Some key concerns. *Topics in Language Disorders* 5:40-57.

Garvey, C. 1975. Contingent queries. Unpublished master's thesis. Johns Hopkins University.

———. 1977. The contingent query: A dependent act in conversation. In *Interaction conversation and the development of language,* edited by M. Lewis and L. Rosenblum. New York: Wiley.

Gleason, J. B. 1973. Code switching in children's language. In *Cognitive development and the acquisition of language,* edited by T. E. Moore, 159-167. New York: Academic Press.

Greenfield, P., and J. Smith. 1976. *The structure of communication in early language development.* New York: Academic Press.

Grossfeld, C., and E. Heller. 1980. Follow the leader: Why a language impaired child can't be "it." *Working papers in experimental speech pathology and audiology,* #9. New York: Department of Communication, Arts, and Sciences, Queens College of the City of New York.

Guralnick, M. J., and D. Paul-Brown. 1977. The nature of verbal interactions among handicapped and non-handicapped preschool children. *Child Development* 48:254-260.

———. 1980. Functional and discourse analysis of non-handicapped children's speech to handicapped children. *American Journal of Mental Deficiency* 84:444-454.

Halle, J. W. 1984. Arranging the natural environment to occasion language: Giving severely language-delayed children reasons to communicate. *Seminars in Speech and Language* 5(3):185-197.

Halliday, M. A. K. 1975. *Learning how to mean—Explorations in the development of language.* London: Edward Arnold.

———. 1977. *Learning how to mean—Explorations in the development of language.* New York: Elsevier North-Holland.

Hart, B. 1982. Language skills in young children and the management of common problems. In *Early childhood education: Special problems, special solutions,* edited by K. E. Allen and E. M. Goetz, 173-199. Aspen Systems Corporation.

———. 1984. Environmental techniques that may facilitate generalization and acquisition. In *Teaching functional language,* edited by S. F. Warren and A. K. Rogers-Warren. Baltimore: University Park Press.

Hart, B., and A. K. Rogers-Warren. 1978. A milieu approach to teaching language. In *Language intervention strategies,* edited by R. L. Schiefelbusch. Baltimore: University Park Press.

Hastings, P., and B. Hayes. 1981. *Encouraging language development.* Cambridge, MA: Ware Press.

Haynes, O., E. Purcell, and M. D. Haynes. 1979. A pragmatic aspect of language sampling. *Language, Speech and Hearing Services in Schools* 10:104-110.

Hodges, W. L., and R. Sheenan. 1978. Follow through as ten years of experimentation: What have we learned? *Young Children* 34:4-14.

Hubbell, R. D. 1977. On facilitating spontaneous talking in young children. *Journal of Speech and Hearing Disorders* 42:216-231.

James, S. L., and M. A. Seebach. 1982. The pragmatic function of children's questions. *Journal of Speech and Hearing Research* 25:2-11.

Johnson, A. R., E. B. Johnson, and B. D. Weinrich. 1984. Assessing pragmatic skills in children. *Language, Speech and Hearing Services in Schools* 15:2-9.

Johnston, J. R. 1988. Generalization: The nature of change. *Language, Speech and Hearing Services in Schools* 19(3): 314-329.

Kaczmarek, L. S. 1985. Integrating language/communication objectives into the total preschool curriculum. *Teaching Exceptional Children* March: 183-189.

Kahmi, A., and L. Koenig. 1985. Metalinguistic awareness in language disordered children. *Language, Speech and Hearing Services in Schools* 16:199-210.

Keenan, E. 1974. Conversational competence in children. *Journal of Child Language* 1:163-183.

Keenan, E., and B. Schieffelin. 1976. Topic as a discourse notion: A study of topic in the conversation of children and adults. In *Subject and topic,* edited by C. Li. New York: Academic Press.

Kemp, J. C. 1983. The timing of language intervention for the pediatric population. In *Contemporary issues in language intervention,* edited by J. Miller, D. E. Yoder, and R. Schiefelbush. Rockville, MD: American Speech-Language-Hearing Association.

Kemper, R. L. 1980. A parent-assisted early childhood environmental language intervention program. *Language, Speech and Hearing Services in Schools* 11:229-235.

Kwiatkowski, J. 1984. Language development for classroom instruction. In *Current therapy of communication disorders: Language handicaps in children,* edited by W. H. Perkins, 83-93. New York: Thieme-Stratton.

Lasky, E. Z. 1985. Comprehending and processing of information in clinic and classroom. In *Communication skills and classroom success,* edited by C. S. Simon, 113-133. San Diego, CA: College Hill Press.

Leonard, L., and L. Reid. 1979. Children's judgments of utterance appropriateness. *Journal of Speech and Hearing Research* 22:500-515.

Leonard, L. B. 1973. Teaching by the rules. *Journal of Speech and Hearing Disorders* 38:174-183.

Maratsos, M. 1973. Nonegocentric communicative abilities in preschool children. *Child Development* 44:697-700.

Masur, E. 1978. Preschool boys' speech modifications: The effect of listeners' linguistic levels and conversational responsiveness. *Child Development* 49:924-927.

McCune-Nicholich, L., and S. Carroll. 1981. Development of symbolic play: Implications for the language specialist. *Topics in Language Disorders* 2:1-15.

McLean, J. E., and L. K. Snyder-McLean. 1978. *A transactional approach to early language training.* Columbus, OH: Charles E. Merrill.

Miles, M. J. 1978. *A comparison of children's language behavior during three art activities.* Unpublished master's thesis. Arizona State University.

Mueller, E. 1972. The maintenance of verbal exchange between young children. *Child Development* 43:930-938.

Muma, J. R. 1978. *Language handbook: Concepts, assessment, intervention.* Englewood Cliffs, NJ: Prentice Hall, Inc.

_____. 1983. Speech-language pathology: Emerging clinical expertise in language. In *Pragmatic assessment and intervention issues in language,* edited by T. M. Gallagher and C. A. Prutting. San Diego, CA: College Hill Press.

Nelson, K. 1973. Structure and strategy in learning to talk. *Monographs of the Society for Research in Child Development* 38(149, Serial 1,2).

Newhoff, M., and J. Browning. 1983. Interactional variation: A view from the language-disordered child's world. *Topics in Language Disorders* 4:49-60.

Page, J. L., and B. Culatta. 1986. Incorporating relational vocabulary teaching into daily classroom activities. *Journal of Childhood Communication Disorders: The Division for Children with Communication Disorders* 9(2):157-167.

Prutting, C. A. 1982. Pragmatics as social competence. *Journal of Speech and Hearing Disorders* 47:123-134.

Pylyshyn, Z. 1977. What does it take to bootstrap a language? In Language learning and thought, edited by J. MacNamara, 37-45. New York: Academic Press.

Reeder, K. 1980. The emergence of illocutionary skills. *Journal of Child Language* 7:13-28.

Rees, 1978. Pragmatics of language: Applications to normal and disordered language development. In *Bases of language intervention,* edited by E. F. Schiefelbusch. Baltimore, MD: University Park Press.

Roth, F. P., and N. J. Spekman. 1984. Assessing the pragmatic abilities of children: Part I. Organizational framework and assessment parameters. *Journal of Speech and Hearing Disorders* 49:2-11.

Sachs, J. 1977. Talking about there and that. *Papers and Reports on Child Language Development, 3.* Palo Alto, CA: Stanford University Press.

Sachs, J., and J. Devlin. 1976. Young children's use of age-appropriate speech styles in social interaction and role playing. *Journal of Child Language* 3:81-98.

Savich, P. A. 1983. Improving communicative competence: The role of metapragmatic awareness. *Topics in Language Disorders* 4(Dec.):38-48.

Schirmer, L. 1984. Dynamic model of oral and/or signed language diagnosis. *Language, Speech and Hearing Services in Schools* 15:76-82.

Schober, D. L., and C. J. Johnson. 1985. Speech act distribution in preschoolers' conversation. Paper presented to the annual meeting of the American Speech-Language-Hearing Association, Washington, DC.

Shatz, M., and R. Gelman. 1978. Beyond syntax: The influence of conversational constraints on speech modification. In *Talking to children: Language impact and acquisition,* edited by C. Snow and C. Ferguson, 189-198. New York: Cambridge University Press.

Snow, C., S. Midkiff-Borunda, A. Small, and A. Procter. 1984. Therapy as social interaction: Analyzing the contexts for language remediation. *Topics in Language Disorders* 4:72-85.

Snyder-McLean, L. K., B. Solomson, J. McLean, and S. Sack. 1984. Structuring joint action routines: A strategy for facilitating communication and language development in the classroom. *Seminars in Speech and Language* 5:213-228.

Staab, C. F. 1983. Language functions elicited by meaningful activities: A new dimension in language problems. *Language, Speech and Hearing Services in Schools* 14:164-170.

Steckol, K. 1983. Are we training young language delayed children for future academic failure? In *Treating language disorders,* edited by H. Winitz. Baltimore, MD: University Park Press.

Tourdot, S., and K. Retherford-Stickler. 1985. Children's revisions of directives to younger siblings and a language delayed child. Paper presented at the annual convention of the American Speech-Language-Hearing Association, Washington, DC.

Umiker-Sebeok, D. 1979. Preschool children's interconversational narratives. *Journal of Child Language* 6:91-109.

Wanska, S. K., and J. L. Bedrosian. 1985. Conversational structure and topic performance in mother-child interaction. *Journal of Speech and Hearing Research* 28:579-584.

Warren, S. F., and A. P. Kaiser. 1986. Incidental language teaching: A critical review. *American Speech-Language-Hearing Association* 51(4):291-299.

White, K., and G. Casto. 1985. An integrative review of early intervention efficacy studies with at-risk children: Implications for the handicapped. *Analysis and Intervention in Developmental Disabilities* 5:7-31.

Wollner, S. G. 1983. Communication intentions: How well do language-impaired children do? *Topics in Language Disorders* 4(Dec.):1-14.

Additional Readings:
Annotated Early Childhood Bibliography

Breznau, C. 1981. *Container crafts.* Malver, PA: Instructo/McGraw Hill.

This paperback book contains 20 duplicated designs to be colored, cut, and pasted on half-pint milk cartons. It has easy-to-do projects that can be used for party snacks, crayon holders, desk organizers, or just for fun. This author also has many other paperback books dealing with cutting, pasting, and coloring.

Brigance, A. H. 1978. *Diagnostic inventory of early development.* North Billerica, MA: Curriculum Associates, Inc.

This is an excellent diagnostic test and is easily administered to young children.

Brophy, J. E., T. L. Good, and S. E. Nedler. 1975. *Teaching in the preschool.* New York: Harper and Row.

This book is an excellent source of information for any teacher who is interested in setting up and effectively managing a classroom. It also has chapters on all aspects of child development, assessment, and diagnosis.

Broman, B. 1978. *The early years in childhood education.* Chicago, IL: Rand McNally.

This book discusses many aspects of early childhood education and is very useful to any preschool teacher.

Caplan, T., and F. Caplan. 1983. *The early childhood years: The two- to six-year-old.* New York: Putnam.

This book is a mini-course in child development, an excellent resource for teachers, aides, and parents. It highlights the major theories of leading professionals on early childhood growth and gives extensive information on the landmarks in physical, psychological, and social development of the child between the ages of two and six years.

Cook, R. E., and V. B. Armbruster. 1983. *Adapting early childhood curricula: Suggestions for meeting special needs.* St. Louis, MO: M. V. Mosby.

This book provides teachers, paraprofessionals, and parents with information and techniques needed to help develop curricula and instruction to meet unique needs of individual children within any preschool classroom. It also has extensive annotated references following each chapter.

Decker, C., A. Decker, and J. R. Decker. 1980. *Planning and administering early childhood programs,* 2d ed. Columbus, OH: Charles E. Merrill.

This second-edition volume is an excellent book which states with conviction that thoughtful planning and administration are essential to the success of early childhood programs. It serves as a guide for initial planning of early childhood programs and contains much helpful information.

Doan, R. L. 1979. *Arts and crafts achievement activities, early childhood achievement units.* West Nyack, NY: The Center for Applied Research in Education, Inc.

This book, together with five other units in the series, offers over 250 classroom-tested activities. Other units deal with body awareness, language development, number readiness, science discovery, and social living. Activities are written in lesson plan form for easy adaptation.

Fleming, B., and D. Hamilton. 1977. *Resources for creative teaching in early childhood education.* New York: Harcourt Brace Jovanich.

This perforated, three-hole-punched book provides a quick reference for basic information about many subjects in a practical, scannable format. This book uniquely integrates curriculum ideas and learning opportunities for a given subject into every part of a preschool program.

Forte, I. 1982. *The kid's stuff book of patterns, projects, and plans to perk up early learning programs.* Nashville, TN: Incentive Publications, Inc.

This book contains over 175 reproducible patterns backed with teaching ideas, lesson plans, recipes, art, drama, math, and music activities, as well as language activities.

Hess, R. D., and J. Croft. 1981. *Teachers of young children,* 3d ed. Boston, MA: Houghton Mifflin Co.

This third edition text is an excellent introductory text for anyone entering the field of preschool education. It provides knowledge about characteristics of children in the preschool years, describes curriculum elements of a preschool program, and gives suggestions for situations that might arise in a preschool setting.

Hildebrand, V. 1976. *Introduction to early childhood education*, 2d ed. New York: MacMillan Publishing Company.

This textbook was written especially for teachers who are concerned with teaching children ages three to six years. This book is highly relevant for any person concerned with planning sound programs that foster children's growth and development.

Hohmann, M., B. Banet, and D. P. Weikart. 1979. *Young children in action*. Ypsilanti, MI: The High Scope Press.

This is a cognitively oriented preschool curriculum that can be used as a manual for preschool educators. The authors utilized research and developmental theory to identify the young child's changing characteristics, emerging abilities, developmental limitations, and psychological makeup.

Language Development Program of Western New York, Inc. *Language development profile* (revised in 1983). Tonawanda, NY: unpublished.

This is a notebook written by staff and administration to help incoming teachers, aides, and visitors to better understand the nature and needs of language impaired children. Many good ideas are presented to help staff better execute early childhood programs.

Lundsteen, S. W., and N. B. Tarrow. 1981. *Guiding young children's learning: A comprehensive approach to early childhood education*. New York: McGraw-Hill Book Company.

This book covers early childhood education from infancy through the primary grades. It consists of four parts: background history in early childhood education; developmental stages of the child; curriculum designed to promote cognitive, effective, and psycho-physical-motor abilities; and strategies teachers will need to create a special world for young children.

National Association for Education of Young Children. 1984. *Program standards written for criteria for high quality early childhood programs with interpretations*. Washington, DC: NAEYC.

The National Academy of Early Childhood Program's Criteria for High Quality Early Childhood Programs is a paper representing the consensus of the early childhood profession regarding the definition of a good quality group program for young children. The criteria were developed over a three-year period by reviewing fifty documents and research literature on the effects on children of various components of an early childhood program. It is an excellent source for anyone planning an early childhood program.

Pratt-Butler, G. K. 1975. *The three-, four-, and five-year-old in a school setting*. Columbus, OH: Charles E. Merrill.

This book is an introduction to preschool education. It is designed to help teacher, parent, or aide better understand young children and how they learn in a group setting. Many suggestions are given for implementing optimum learning experiences.

Warren, J. 1983. *Crafts: Early learning activities*. Carthage, IL: Monday Morning Books.

This full-size paperback book gives excellent holiday and seasonal ideas for easy-to-do early learning projects for teachers as well as parents of preschool and primary-age children. To order: Good Apple, Inc., Box 299, Carthage, IL 62321-0299.

Wasserman, F., and S. Medow. 1984. *Early childhood seasonal and holiday activities.* Compton, CA: Education Insights.

This book is an excellent resource for activities for all seasons and holidays. It comes in card-file form for easy reference.

Wilmes, L., and D. Wilmes. 1982. *The circle time book.* Dundee, IL: A Building Blocks Publication.

This book is a collection of activities for special events which introduce young children to a variety of holidays, festivals, and special occurrences. It gives excellent ideas for circle time activities.

_____. 1983. *Everyday circle time.* Dundee, IL: A Building Blocks Publication.

This book is a "must" in any preschool classroom. It is a collection of many units, each introduced with an opening activity and then expanded through language and games, fingerplays, stories, recipes, books, and more.

The following journals and magazines may be helpful resources for use with any topic in early childhood education.

Childhood Education. Published by the Association for Childhood Education International, 3615 Wisconsin Avenue NW, Washington, DC 20016.

Children Today. Published by the Children's Bureau, Department of Health, Education, and Welfare, Washington, DC 20013.

Educating Children. Published by the Department of Elementary, Kindergarten, and Nursery Educators of the National Education Association, 1201 Sixteenth Street NW, Washington, DC 20036.

International Journal of Early Childhood. Published by the Organization Mondiale pour l'Education Prescolaire (O.M.E.P.), The United States Committee, 81 Irving Place, New York, NY 10003.

Offspring. Published by Michigan Council of Cooperative Nurseries, Box 1734, East Lansing, MI 48823.

Pre-K Today. Published by Scholastic, Inc., 730 Broadway, New York, NY 10003.

Voice for Children. Published by the Day Care and Child Development Council of America, 1012 Fourteenth Street NW, Washington, DC 20005.

Young Children. Published by the National Association for Education of Young Children, 12834 Connecticut Avenue NW, Washington, DC 20001.

Preparing the Classroom: Use of Space, Furniture, and Learning Materials

Mary Ann Gianni, B.S.E.

Creating the Optimal Physical Environment

The physical environment of the preschool classroom can have a profound effect on the behavior, learning ability, and development of the children who work and play in it. Good learning environments foster optimal growth and development, exercising and challenging children's developing potentials. Poor learning environments do not permit newly developed skills to be used, or they demand that these skills be employed at a level of competence too far beyond the learner's reach (Hohmann et al. 1979).

For language-impaired children, it is critical that there be space for creative interaction as well as an environment that is appropriate for facilitating and recording language change. The classroom setting has been defined as a "treatment context" which "provides a high probability of children's actions upon and within it" (McLean and Snyder-McLean 1978). An optimal setting contains enough space for children to move around and a variety of interesting objects, as well as different people, for the child to interact with (Cole 1982).

Each setting within the classroom should be evaluated in terms of what it offers children and how interesting and "compelling to talk" the classroom and activities are. Activity areas should promote face-to-face interaction with ample free playtime for children to choose topics and conversational partners. When children have opportunity to talk, they become more adept at exploring what language can do.

Clinicians who are new to the management of self-contained classrooms need to be aware of the specific ways in which the environment affects children's behavior. For example, the simple act of making materials visible yet inaccessible may promote use of requesting. Interaction with the physical environment is a very important part of learning for preschool children. They explore and discover most things with their bodies, experiencing the excitement of high places, the motion of tricycles, riding toys and swings, and the texture and shape of the objects in this environment. Children need room to move freely. They need corners where they can be quiet and have a chance to be alone. They also need areas to play, to eat, to clean up, to rest, and to explore objects and books.

Studies have found that there is marked increase of negative and idle behavior under conditions of high density and low resources or equipment. On the other hand, positive and constructive behavior is prevalent in programs with low density and high resources. If high density is unavoidable, the quality and quantity of equipment should be at its maximum (Decker et al. 1980).

Modifying the environment

Careful planning of room arrangement, storage spaces, and equipment is essential to both the smooth mechanical functioning of the class and to the clinician's ability to manage the children's behavior. If facilities are carefully arranged, children will be able to function independently, learning favorable attitudes toward helping, cooperation, and care of materials. For example, children can help clean up after an easel-painting session if sinks are near the art area and they are at the right height. Bathroom lavatories or sinks adjacent to art areas should be about 22 inches high (Hildebrand 1976). While you may not have control over the design of these facilities, you can certainly modify the environment by acquiring stools and appropriate-sized furniture. Children feel more self-sufficient if the handles on the sinks are easily manipulated and they can do a cleanup job without any help from an adult.

Similarly, everything in the room should be planned with the ages of the children in mind. When a program has two-and-a-half-, three-, four-, and five-year-olds in the same classroom, a clinician must remember both extremes. This means small chairs, low tables and shelving, and cubbies that extend to the floor. Most of the storage space should line up with or be built into the walls, although it should be supplemented with portable bookcases and cubbyhole shelving that can be used as dividers between activity areas (Broghy et al. 1975). A good deal of thought must also go into deciding where the children will place their outer clothing, where they will go when they enter the room, how tables are grouped, how individual areas are to be created within the room, and how traffic lanes can be kept clear to avoid bumping into furniture or each other.

Preschool children need more room for unimpeded movement due to their more volatile, emotional nature, immature social skills, and propensity to follow where their spontaneous inquisitiveness leads them. Many behavior problems can be avoided by limiting the stress of forced contact due to cramped space conditions. This will also mean limiting the number of children in the various areas of the room (for example, four children in the block area, two in the home area, two in the book/listening area, three in the water play area, etc.).

Storage space for children's personal items

It is important for preschool children to learn responsibility for the care and organization of their personal possessions and themselves. The classroom arrangement can help facilitate learning this trait.

A typical classroom might have a cloakroom with individual hooks and a bench. However, cloakrooms are not always found in classrooms, particularly in moderate climates. It is often up to the teacher/clinician to provide creative solutions to this organizational problem. Many classrooms have individual cupboards under a counter along one wall, which could be used for storage of coats, lunches, and show-and-tell materials; however, the use of a single space as sole storage for all the children's belongings will likely lead to chaos and coats on the floor, breakage of special items, and hurt feelings. Optimal is a separate place for coats and lunch boxes. A portable coat/lunch rack can be constructed from a metal clothes rack on wheels and two large sheets of pegboard. Put large hooks in the pegboard, securing the hooks on the back side of the pegboard with strong tape to keep the hooks from lifting out. Then attach the pegboard sheets to either side of the rack's upright supports, resting the bottom edges on the wheel bars. The rack can be moved out of the way, even out of the classroom if possible.

Shelf brackets can be hooked into the pegboard near the bottom of the coat rack to provide lunch-box storage space for children in full-day programs. This way, coats and lunches can be kept together. Outside the room, there should be a storage box where children can leave lunch boxes while they play after lunch. Each week, assign one or two children the "work job" of bringing the lunch boxes in after lunch.

There also needs to be "mailbox" space by the door for small personal "show-and-tell" items, notes, and papers coming from or going to each child's home. Particle-board units with many compartments are inexpensive and easily painted. An even less expensive cubby divider can be made with empty cardboard ice cream buckets stacked in a honeycomb pattern. Alternately, label five-quart ice cream pails with each child's name and symbol and line these up on the floor by (or outside) the door. Many clinicians also use folders and notebooks for each child to transport information to and from school.

Keep a stapler and safety pins within reach of the cubby area. Papers should be stapled together before putting them in the children's bins, and very important notes can be pinned directly onto the children's clothing as they leave the room.

Children should have a pattern of getting coats and lunch boxes first, then gathering personal belongings and papers to go home. Children cannot put on their coats while handling other things. Buttoning and zipping are important learning activities in themselves. As children are dismissed to collect their belongings, an aide can direct the children in procedure as well as help teach dressing skills. Arrival and dismissal times are a rich source for practicing self-help skills. Sample activities to employ during these times are presented in the chapter on behavior management.

All personal spaces should be labeled with the child's name and a symbol which combines shape and color for reinforcement of those concepts (for example, Tecia = red circle, Brad = blue triangle). At the beginning of the year, include a photograph or photocopy of a picture of the child on these spaces for initial success, security, and self-concept. As the children are able to recognize their names, let them place their photographs on a special "I Can Read My Name" poster.

Because preschoolers are very accident-prone—during water play, painting, or even just having a snack—all children, even those who are toilet trained, should have a complete change of clothing available. This should include a shirt, long pants, underwear, socks, and shoes, if possible. These should be clearly labeled and accessible, although they don't need to take up room in the children's cubbies. A cardboard box with labeled bags works well. Keep an inexpensive sweatsuit or sweater on hand for children who come to school inadequately dressed. Additional socks and underwear also should be kept for emergencies when parents fail to replace items that have been used.

Room layout

Many of the physical layout suggestions below are taken from Decker et al. (1980). According to their recommendations, a rectangular room is less formal and easier to arrange. Rooms should not have hidden areas where supervision is impossible. To create this ideal situation, dividers and storage cabinets should be no more than 4' high. This type of room arrangement cuts down on discipline problems and reduces confusion in both adults and children. For example, if there are no wide-open runways for children to run, little running will take place, and the problem of running in the classroom and reprimanding for this behavior will be virtually nonexistent.

In addition to tables and chairs, the room should be designed with ample bulletin board space and display areas for the children's work. All areas of display should be at their eye level to encourage children to comment on, admire, and model from other children's work as well as their own. Space for structured group activities (story hour, films, snack, etc.) should be designed so that there is a minimum of rearranging either before or after an activity (Hess and Croft 1981). It is also very important to follow basically the same routine for most activities. Young children respond to structure very well and thrive on repetition.

Consistent with the nature of language remediation programs, interest centers or "work stations" often are the basis for room arrangements. Such centers are a series of working areas that have a degree of privacy but nonetheless are related to the whole classroom operation. The distinctiveness and integrity of each interest center can be maintained by defining space, allowing sufficient room, and providing acoustical seclusion. It is important that each interest center be well defined with clear boundaries and sufficient space. Space can be defined by many types of barriers. Use shelving, cubbies, boxes, desks, and storage units in conjunction with the walls and corners of the room. Different colored walls or dividers also may be used if the center is to be permanent.

Before deciding on how to define space for an interest center, decide whether or not the space is to be permanent. Most interest centers can be permanent, with perhaps one or two temporary centers that are changed every three or four weeks. Suggestions for these special centers include hospital emergency room (for doctor and nurse activities), fire station, post office, grocery store, beauty shop, fast-food restaurant, department store, movie theater, and construction center. These temporary centers can be designed to help children learn more about the community around them while reinforcing all of the language needed to enjoy this interest center. (See "Theme areas" in the chapter on Planning and Scheduling, and the Lesson Plans sections on Theme Areas and Theme Days and Weeks.)

There should always be sufficient space for the type of activity the interest center is intended to accommodate. More space is required where group play is encouraged and large items are to be spread out, or aggressive acts may take place.

Noise levels from one center should not interfere with work in any other activity center. Adequate acoustical material should be used on floors, walls, and ceilings; headsets may be used with music and listening centers; and centers with similar noise levels should be located near each other. Most literature suggests that noisy and quiet areas should be separated. However, mixing noisy and quiet areas on occasion would resemble more accurately a real-life situation and help keep certain interest areas from appearing to be "boys only" or "girls only."

Many factors enter into the arrangement of interest centers and their equipment and materials, including floor covering, electrical outlets, water source, light intensity, storage requirements, noise level, population requirement for each center, and size and amount of equipment in each center. Specific recommendations are included below for each interest center.

Specific Interest Areas

There can be many different learning centers in a preschool classroom, depending on the nature and needs of the children served. The only limit on the variety of learning centers in a classroom is the imagination of the teachers, aides, and parents who create them. An exhaustive list is provided in *The early years in childhood education* (Broman 1978). Decker et al. (1980) also give much pertinent information in arranging interest centers, some of which is included in the discussions below.

Block area

Since block constructions are easily knocked over by fast-moving traffic, this center should be placed in areas of little or no traffic and should have protection with storage units or dividers that almost completely enclose the area. Hohmann et al. (1979) recommend that the block area and the home center be located near each other to facilitate interaction of the two centers. Additionally, the block area should be covered with low pile carpet if possible, and block shelves also should be carpeted to reduce noise. It is helpful to have pictures of the shapes of blocks as well as the wooden toys that go on the open shelves. Children will put things back in a more orderly fashion when they know where each item belongs; therefore, cleanup time is reduced.

Block-area equipment includes things to build with, to put together and take apart, to fill and empty, and to pretend with. Riding toys, construction benches, tables, chairs, and sand tables should not be included in this area, to give as much space as possible for block building. The block area should be able to accommodate a single child who wants to work alone, with another child, or with a group of children.

Home area

The most common type of dramatic center is the home center. Because children love to pretend to be in an adult world where they can work, play, express their ideas and feelings, and, most importantly, use their language to communicate rules and respond to others' requests, the home center is a most important area in any preschool.

The home area usually requires more space than other areas because of the size of the furniture (stove, refrigerator, sink, chairs, table, doll beds). Additional space is needed if a dress-up area is included. Carpeting is not necessary for acoustical control in this area and is not recommended if children use water in their mini-kitchen.

The boundaries of the home area can be defined by low storage shelves, child-size furniture, storage boxes, a low, versatile block-and-board shelf, or a free-standing mirror.

Identical and similar materials need to be stored together in all work areas where children can see and reach them, and storage places for materials need to be clearly labeled with samples of the materials or with pictures, photographs, or outlines (Hohmann et al. 1979).

Children's backgrounds and experiences must be taken into account when attempting to equip a home area. In order for young children to pretend to be adults, they must have the same materials adults use or similar ones. Keep in mind the cultural backgrounds of children, and include items they would see their families use in preparing special foods and celebrating holidays. Ethnic clothing is an exciting conversational stimulus, and cultural themes can be developed into units that correspond with key holidays or community events.

All home areas should have a table and chairs. Hohmann et al. (1979) recommend a regular round table as being more versatile than a child-sized tea table; such a table can accommodate both real and pretend cooking episodes and "family meals" as well as small group activities.

Art area

The art center should have places for individual and group work. Work surfaces should include the wall (chalkboards and murals), tilted easels for painting, and flat surfaces (tables). Easels located side by side help to foster spontaneous conversation among children.

Consider the convenience of a water supply and an easily cleanable floor surface when determining where to locate an art area. If the area near a sink is not tiled or is not covered with a washable surface, cover the floor with plastic sheeting, an old rug, or newspaper.

An art area should have space for hanging smocks, drying paintings, storing materials, storing projects in progress, and hanging completed projects. If space is limited, cover a blackboard with burlap and attach bulldog clips to hang wet paintings. Clothesline and clips are also handy and drying artwork is raised up out of the way, making use of often-wasted overhead space.

The art center needs many storage shelves for art supplies. Poster and construction paper should be kept from the light, and expendable materials should be restocked constantly. Keep a box of construction paper scraps; the small and odd-shaped pieces are often easy to handle and inspire ideas.

Not all 3- and 4-year-olds will use art materials in the same way (Hohmann et al. 1979). Some will be more interested in exploring them, in learning how they work, and what can be done with them. These authors state that the children's main interest is in the *process* of experimentation rather than in the results of their experimentation. Allow children to make their own objects in their own way, and emphasize process rather than product.

Because much language can be pragmatically taught through making art projects, specific lesson plans have been prepared to demonstrate the many language intervention targets to model, prompt, and elicit during an art session (see Sample Lesson Plans section). Keep in mind that children should not be forced to start or complete any projects in which they do not want to participate. Usually a child will see another child's completed project and then decide to make one also.

Music area

If finances allow, children can listen to music in any of the quiet areas of the classroom with the use of listening stations and headsets. Keep tapes and records available, adding music that fits in with the season or any special classroom theme.

The area for dancing and singing should be physically separate or, ideally, acoustically treated to focus sound within. Carpeting the dance area does not permit as much movement as vinyl flooring but does minimize danger from slipping and falling.

Sand-and-water area

A sand-and-water table is a most enjoyable area for all three- and four-year-olds. This center is usually a large, wheeled, wooden table, with a metal or plastic lining and a stoppered hole for drainage. Most tables have a sturdy cover that turns the table into another work surface, a display table, or an exam table for the hospital theme center. When used for sand play, the table should be located on carpeted surfaces; for water play, table should be located on tile and near a water supply.

Circle area

This area is used for weather and calendar activities at the beginning of the day, closing activities at the end of the day, and whole-group language activities. The morning calendar time should be a clear routine incorporating individual and group practice of time concepts (seasons, days, weeks, months, years, birthdays, holidays, special events, today, yesterday, this week, last week); number concepts (how many children are here, number of days in a week, how many days to Christmas, etc.); and self-concept (name recognition, job responsibility, citizenship, "all about me" display boards, show and tell). (See Sample Lesson Plans section for detailed information about Circle Time.)

Post an interactive calendar board with many individual tasks to be assigned as "jobs." In the first two weeks of the school year, work through the calendar and daily agenda with the children each day. List the agenda on a board for the children to refer to, with pictures placed next to words and each step numbered. A simple daily class schedule also should be set up with movable cards in a pocket chart and be reviewed as part of the morning agenda. Use a pocket chart also to assign the various jobs listed on the calendar.

Children will rapidly become familiar with schedules and lists, memorizing them and occasionally correcting the adults when the schedule is "violated." They enjoy "reading" the schedule as time goes on. The schedule becomes an event menu, and reading the "menu" can be assigned as a job for older children in the group. This provides excellent practice in beginning phonetic associations, guessing as a reading strategy, and memory training.

Concept and manipulation areas

These areas are characterized by children working alone or in a group with staff members' assistance.

Puzzle and game center. Because this is considered a quiet area, it should be located as far as possible from noisy areas of the room. Hohmann et al. (1979) contend that while most children don't mind noise, they do need a quiet place to go when they choose. Low storage shelves can help define a quiet area, with some of the shelves facing into the activity center so children can see the games and puzzles easily and make their selections. Small tables and chairs can be used for children to work on, but most children prefer to spread out on the floor. A rug or joined carpet squares make working on the floor especially inviting. As in other learning areas, materials in the puzzles and games center should be stored in designated areas with clear pictures and labels. Training the children to put items back in their designated places facilitates cleanup and leaves the materials arranged for other children who will be coming into the center.

Book and listening area. Include pillows or beanbag chairs to make the book nook more inviting. Stuffed animals are cozy to read to and talk to when adults cannot be with each child. Store books on slanted racks which display the covers of the books, so children can readily see what is available. (Librarians have long known that books whose covers are displayed are checked out more frequently than those with just the binding edge visible.)

Familiarize yourself with good children's literature. Reading to children has a profound impact on the development of listening skills, receptive language knowledge, and story grammar. In terms of format and context, include a wide range of reading material. Keep on hand patterned language books, cumulative tales, magazines, children's and adult newspapers, books, old and modern classics, fiction and nonfiction, wordless class-made books, and big books that you can use for group reading. Pull interesting and interrelated books from school and public libraries. Always have a theme or concept display of books with associated objects and pictures. Be careful that the collection of books is not simply a gleaning of worn-out garage sale rejects, or only popular TV themes.

Writing and bookmaking area. A separate writing and bookmaking center encourages the simultaneous developmental process of writing. It should always be open as a choice and attended by an adult who can listen and write down stories and words to accompany art work, letters and cards, signs for the home center, and story activities. This adult (clinician, teacher, aide, or parent volunteer) should encourage invented spelling and spontaneous writing. Display examples of all kinds of writing (posters, signs, notes, letters, ads, lists, etc.). Since spelling, writing, reading, and oral language are all developmental and interrelated, they have a special place in the self-contained classroom. Approximations to literacy should be encouraged, just as approximations to oral language are accepted. This means not requiring exact spellings but modeling dictionary adult spelling where possible. Encourage phonetic attempts at spelling for those children who are able, even if they know only one sound/symbol relation.

Make an important space for an individual journal or diary for each child to draw and write in. This records the year-long progress of these skills. Model the use of this journal in front of the group by drawing a picture about yourself or an experience you've had; write about it and label the picture. Children more easily value what their adult role models value.

Provide reasons to write: cards to sick friends, signs for classroom areas, observations about classroom projects and activities. Make classroom books from language experience stories the children dictate. When this center can't be staffed by an adult, encourage independence. In areas such as the science center, tape-record a simple stimulus question for the child to listen to. The child then observes the experiment or display and records an answer. These answers then can be written into a class journal to be read at other times.

Stock the writing center with a variety of papers, writing tools, and writing samples:

- writing tools: pens, pencils, markers
- paper: lined and unlined newsprint, memos, self-stick removable notes, blank checks, spiral notebooks, receipt books, blank forms, blank books, teacher-made cards
- envelopes: all kinds and sizes
- cardboard: oaktag, index cards

- stamps: magazine, book, and record club stamps; wildlife stamps; Christmas seals
- labels and stickers: blanks to design and apply
- typewriter or word processor
- stamps and inkpads
- writing samples: alphabet, examples of different kinds of calligraphy
- magazines, newspapers, and catalogs to cut up
- samples of cards and books to make

For more information on "whole language" approaches to reading, spelling, and writing in a preschool environment, consult *Young Children Can Write: The Beginnings* (Milz 1982), and such authors as Kenneth and Yvetta Goodman, Charles Reed, Carol Chomsky, Marie Clay, and Glenda Bissex.

Treatment area. This is the area for individual or small group therapy. It is also the area where testing can be performed. Obviously, acoustic considerations are critical. Appropriate recording devices (language master, tape recorder, videocassette recorder) should be maintained here. Allocation of space for individual treatment materials (bookshelves, cabinets) can serve the dual purpose of easy access and storage as well as dividing this area from the remaining classroom. If the facility is equipped with a remote-controlled video recording system, it is here that the console and main controls should be located. An ideal setup would include two wall-mounted cameras, along with strategically placed microphones feeding into this video unit.

Additionally, closed-circuit TV or a one-way mirror into the classroom from an adjacent room would allow parents and professionals to observe the children unobtrusively.

Conclusion

The physical arrangement of any classroom stimulates a child's ability to make choices independently and then act upon these choices. A classroom which is divided into well-defined work and play areas, with materials logically arranged and labeled, enables children to have control over their environment, and lets children act as independently as possible. Each area should provide a unique set of materials to be worked with or played with. Then the child knows exactly what is available at all times and what can be done with this material. Decisive, thoughtful planning can be done when an area is chosen by a child, rather than spur-of-the-moment decisions in an unorganized environment.

Children need space—to pretend, to create, to imagine, to sort, to build, to meditate, to work in groups, or to work by themselves. They need space to learn through their actions as well as their peers' actions. They especially need space for their own personal belongings. In this very big world of adults, they need to know there is a special space for *only them.*

A well-arranged classroom reflects the imagination and educational philosophy of the teachers and aides responsible for that classroom. This arrangement, in turn, reflects the success of the relationships between the children and the adults in the classroom, as well as the ways in which children use materials in this ordered environment.

40 / CLASSROOM LAYOUT AND EQUIPMENT

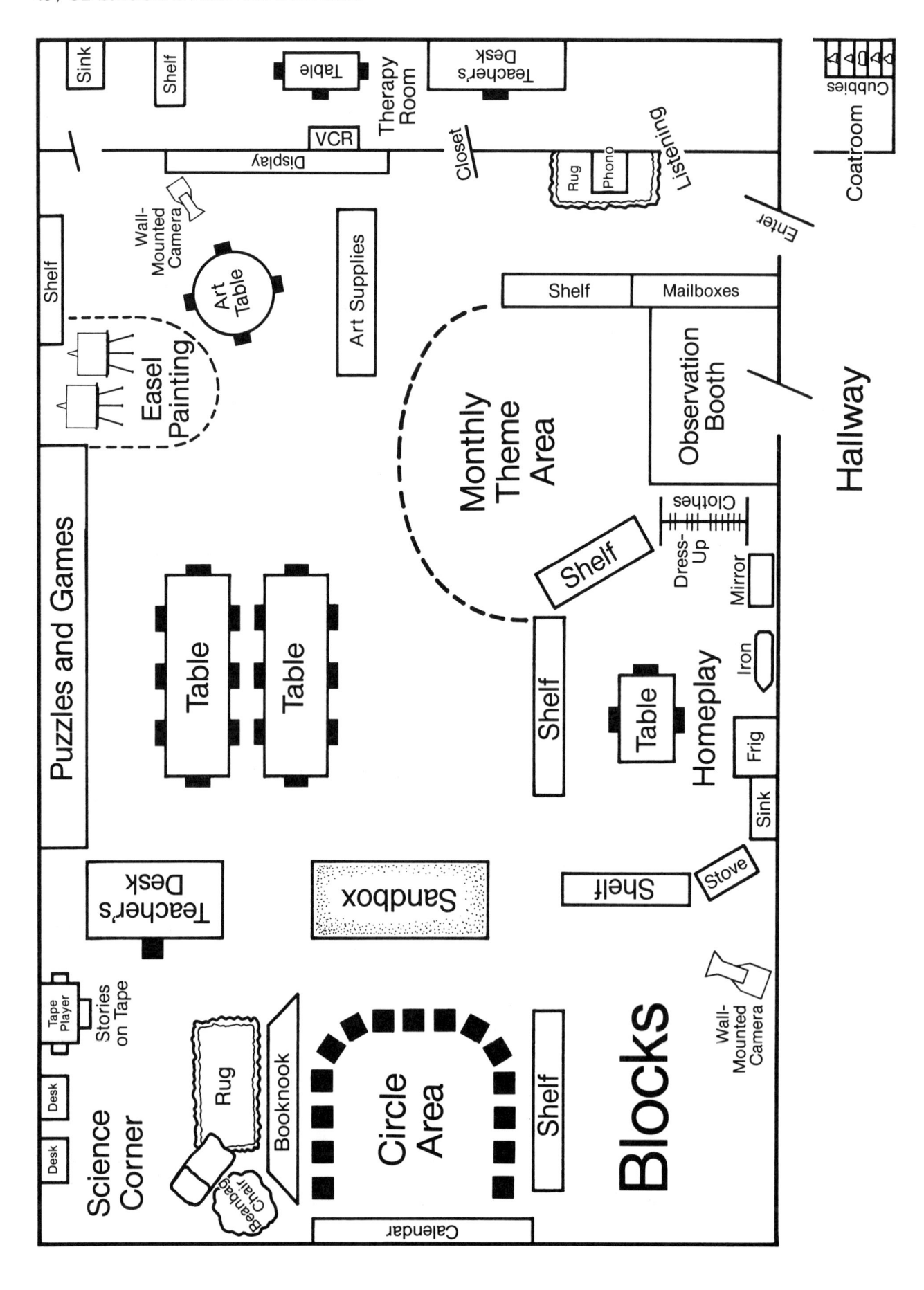

Appendix
Checklist for Arranging and Equipping a Classroom

The following list is one of many taken from Hohmann et al. (1979) and is an excellent reference for any teacher, new or experienced, to refer to at the beginning of each school year.

Room Layout

- The room is divided into several distinct areas or interest centers (such as house, art, block, quiet, construction, sand, music, animal, plant).
- Boundaries are well defined by low shelves, stable screens, or walls with openings so that children and adults can see into the different areas.
- The art area is near a sink.
- Work areas are not cluttered with unnecessary furniture or materials.
- The areas are in corners or on the edges of the room and open into a central planning or meeting area.
- If possible, the art area floor is tiled and the block area is carpeted.
- Traffic flow permits children to work without interruption.
- The house and block areas are adjacent to each other for interrelated play.
- The noisier areas are not close to the quieter areas.

Storage of Materials

- Materials are stored in the area where they are used.
- Shelves, drawers, and containers are labeled with objects, pictures, photographs, or outlines of the contents.
- Identical and similar items are stored together.
- Sets of materials in different sizes are hung or stored so that size differences are apparent.
- Materials within each area are easily accessible to children.
- All materials within children's sight and reach can be used by children.
- The planning board for each area is easily reached and seen within that area. Objects or pictures representative of the area are displayed on the board.
- Materials are stored so that some materials in each area are visible from where the children plan.

Materials

- There is an adequate amount and variety of materials in each area.
- There are unstructured materials in each area that can be used in many ways. For example, poker chips can be used for counting, stacking, matching, sorting, representing food, and money.

- There are a variety of materials available to children to achieve their goals. Examples: papers can be put together with glue, paste, tape, staples, paper clips, string, rubber bands; a house can be made with blocks, paper, wood at workbench, playdough, paint.
- There are materials which can be used for pretending or making representations in each area.
- There are enough materials in each area for children to work simultaneously.
- There are materials which can be manipulated and actively explored in each area.
- There are many real things (plants, animals, real utensils, tools, and instruments) which children can explore.
- Each adult familiarizes children with names and contents of areas.

Personal Storage

- Space is provided for displaying and storing children's work and belongings.
- Display spaces are at child's eye level as much as possible.
- Display space is provided for children's work in each area.
- Individual storage (dish tubs, empty gallon containers, shoe boxes, baskets, vegetable bins) and coat space is provided for each child to store personal belongings. These storage spaces are labeled and placed low enough so that children can use them independently.

Decision Making about Materials

- As equipment is changed or added throughout the year, children should help decide where the new materials should go.
- Children can help make labels for the new items.
- Classroom adults should talk with the children about room arrangements.

Materials for Specific Areas

Block area

The block area includes an ample supply of the following:
building materials
take-apart, put-together materials
materials for filling and emptying
materials for pretending

Riding toys, a workbench, a sand table, table, and chairs are NOT included in the block area.

Home center

The housekeeping area includes an ample supply of the following:
    kitchen equipment for manipulating, sorting, filing, emptying
    materials for dramatic play
    materials for real cooking activities (while adult supervises)

There is a workable clothes storage system for dress-up clothes.

A section of the home area is undefined, allowing for other kinds of role play.

Art area

Include ample supplies of the following types of materials:
    paper of different sizes, textures, colors
    materials for mixing and painting
    materials for holding things together and taking them apart
    materials for making two- and three-dimensional representations

The art area also includes:
    a variety of work surfaces
    workable smock storage
    a place for drying pictures
    a place for storing projects in progress

Introduce art area materials gradually.

Keep the supply of expendable art materials constant.

Quiet area

Include an ample supply of the following kinds of materials:
    materials to sort and build with
    materials to order and build with
    materials to fit together and take apart
    materials for decoding and pretending
    books

Store books in forward-facing racks and change them periodically.

Construction area

Include the following items:
    a sturdy work surface
    tools and wood storage
    tools
    wood, cardboard, styrofoam, etc.

Music area

Include the following items:
    space for movement
    instruments
    a simple record player and/or tape recorder
    records and/or tapes

Sand-and-water area

Include the following items:
- an appropriate sand/water vessel
- a cleanable floor surface
- materials for pretending, scooping, digging, filling, emptying
- additional sand-like materials for variety (beans, styrofoam bits, teddy bear counters, etc.)

Locate the water table near a water source.

Outdoor area

The outdoor area (or large room used exclusively for outdoor activities) includes the following:
- things to climb and balance on
- things to swing on
- things to slide on
- things to get into and under
- things to jump on and over
- things to push, pull, and ride on
- things to kick, throw, and aim for

References

Broman, B. 1978. *The early years in childhood education.* Chicago, IL: Rand McNally.

Brophy, J. E., T. L. Good, and S. E. Nedler. 1975. *Teaching in the preschool.* New York: Harper and Row.

Cole, P. R. 1982. *Language disorders in preschool children.* Englewood Cliffs, NJ: Prentice Hall.

Decker, C., A. Decker, and J. R. Decker. 1980. *Planning and administering early childhood programs,* 2d ed. Columbus, OH: Charles E. Merrill.

Hess, R. D., and D. J. Croft. 1981. *Teachers of young children.* Boston, MA: Houghton Mifflin Co.

Hildebrand, V. 1976. *Introduction to early childhood education,* 2d ed. New York: MacMillan Publishing Co.

Hohmann, M., B. Banet, and D. Weikart. 1979. *Young children in action.* Ypsilanti, MI: The High Scope Press.

McLean, J. E., and L. F. Snyder-McLean. 1978. *A transactional approach to early language training.* Columbus: Charles E. Merrill.

Milz, V. E. 1982. *Young children can write: The beginnings.* Occasional Papers published by the Arizona Center for Research and Development, Tucson, AZ: University of Arizona.

Staffing and Training in the Preschool Language Classroom

Paul E. Quin, M.S., CCC/SLP
Judith L. Bergman, M.S., CCC/SLP
Barbara Zellan, M.S.W., A.C.S.W.

This chapter gives specific recommendations for the staffing requirements of the preschool language classroom. A speech-language pathologist, an early childhood educator, and, assuming a class size of twelve children, one or two instructional aides are suggested. Ancillary staff might also include a social worker, a psychologist, and other learning disabilities specialists. A discussion of peer models, while not strictly considered "classroom staff," is also included.

A large section of this chapter discusses the philosophy of role releasing, where all classroom adults collaborate in training, expertise, and efforts across disciplinary boundaries to provide effective intervention in the classroom setting.

The role of parents in cooperating with intervention efforts is discussed, as well as suggestions on how to elicit parental support and involvement.

Staffing Recommendations

Speech-language pathologist

The role of head teacher in the preschool language classroom needs to be filled by a speech-language pathologist, because more highly trained intervenors are more effective in early childhood training than intervenors without such training (White and Casto 1985). Rather than being an outside resource, the SLP is actively engaged within the classroom setting, planning lessons, evaluating children, and training other classroom adults.

In addition, the SLP trains all classroom adults (early childhood educator, aides, interns, parents) in procedures for cuing, guiding, and prompting children in what to say, when, and to whom, so that the children can gain experience in how language serves them in that particular activity or setting. By including the other classroom adults as trained intervenors, the SLP no longer must function as the primary intervention agent (Craig 1983). Sections later in this chapter offer suggestions for training of parents and classroom staff.

Another aspect of the SLP's role is to determine optimal group size for language intervention with a particular population. In every case, smaller groups have consistently been associated with higher gains on standardized developmental tests (Ruopp 1979), and it is suggested that overall group size, rather than the teacher-child ratio, is the critical factor. When a room is too noisy, little voices cannot be heard even in one-to-one conversations at close range, and those conversations that do get started are often cut short by noise or interruptions. Therefore, three adults for twelve children would promote more effective language intervention than four adults for sixteen, even with the same teacher-to-child and normal-language-peer-to-language-impaired-child ratio. Even smaller total class sizes would be appropriate for more severely language-impaired children.

The importance of maintaining a low adult-to-child ratio to promote verbal interactions with adults should not be minimized, in spite of the contribution of normal language peers. Research shows that verbal interaction with adults significantly influences the development of communicative competence (McCartney 1984).

Early childhood educator

Because an important goal of the self-contained language classroom is to provide language remediation in a social and preacademic environment, it is necessary to have an early childhood educator as part of the team. This professional is able to plan appropriate activities for cognitive, social, and preacademic skills. A speech-language pathologist usually has less training and experience in classroom management and development of skill areas other than language, and with both professionals serving as planners and teachers, the children will develop all skills appropriately and activities can accomplish multiple objectives.

Classroom aides

To encourage interaction, provide more individualized attention, and to provide additional adult models, one or two instructional aides are included. Extensive training in language remediation, provided by the speech-language pathologist (detailed below in the section describing transdisciplinary staffing), allows the aides to take an active and effective role in language intervention throughout the day.

Parents

Parents, with their tremendous emotional investment and expertise and perspectives in dealing with their children, are an invaluable resource to the "official" staff of the preschool language classroom. Positive parent involvement is critical both for the future well-being of the communication-disordered child and for many aspects of the functioning of the classroom. The section in this chapter on parental involvement includes specifics on home visits, written correspondence, discussion groups and workshops, and parents as volunteers in the classroom.

Ancillary staff

Additional staff will probably be involved in classroom activities on a part-time basis. These professionals may include a social worker, a psychologist, and other learning disabilities specialists, as the children's needs dictate. The social worker, particularly, is useful in sharing expertise in child development and social-emotional issues, and in conducting home visits and parent-support groups.

Peer models

Normal-language children in self-contained language classrooms provide powerful models for language-impaired children. While students need interaction with adult models of language, exposure to adult models exclusively may inhibit development of pragmatic skills because adult pragmatics varies from children's pragmatic usage. Children have certain interactions among themselves that do not tend to occur with adults, such as issuing demands, engaging in arguments, making accommodations, and inviting another child to participate in a joint activity (Cole 1982). Peer interactions in nursery school and informal play groups also provide experiences not always available in family units, as children are placed into "same-status alignments" with each other (Corsaro 1981).

The normal-language peers also provide opportunities for staff and parents to observe normal children behaving normally. Tantrums, aggression, and other "undesirable" behaviors are not necessarily attributable to the language disorder in the language-impaired child, but are normal for the child's level of social-emotional development. Behaviors that parents believed to stem from lack of sufficient communication skills are displayed by the peer models in the class, and this observation may help to reduce parental frustration.

The use of peer models usually does not require specific training of peers as long as children with good to excellent language skills and typical social-emotional development are selected. The recommended ratio of normal-language peers to language-impaired children is one to three (three peers and nine language-impaired children for a class of no more than twelve preschoolers).

Training Classroom Adults to Facilitate Language

The number and types of adults available to staff a language classroom depend on staffing patterns and the philosophy of the individual early education program. Some programs have a true transdisciplinary approach to the management of children with language disorders. Psychologists, social workers, early childhood educators, and learning disabilities specialists team with the speech-language pathologist in assessing and treating children who are enrolled in special language classrooms. All these adults regularly observe and interact with the children. Other options include such specialists as consultants, engaging the children periodically.

Other adults are also present in the preschool language classroom. In almost all programs, one or more paraprofessionals are assigned to classrooms for language-impaired children and they, in effect, become part of the teaching team, serving as co-clinicians. Graduate student interns may also assist the SLP in managing the language curriculum. Support staff such as custodians, nurses, and adaptive physical education specialists also can make a contribution to the program. It is expedient to consider training these individuals so that they can function as "active, careful speakers and . . . active, creative listeners" (Friel-Patti and Lougeay-Mottinger 1985, p. 48).

Role releasing

The concept of *role releasing* is helpful in guiding the training of co-teachers, aides, parents, and ancillary staff who come in contact with children in self-contained classrooms. This transdisciplinary role-sharing model promotes cooperation among staff, as well as benefitting the children served. Role releasing means that you will relinquish sole responsibility for language facilitation as the other classroom adults are trained to act as language intervention agents, learning techniques of modeling, expansion, and cuing of selected language targets when interacting with the children. At the same time, role releasing implies that you will assume responsibilities of others (for example, cleaning up, escorting children to the bathroom, organizing materials) who are committed to sharing your role as language facilitator.

Every classroom adult must be perceived as belonging to an authoritative discipline. Each has something important to contribute and each can role-release certain functions with appropriate training and monitoring, while still retaining certain functions. Chart 1 gives examples of the functions retained and released by each classroom adult.

Staff training

Training of classroom adults, critical to the success of role releasing and actually doing language therapy in the classroom context, can take place during specific training sessions and role playing when children are not present, and with feedback in the classroom as the adults engage in language intervention. Charts interspersed throughout this chapter are designed to be reproduced for distribution during training sessions.

Chart 2, "Language intervention in a naturalistic setting," can be used in training classroom adults in the use of appropriate levels of prompt and situational cues to develop (1) comprehension, (2) modeled use, (3) cued use, and (4) independent use of targeted language skills in context. Discuss the first part of the chart with the staff, then use the examples in the second part for role-playing situations during a training session.

Chart 1
Roles retained and released in the preschool language classroom

Authoritative discipline	Retained roles	Released roles
Speech language pathologist	Language assessment Targeting objectives Data interpretation Periodic reassessment Phonological/articulation therapy (occasionally released to graduate student interns) Planning language content of all lessons	Language intervention Data collection Gathering language samples
Early childhood educator	Visual perceptual motor skills assessment Planning arts and crafts projects; gathering materials Planning field trips Ordering consumables	"Teaching" activities (calendar, attendance, arts and crafts, etc.) Setting up the classroom Scheduling (shared with SLP)
Social worker	Diagnostic assessment of family interaction Parental counseling Referrals related to psychological issues Assessment of appropriate disciplinary measures	Observation of child interaction Observation of parent/child, sibling interactions
Classroom aide	Door greeting	Helping change wet or soiled children Cleanup after sessions Accompanying children to bathroom Other maintenance tasks
Parents (The parent is considered an authoritative discipline, though not necessarily functioning in the classroom.)	Primary care of the child	Hugging, holding, praising, comforting as necessary and desirable Guiding, protecting, limiting

© 1990 by Communication Skill Builders, Inc. This page may be reproduced for instructional use.

Chart 2
Language Intervention in a Naturalistic Setting

The four phases

I	II	III	IV
Antecedent			
Therapist* models target form in useful context which demonstrates its meaning (using self-talk or parallel talk).	Therapist models target form; asks child to repeat it at a crucial point in a communicative exchange (when it is most useful to child). Correct production is shaped through modeling and expansion, not by directly correcting the child.	Therapist elicits child's production of target form through verbal prompts that do not contain any part of target form, and/or through other situational cues.	Therapist or peers interact socially with child.
Behavior			
Child performs action, attends to object or another's action while target is modeled.	Child repeats target form, alone or in a phrase or sentence, as functionally appropriate.	Child produces target form, alone or in a phrase or sentence, as is functionally appropriate.	Child produces target form spontaneously, appropriately, and in a generalized context.
Consequence			
Child develops comprehension of target form and of its function in expressing a communicative intent.	Child's production is rewarded by realization of communicative intent.	Child's production achieves the communicative intent.	Child's production achieves the communicative intent.
Data			
Percent of behaviors demonstrating this comprehension	Percent correct production given a complete verbal model	Percent correct productions given a verbal prompt or situational cue	Percent correct use in obligatory contexts

*"Therapist" may include a peer, a parent, or other person. However, additional training is needed to implement Phases II and III.

© 1990 by Communication Skill Builders, Inc. This page may be reproduced for instructional use.

Chart 2 (continued)

Examples

The child in the following examples is 3-1, MLU 2.90. Does not use "under." Target: UNDER. Setting: preschool classroom.

Phase I

Adult is playing a game with the child in the playroom using a large upturned box. Child hides under it. Adult: "Oh, dear, Jimmy is lost. Where are you, Jimmy?" Adult knocks on box. "Aha! You're UNDER this box." Game is repeated over and over. Desks and tables can also be used. Adult also plays this game with other children while Jimmy watches.

Adult builds a block bridge with Jimmy. He pushes cars under it, and the adult pushes them back. Adult: "Here comes the car. It's going UNDER the bridge. Now it's UNDER. Here it is."

Puzzle piece falls to the floor. Adult to Jimmy: "There it is. Please get it. It's right there UNDER the table."

Measurement: Ask the child to put something else under a different box, to put a napkin under a cookie at snack, to find something hidden under a cloth.

Phase II

Adult instructs Jimmy, "Tell Matt (new student) where this goes (showing placement). Tell him, 'Put it UNDER your mailbox.'" Jimmy: "Under your box." Adult: "Thank you, Jimmy, for helping." Jimmy can be asked to tell other children to put items under things at appropriate times throughout the day.

Phase III

Adult is playing a game in which Jimmy has to hide something so another child who is IT can't find it. Adult cues by pointing to the spot under a small chair. "Where can we hide this, Jimmy?" Jimmy: "Right there." Adult puts object on top of chair. Jimmy: "No, no, un...there." Adult: "Oh, UNDER the chair? You want it UNDER?" Jimmy: "Yeah, under chair." (This is Phase III with backup to Phase II, complete model of target form.)

Phase IV

Jimmy to adult: "Help me. I can't get my ball." Adult: "Where is it?" Jimmy: "It roll under that table." Hide/seek games and activities with cars and blocks can be choreographed so that there is a high probability that Jimmy will need to use the target form.

Measurement: Record a very large sample of spontaneous language in segments throughout the morning, observing guidelines so that no verbal prompts or structured teaching occurs. Measure the percentage of correct use in obligatory contexts. Ninety percent or better correct use in even a small number of contexts would be highly significant and would indicate mastery of the target.

© 1990 by Communication Skill Builders, Inc. This page may be reproduced for instructional use.

The desired responses at each of the four levels presented in Chart 2 meet the criteria of behavioral functionality outlined by Guess et al. (1978, cited in Kaczmarek 1985). These responses "(a) produce immediate consequences for the child, (b) have consequences which are potentially reinforcing, (c) have consequences which are specific to the response, and (d) are natural and appropriate to the child's interaction with his environment" (p. 184).

The guidelines listed in Charts 3 and 4 are also useful as staff training tools. Again, these can be demonstrated with role play or by discussing videotaped interactions. Encourage staff to practice these specific techniques with children during interactive- and free-play periods.

Intervention must be seen in terms of *process* as well as *content*. The staff must decide to what extent conversational encounters should be preplanned and how much they can rely on responding to children or initiating spontaneously during work or play interactions. Training also should address the tendency of adults to talk more to the children who talk most to them (Cazden 1981).

The fundamental strategy in the classroom is to promote the child's experience of language "paying off" when it is used appropriately and works as intended. However, classroom staff should not continue to respond to "old inappropriate uses of language in ways that make the language continue to work for the child" (Hart 1982, p. 180). This creates a fine line to tread, since direct correction has been found to slow the acquisition of language skills (Cardoso-Martins and Mervis 1981; Grossfeld and Heller 1980). Charts 3 and 4 offer some classroom language intervention guidelines that may be useful to share with the classroom adults you will be training.

Chart 3
Guidelines for Language Intervention
During Interactive and Free Play Periods

1. Let the child decide what to do (free play).

2. Respond to topics brought up by the child or comment on what the child is doing.

3. For children with MLUs of 3.0 and under, use simple, active, affirmative, declarative sentences most of the time.

4. Express one thought at a time. If your language includes such words as *when, if, and, so,* or *but,* you are using sentence forms which are too complex for children with MLUs of 3.0 and under.

5. Think and formulate phrases BEFORE you speak. You don't always have to speak in complete sentences if it is not conversationally natural.

6. Watch and listen. Don't overload the child with verbiage.

7. If it is appropriate to express negation or to ask a question, check with the goals posted on the walls for each child. In general, questions starting with *who, what,* and *where* are appropriate for all children.

8. Remember that communication has not been rewarding for many of these children. When they talk, give them your full attention, comment on what they say, and don't be afraid to ask for clarification if you can't understand them. At least try to establish what they are talking about, perhaps asking them to show you.

© 1990 by Communication Skill Builders, Inc. This page may be reproduced for instructional use.

Chart 4
Language Intervention Procedures
for Preschool Classroom Adults

The general goal for all adults in the preschool language classroom is to cue, guide, and prompt children in what they say, when, and to whom, so that the children can experience *how language works,* how it can be useful to them in social interactions in the preschool setting.

1. Become a "positive cue" for the child. Give a lot of positive feedback. Catch the child doing the right things, and frequently and openly approve.

2. Remember to:
   - establish eye contact
   - place yourself at the child's level
   - speak naturally but slowly
   - use a firm but gentle tone of voice
   - use simple, short sentences unless otherwise instructed

3. If the child is talking (to self or others):
   - Go to the child and listen. Model good listening.
   - Stay on the child's topic of conversation when you take your "conversational turn." Model topic maintenance.
   - Bring another child into the conversation and encourage children to talk to each other.

4. If the child is not talking:
   - Talk about what the child is doing, just did, or will do next.
   - Comment on the toys and materials the child is using.

5. If the child talks and the utterance is unclear, imprecise, incorrect, or incomplete:
   - Be aware of the correct expectations for this child. If it is appropriate, try to elicit a more effective form without "correcting" the child, that is, without implying that the child did something wrong:
     a. Pause. Ask a clarification question. "Huh? You want the what?" If children have the correct form in their repertoire, they will say it. If not, go on to (b) below.
     b. Repeat what the child said using the correct form, and pause so the child can repeat this if desired.
     c. You may also expand or rephrase what the child says.
     d. Then respond to the content of the child's utterance.

6. If the child is in a situation where language would be useful and is not talking but rather creating a disturbance, cue, model, or prompt the useful language:

Example:

Mary grabs Johnny's block. Johnny pushes Mary away and grabs it back.

Say to Mary, "Mary, Johnny had the block. It was his turn. You need to say [pause], 'I want your block, please,' or 'Can I have your block?'" Mary then says this to Johnny.

Say to Johnny, "Johnny, you can keep the block or you can let Mary have a turn. What will you say to her?" Give him a model if necessary.

Definitions:

Cue: "Mary, what do you need to say?"

Model: "Mary, say 'Johnny, can I have your block?'"

Prompt: "Mary, ask Johnny for the block."

© 1990 by Communication Skill Builders, Inc. This page may be reproduced for instructional use.

Involving Parents in the Treatment Process and in Classroom Dynamics

> Given . . . evidence that children whose parents receive specialized training make greater progress in therapy than those whose parents do not, the question is no longer, "Should parents become involved in the intervention process?" but rather, *HOW* should parents become involved in the intervention process. (Cross 1984, p. 1)

There are several excellent reasons for including parents in self-contained classrooms for language-impaired children. Drawing from a large body of evidence involving normally developing children, it is clear that parents spontaneously modify their input to language-normal children and are responsive language models. "Motherese," the speech patterns mothers tend to use with young children, has been characterized as "the ideal teaching language—syntactically simple, highly repetitive and fluent, containing a large proportion of interrogatives and imperatives, delivered in a higher pitch with exaggerated intonation contours" (Newhoff and Browning 1983, pp. 50-51). In some instances, this style of language tends to help the limited and inattentive child-listener to maintain dialogue and keep conversational focus.

Parent involvement in the treatment process often begins with the clinician analyzing a parent-child interaction in an effort to assess the adequacy of the verbal exchange. Though most parents demonstrate a linguistically nurturing style, not all parents of language-impaired children engage in facilitative dialogue or positive "motherese." Interactions between parents and children who are language impaired may differ from those of normal users (Cross 1978, 1984). Parents of language-impaired children may tend to be more directive and controlling of the child's verbal and nonverbal behaviors by using more imperatives, fewer questions, and more corrections. For these parents, involvement in the treatment process might begin with specific training to alter their manner of verbal interaction. There is a growing body of literature pointing to the positive influence that trained parents can have on the linguistic and communicative competence of their language impaired children (Blodgett et al. 1979; Fey et al. 1978; McLean and Vincent 1984; Sherer and Olswang 1984; Tizard and Rees 1974). Several investigations and collections of research have shown that parents' application of such techniques as expansion of utterances, semantic contingency, and purposeful repetitions accelerated syntactic and vocabulary development in the children studied (Nelson et al. 1983; Newhoff and Browning 1983; Snow and Ferguson 1978).

Involving the parent as a "co-clinician" also has the benefit of supplementing and helping generalize the effects of treatment brought about by clinician-directed intervention. Parents spend considerably more time with their children than do clinicians, and parents generally maintain a positive, nurturing rapport with their children. "The most productive loci of learning may be those times when the child is highly motivated to communicate. If language skills are facilitated in the child's home by the child's family members, problems of extraclinic generalization that may have been the nemesis of language interventionists possibly could be circumvented" (Fey 1986, p. 291).

It seems only natural to deploy parents as "carryover agents" in the child's everyday environment. Train parents to simplify their input, model a target, elaborate the child's language, to find real reasons to model any targeted language form and to repeat it, and to avoid the use of relative or embedded clauses. In programs where such training has taken place, results showed that the procedures were easy for the parents to assimilate, did not change their usual routines, and had a great impact on the child's acquisition of target rules (Culatta 1984).

Additionally, parental involvement may be critical in terms of the child's general adjustment and behavior. Studies have demonstrated that language impaired children are at a higher risk for developing psychiatric and behavior disorders than are other children (Cantwell and Baker 1980; Mattison et al. 1980). These authors considered possible mechanisms "through which speech and language disorders could produce or intensify behavioral disorders. These included impaired peer relationships, reading retardation, or stressful parent-child interaction. Therefore, a child may need one or more of these areas focused on in addition to the speech and language therapy" (Mattison et al. 1980, p. 256). By providing support, education, and counsel, clinicians may help prevent the development of stressful family interactions and, by virtue of establishing the parents' trust, will be able to effect referrals if necessary.

Important attitudes in working with parents

For parent involvement to be a successful component of your program, there must be mutual trust and respect between parent and professional. Too often in the past, parents were viewed as, at best, well meaning but ill informed, or, at worst, ill intentioned and uncaring, when it came to involvement in their child's education. Consider the guidelines below in working to involve parents in the treatment process (adapted from Hetznecker et al. 1978).

1. The extent and type of parent involvement must be determined on an individual basis; an effective program must meet the needs of each parent and child. Not all activities are right for all families.

2. Keep a realistic perspective in terms of parents' commitment. Today's lifestyles often require that both parents work full time, and single parents frequently function as the sole support for the family. Time constraints and the families' priorities may make it difficult for them to commit to all aspects of your program.

3. Cultural factors must be identified. Differences in values and child-rearing styles must be honored.

4. Assume that parents are accurate, truthful informants, capable of changing if presented with a reasonable set of objectives.

5. Give each parent the opportunity to contribute at some level. By being flexible in the roles that parents can perform, you will lessen the chance of certain parents feeling that they are not contributing because of time or logistical constraints.

6. Know that parents have a great emotional investment in their children's success or failure, no matter how indifferent they may appear to be. Judgments about the child may be viewed by the parents as judgments about themselves.

7. Be cognizant of the fact that parents may be experiencing one or more stages of grieving. To them, the child's language disorder may represent a "broken dream" of normality, and parents may be working through anger, indifference, conflict, or denial as a temporary stage of adjustment.

8. Specifically with respect to linguistic aspects of the parent-child interaction, the determination of cause-effect is elusive. "Undesirable" parent behaviors

may be the result of the child's limited communication, not the basis of it. Do not transmit an attitude that the child's parents have caused the problem.

9. Be sensitive to the possibility that using parents as co-clinicians may exert undue pressure on the child or the adult. Each parent-child relationship is different, and not all parents are candidates for this role.

Degree of parental involvement

The structure and style of your parent program will depend on a number of factors. Availability of ancillary personnel is a major determinant of what you will design. For instance, if a social worker is part of the team, the number of home visits, the depth of home-based assessment, and the breadth of family management is likely to be greater than what you can accomplish by yourself. Similarly, your own time constraints, as well as those of the parents, influence the strategies to be chosen. Finally, and most importantly, choose parent training activities on the basis of what you perceive to be the individual need of each child.

It may be helpful to consider the range of parent activities and degree of parent involvement on a continuum. The figure below illustrates this range of involvement. A given parent may participate in a majority of these activities; others may contribute in only a few of these roles. Matching of parents to activities will depend on the objectives you set. As these will change over time, so too will the contributions of the parents.

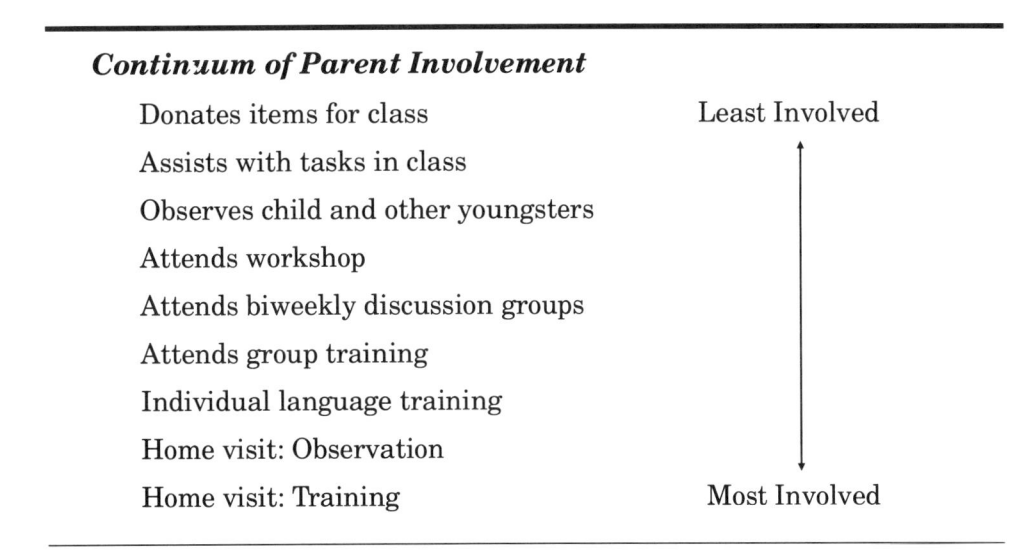

Continuum of Parent Involvement

Donates items for class	Least Involved
Assists with tasks in class	
Observes child and other youngsters	
Attends workshop	
Attends biweekly discussion groups	
Attends group training	
Individual language training	
Home visit: Observation	
Home visit: Training	Most Involved

School-home communication

Frequent and reliable communication should be an ongoing component of your parent program. Several strategies are helpful to consider here.

Daily communication. Daily interaction with parents can be accomplished with a simple note the child takes home, by comments you write on work the child has completed, through reward comments or stickers the child has earned, and, if necessary, with a phone call. This type of casual contact opens up the lines of communication. The exchange of home-school notes can be integrated with classroom activities that emphasize written communication. A designated "mailbox" for such material can become the center for a daily activity that is fun, educational, and stimulating for the child. An additional benefit of daily communication (even a simple listing of the day's activities) is realized when one considers the first question most parents ask of their children when they arrive home: "What did you do in school today?" The usual response is "I don't know," or "I don't remember." With these reports of the day, the parent can review events while they are fresh in the child's memory.

Weekly newsletter. A newsletter is a common feature in many classrooms. The basic format can remain the same from week to week, and a paraprofessional aide could be given the responsibility of updating these each week. Whenever possible, feature children's first names and use direct quotes to add interest to the information.

A newsletter that recalls activities of the past week (perhaps sent home on Fridays) is a good source of information from which the parents can engage in dialogue with the child. The newsletter might be written in a style that contains key language forms (capitalize these for emphasis) at a relatively low reading level so that it is comprehensible when read aloud to the child. A weekly (or bi-daily) newsletter is probably best suited for reinforcing past-tense forms. Sample newsletters that review past classroom events are included in Appendix A at the end of this chapter.

A newsletter that summarizes events planned for the upcoming week is also very helpful. This might include the "theme" being planned, a listing of core vocabulary or relevant concepts parents can preview at home, requests for materials the child should bring, and a few suggested home activities. A distinct advantage of this newsletter-in-advance is that parents can plan activities that are relevant to what will be done in class. For instance, they may visit a zoo if animals are on the agenda, they might plan to watch a relevant television program, accompany the child to the library to select related books, etc. From a cognitive-linguistic standpoint, such activities help build a mental framework which the child brings to the upcoming lessons in school. A sample of this type of newsletter is also included in Appendix A.

Home visits

Using parents to supplement or extend treatment objectives generally involves some degree of assessment followed by parent training. This usually can be accomplished with a home visit, direct training that takes place in the classroom, and occasional one-to-one meetings with the parents.

A home visit, particularly if conducted early in the school year, can yield insights regarding family dynamics, the type and effectiveness of language stimulation in the natural environment, and the nature of the parent-child interaction. In some cases, it may be the site of choice for training the parents in general language stimulation or home-based language activities. While it is ideal to make more than one visit per year, this may place an unreasonable constraint on the clinician's time and often is inconvenient to the parent. However, periodic visits are appropriate for those children who may be living in unusual circumstances or if a social worker or psychologist plans such visits as part of his or her role on the team.

Parents should have a general understanding of purpose and mechanics of the home visit program. This can be explained to them in an initial meeting when they are given health forms and other permission slips to sign when their child first enters a program, or in a preliminary letter and/or parent meeting prior to beginning home visits in an ongoing program.

Scheduling home visits. Form 1 in Appendix B at the end of this chapter is an example of a preliminary information form on which parents indicate preferred days and times among the choices given and also indicate driving directions to their homes. You may reproduce this form and distribute it to each child's parents at the beginning of the year, filing the returned sheets for reference later in the year.

Two to three weeks prior to each home visit, send home an appointment form with a confirmation section to be returned to you (Form 2 in Appendix B). Fill out the top half of each sheet after scheduling visits for the entire class, referring to the parents' preferences you have on file.

What to bring for a home visit. The following is a convenient checklist of documents (and their location in Appendix B) which are useful to have when conducting a home visit:

_____ Driving directions with parents' phone number and address (Form 1)

_____ List of child's current language objectives

_____ Parent evaluation form (Form 3)

_____ Home visit contact record (Form 4)

_____ Blank "Suggestions for Language Enrichment" sheet (Form 5) if this is the first visit. If this is not the first home visit, bring a copy of the "Suggestions" form, completed after the last visit.

_____ Clipboard or notebook, pen

Have the list of the child's current objectives under a blank sheet of paper for ready reference. Use the paper for jotting down notes on what transpired during the visit, specific games the child engaged in, toys brought out, specific techniques demonstrated, and targets addressed. These notations will help later in documenting the visit and completing a new "Suggestions" form for the parents' reference.

Psychological dimensions. An important aspect of the clinician's preparation for the home visit is to be aware of certain psychological issues and to reflect thoughtfully on how you will deal with them. As a new adult and "specialist" coming into the home, you may be considered as a "judge" of both the parents and their home. They have a child with a "handicap" or "problem." They naturally will want to demonstrate, in many ways, often including a spotless house with not a toy out of place, that it really wasn't their "fault" (although they may feel guilty) and that they are really very good parents (which they most likely are). They may or may not be aware of these feelings but will watch you carefully for any verbal or nonverbal signs of approval or disapproval.

The following guidelines can help in relaxing parents and creating a natural and spontaneous atmosphere conducive to a productive home visit. After greeting everyone, give parents the parents' evaluation form. Mention the importance of receiving their feedback and evaluation of the visit. Ask them to complete it after the visit and to bring it to school the next day with their child.

This immediately puts them in the position of evaluating you and may help in removing some of the barriers parents perceive between themselves and the professional.

Second, remember that people do their best in dealing with life's problems and challenges based on their current belief system and level of knowledge. Acknowledge, even nonverbally, that these parents are doing their best.

Third, reiterate that the purpose of the visit is to observe the family engaged together in the child's favorite activities and perhaps to demonstrate additional ways to talk and play with the child that will best stimulate language development. (Keep in mind that to "observe" means to "make note of" without necessarily being critical or judgmental.) Be ready to answer parents' questions, but reserve extended discussions for parent conferences when the child is not present. Indicate that there will be many opportunities during classroom visits, parent discussion groups, and workshops, where they can pursue discussions about their child and about speech and language development.

Finally, refrain from making evaluative comments during the visit except, perhaps, to comment positively on the suitability of a game, toy, technique, or activity. Note: Don't comment on the immaculate house or the mother may exhaust herself getting ready for each succeeding visit, and even cancel if she doesn't have time to clean up beforehand. Also, avoid assuming the role of classroom teacher, therapist, or disciplinarian. You are there as a special guest, in a helping—not directing—role.

Conducting the home visit. If this is the first visit, the child will be very excited to see a familiar staff member "out of context" and probably will want to show off the bedroom. After giving the mother or father the parent evaluation form, follow the child willingly, inviting the parent to come. Remember, you are modeling the best communication style for this child from the moment you arrive. Be spontaneous, but also be mindful of modeling for the parent.

Invite the child to select a favorite toy or game and to bring it out to the playroom, living room, or kitchen, unless the parent seems to indicate that something else has been planned. It doesn't really matter what the agenda is; *everything* will provide opportunities for language stimulation. Be flexible, be observant, and be creative, referring frequently and unobtrusively to the list of the child's objectives to see what could be modeled naturally and expanded for any activity that occurs.

Model and expand the child's utterances. Use parallel talk if appropriate, commenting on ongoing activities. While interacting with the child, comment aside to the parents or glance to see that they are aware of what language technique is being used. Be direct in noting that correcting is NOT recommended, and that research has shown this slows down learning. Be understanding if parents admit that they have been doing this, thinking it was the right thing to do, but demonstrate other techniques that may work better. Do not directly correct the parents' way of responding to the child. Model "not correcting the child" by not directly correcting the parent. Just respond to the child in a better way and point it out as a good technique.

When a child is finished with a chosen activity, feel free to suggest others. When you are familiar with the toys and materials available in the house and the types of activities favored by the child, go ahead and suggest a particular activity that will permit modeling of a specific language target form or skill.

Encourage other family members to join in, but do not insist. In one family, the father may be home specifically to take care of the toddler-aged sibling so the mother can give the home visit her full attention. In another, an older brother or sister may come home from school in the middle of a visit and compete for attention unless readily included. A grandparent may want to sit and watch but is reluctant to participate. Be nondirective and flexible, but remember that this is the *child's* time, and you are that child's special visitor.

Documenting the home visit. As soon after the visit as possible, complete the Home Visit Contact Record (Form 4 in Appendix B), making candid notes about what occurred, and the Suggestions form (Form 5 in Appendix B). In completing the Suggestions form, remember that it is to be written for the parents to use. Suggest that they post it on the inside of a kitchen cabinet where it will be unobtrusive but available for ready reference, or on the refrigerator. Ask parents to save all Suggestions forms, since some forms will refer to information on earlier sheets if work with a specific technique or target is still indicated.

At the end of the school year, three documentation files will exist: the parents' evaluations of the visits, candid notes about the visits, and all the Suggestions forms.

If advisable, share some or all of these with the social worker, if one is part of the team. This information is very helpful in instances where stressful interactions are observed during a home visit.

Parent training

It is unrealistic to expect parents to remember what was demonstrated to them or to learn to use any technique with ease after only one visit. The purpose of the "Suggestions" form is to give the parents concrete reminders of what transpired and to reinforce your demonstrations. Fill out this form as soon as possible after the visit, making a copy for reference, a copy for the parents, and, if necessary, a copy for the school records. Expect to repeat instructions from one visit to the next and from one Suggestions form to the next.

The core of parent training is likely to occur in the treatment setting. You may have had an opportunity to assess the parent-child interaction as part of your initial evaluation. Many observational forms exist for this purpose. Of particular merit is the Russo and Owens protocol (1982).

Training a parent in methods of interactive language stimulation typically is done through live demonstration and active participation, or videotaped observation followed by practice. Observation is critical. Use the same techniques as discussed above in the paragraphs on the home visit: model and expand the child's utterances, use parallel talk if appropriate, comment on ongoing activities, and be explicit about the avoidance of "correction of language form." After the parent has observed you in interaction with the child, have the parent join you in the dialogue and try the particular strategy you modeled. Evaluate the parent's behavior, but be judicious in the verbal feedback given. Again, remember that it is unrealistic to expect parents to remember what was demonstrated or to learn a technique after a single training session.

The list below contains suggestions you might want to share with a parent. Generally, these strategies work best with the language impaired child who has normal or near-normal cognitive abilities. As a clinician, you must make your own judgments as to which parents will benefit from these strategies.

Language Modifications for Adults

1. Use short sentences.
2. Use subject-verb-object word order. Avoid permutations.
3. Exaggerate intonation and stress.
4. Avoid overgeneralizations.
5. Emphasize beginnings and endings of utterances.
6. Make context clear.
7. Point out and name interesting things and events. Comment and expand.
8. Label events as they occur.

If the parent training is more directed toward home-based treatment activities or generalization strategies, the following guidelines might serve to structure the training sessions you design:

Home tasks should be:

- simple
- concrete
- specific
- meaningful
- measurable
- brief

You need to:

- make sure the parent has time to carry out a program.
- make sure the nature of the parent's interaction is supportive. If not, direct parent involvement is contraindicated.
- use clear, plain English. AVOID JARGON.
- give clear, written directions.
- give parents the necessary stimuli and materials to complete the task at home.
- avoid placing undue pressure or inadvertently eliciting a feeling of guilt should they not follow through.

For effectiveness, parents need to:

- clearly understand the task.
- understand why the task will help the child.
- be able to effectively identify and discriminate between desired and undesired responses.
- apply selective, natural reinforcement.
- demonstrate to you that they can carry out the task before being asked to do so at home.

A number of methods can be employed in training parents to carry out specific techniques at home. Observation and videotape demonstration have already been discussed. Consider the use of role playing, with you playing the child. In this format, parents feel more at ease when trying out the activity or strategy because they can make errors without affecting the child. Explanations, handouts, and discussions can be effective during parent conferences, or even small-group training meetings.

Parent workshops and discussion groups. Periodic discussion groups and more formal workshops are excellent vehicles for training and educating parents. Discussion groups also provide a forum for parents to discuss with you and with each other their feelings and attitudes regarding their child's communication disorder. Probably the most important factor for group members is the support received from other parents. Parents suffer serious damage to their self-esteem when their child is less than "perfect." They benefit from empathy, reassurance that they are not alone, alleviation of guilt, and a feeling of caring. Secondly, parents are given an opportunity to discuss feelings, both negative and positive, about their child. With your guidance, and possibly that of the social worker, parents can learn from other parents different techniques for modifying their own methods of language stimulation, discipline, and general interaction with their children. Parents benefit from the closeness that develops in the group and they come to depend and rely on one another in a positive way.

There is no general rule as to how often discussion groups should meet. This is highly variable, ranging anywhere from being required and scheduled every two weeks, to meeting as desired once a month. Staff availability might be a contributing factor in scheduling frequency. If a social worker, an early childhood educator, and/or a psychologist are part of the team, consider rotating the leadership of the group.

One problem that presents a major challenge is involving fathers in the counseling/education process. Part of the difficulty stems from scheduling meetings during the day, but evening meetings, if scheduled too often, may become more of a burden than a benefit. One solution might be to emphasize that attendance by both parents at each meeting is not expected, that a single representative from the family will suffice.

Another format for parental training and involvement is the more formal parent workshop. Rather than serving as a period of open discussion, these workshops, no more than three per year, present a very defined topic of interest. Parent workshops can be tailored to instruct parents in strategies for language interaction, to provide information and education about the development of speech and language, the impact of communication disorders on preacademic and academic success, problems of socialization experienced by this population, aspects of development other than communication (such as motor, cognitive, self-help, etc.), and issues in child health care. Workshops are an excellent means of discussing related speech disorders seen in language-impaired children, particularly the inevitable period of dysfluency they will experience as language development proceeds.

Strive to be as informal and responsive to the audience's questions as possible. Parents enjoy receiving handouts which may be reviewed with them during the workshop and which reiterate the material presented. The workshop should not exceed one and one half hours in length. It is better to cover a few carefully chosen points well, with ample concrete demonstrations and time for discussion, than to cover a lot of material superficially.

You might take advantage of your staff's expertise or that of professionals in the community by inviting guest speakers to the workshop. Broaden attendance by advertising the topic among other schools and agencies in the area.

Evaluation of formal parent workshops is an important source of feedback. Form 6 in Appendix B at the end of this chapter is an example of a nonthreatening and "nonacademic" form that you could encourage parents to complete. A sample of a year-end survey and questionnaire is also provided in Appendix B (Form 7), to obtain more complete parental feedback on the programs and activities of the entire year.

Participation in other classroom activities. Parent volunteers should always be welcome. Parents can participate in your classroom environment and make contributions that, at least initially, go beyond the obvious focus on their child's language and learning disabilities. You might ask a parent volunteer to oversee craft activities, read to the children, lead a group in a song, take playground duty, be "on call" at work stations, organize a field trip, assist during snack time, run off copies, decorate the room or a bulletin board, or be available as a language model by participating in planned activities.

Recruit parents by informing them of upcoming special events, and list what special talents you could use. Parents or grandparents may have avocational interests that would be fascinating to the class (for example, musical talent, special crafts, pets they could bring, special collections such as dolls, stamps, cards, bugs, etc.).

A by-product of involving parents as assistants is that they will gain a sense of ownership toward the program. For parents initially reluctant to participate in language training, the fact that they are now in the classroom becomes a first step toward developing a productive role in their child's language program.

Above all else, keep the doors of your classroom open. Make parents feel that they can walk in any time and simply observe the process. Reduce or eliminate policies that require notification or permission to visit.

In conclusion, no language classroom program will succeed in generalizing improved language usage and form without parent involvement. From helping with snacks to participating in individual training activities, parents can make a contribution and, in turn, acquire strategies for helping their children to unravel the complexities of language learning.

Appendix A
Samples of School Newsletters and Communications

Preschool Postings

A weekly newsletter from the Children's Language Institute Preschool Program – October 11, 1989

We Walked to the Park

This week we all walkED to the park. We lookED for leaves, pine cones, pine needles, and acorns. It is the FALL and the weather is getting COOLER. The leavES ARE turning yellow and orange and brown. SOME leavES are still green. Some leavES are still ON the treeS BUT some leavES are fallING TO the ground.

We FOUND lots of nice things. We FOUND orange, yellow, and brown leavES. We FOUND green leavES too. We FOUND pine needles and pine cones. The colorED leavES WERE smooth and dry. The pine needles were sharp and prickly.

Pine needles are on EVERGREEN trees. EVERGREEN trees stay green all year long. The pine needles DON'T turn colors.

We put our things in big bags and our teacherS BROUGHT THEM back to our classroom.

We Made a Collage

We gluED our leaves, pine cones, walnuts, twigs, and pine needles onto a picture of a tree. Some leaves were ON the tree. Some were ON the ground. We colorED the ground brown and green.

Columbus Was a Sailor

We WILL not have school next Monday. Monday WILL be Columbus Day. Judith TOLD us all about Columbus in our Circle on Friday.

Columbus was a sailor. He sailED with lots of other sailors on three ships ON the ocean. He wantED to find land far across the ocean. Everyone said, there's NO land. You'll just come to the end and fall off! But Columbus was right. He FOUND land. We playED Columbus. We had pretend BINOCULARS and we LOOKED for land. We sang (to "Row, row, row your boat"):

Sail, sail, sail your ship.
Sail it night and day.
Look for land, look for land,
All along the way.

We Learned a New Song

Donna TAUGHT us all a new song all about our HANDS.

We open and shut our hands. We give them a clap. We creep and crawl them up to our chin. We open wide our mouth, BUT we do NOT put them IN. We make our hands go BEHIND our back VERY fast. We love this song. Here are the words:

Open, shut them. Open, shut them.
Give a little clap.
Open, shut them. Open, shut them.
Put them in your lap.
Creep them, crawl them,
Creep them, crawl them,
Right up to your chin.
Open wide your little mouth,
But do not put them in.

Preschool Postings

A weekly newsletter from the Children's Language Institute Preschool Program – April 18, 1990

Teddy Bear Week

This week WAS Teddy Bear Week. We all BROUGHT in our own teddy bearS OR other stuffED animals. We had BIG teddy bears, FAT teddy bears, tiny little teddy bears, sleepy teddy bears, and talking teddy bears. We HAD a ceramic teddy bear, a Winnie-the-Pooh teddy bear, a TALL teddy bear wearing a Calvin Klein shirt, a teddy bear FROM Hawaii, a pink teddy bear, a purple, yellow, and green teddy bear, AND a soft blue teddy bear.

Our teddy bears stayED in a Teddy Bear "House" where our fire station used to be. THEY had a cradle to sleep in. THEY had a high chair to sit in and ATE honey from a make-believe honey pot. OUR teddy bears HAD a lot of seats to sit in.

SOME of our teddy bears did not want to stay in our classroom overnight. They WOULD miss us too much, so we TOOK them home after school and we BROUGHT them back every morning. They WERE commutING teddy bears.

We Played Games with Our Teddy Bears

At play time, we TOOK turns playing with our teddy bears in the Teddy Bear House. We WENT camping WITH them. We MADE a tent WITH a tablecloth OVER a table. We put our teddy bears UNDER the tent AND we WENT under too. WHEN we WOKE up, we cookED a pretend camp breakfast and made believe we ATE it.

We had a tea party WITH our teddy bears in the Teddy Bear House. We had FOUR cups of tea. We pourED the tea. We HAD a lot of fun.

Home News about Our Teddy Bears

Melissa got her teddy bear for her birthday. Alyson has one teddy bear that talks back when you talk to it. Her other teddy bear'S name is Cutie Bear. Emily Ann got her teddy bear FOR Christmas. Sarah got her white bear for Christmas from her Uncle Ronnie and namED it "Mary Ann." Jessica got her Hawaiian bear all the way from—you guessed it—Hawaii. Henry said Richie GAVE him his Teddy Bear Bank for his fourth birthday. Michelle HAD two panda bears and a little ceramic bear.

And the Winner Is . . .

On Thursday we HAD a Teddy Bear Contest. Paul and Kay CAME into our room to give the prizes. Every child WON a first-prize blue ribbon FOR HIS OR HER teddy bear. Here are the winners:

    Jessica's—traveled the farthest
    Henry's—the richest
    Richie's—the chubbiest
    Ryan's—the tallest
    Michelle's—the hardest
    Danielle's—the funniest outfit
    Sarah's—the biggest heart
    Melissa's—the friendliest
    Emily Ann's—the most lovable
    Alyssa's—the cutest
    Alyson's—talks back the most
    Beth's—the softest
    Joey's—the roundest
    Samantha's—the smallest
    Brett's—the longest

Appendix B
Sample Forms for Training and Home Visits

This appendix gives examples of some of the forms you can use in communicating with parents regarding home visits and other training opportunities. You can photocopy these forms as they are, or make modifications suitable to your program. Using your school's letterhead for these forms ensures that your phone number will always be available to the parents, as well as giving the "papers from school" a little more impact and identifiability to prevent their being mislaid.

Form 1
Preschool Program Home Visit Information

To the parent/s of _____ Date _____

I would appreciate your completing this form so that I can schedule home visits at our mutual convenience. I am looking forward to observing your child and home this year, and will be able to make suggestions regarding language stimulation and enrichment activities for you and your child.

Thank you.

_____
(signed)

Address _____

_____

Phone _____

Please check preferred afternoon(s) Please check preferred appointment time:
- ☐ Tuesday
- ☐ Wednesday
- ☐ Thursday
- ☐ Friday

- ☐ 1:00 – 2:00 p.m.
- ☐ 1:30 – 2:30 p.m.
- ☐ 2:00 – 3:00 p.m.
- ☐ Other (specify) _____

For parents of children new to the program, please write driving directions to your home from the school. Thank you.

_____

_____

_____

_____

© 1990 by Communication Skill Builders, Inc. This form may be reproduced for instructional use.

Form 2
Home Visit Appointment

To the parent/s of _____ Date _____

From _____

      I have scheduled a home visit on _____
                                                                          (day)

      _____ at _____
           (date)   (time)

      Please return the bottom half of this form to confirm this appointment, or to reschedule if the date and time are not convenient.

Preschool Program Home Visit Confirmation

From the parents of _____

The home visit scheduled for _____ at _____
                                                      (day)   (time)

    ☐ is convenient
    ☐ needs to be rescheduled.
    Suggested date/time to reschedule:

    _____
        (day)   (date)   (time)

Please return this to the school office. Thank you.

© 1990 by Communication Skill Builders, Inc. This form may be reproduced for instructional use.

Form 3
Parent Evaluation of Conference/Home Visit

Date of visit_____ Date of this report _____

Check one: ☐ Home visit   ☐ School conference   ☐ Other

Staff involved: _____

Parent completing this report: _____

We appreciate your completing this form. It will help us to plan visits and meetings that will be of the most value to you and your child. Please leave the completed form in the office. Thank you very much.

1. The purpose of this meeting or visit was explained to me (check one):
    ___ clearly   ___ fairly well   ___ poorly

2. After this meeting or visit, I had a better understanding of (check all that apply):
    ___ My child's current language and speech skill level
    ___ How language develops in young children and what to expect
    ___ How speech develops in young children and what to expect
    ___ The preschool instructional plans for my child
    ___ What my family and I can do at home to help my child's language or speech to develop
    ___ What my family and I should avoid doing and why

3. I feel I need more information about:

4. Which of the following helped the most? (Check all that apply.)
    ___ Having my questions answered
    ___ Looking at tests and reports with the speech-language pathologist
    ___ Talking about my child's language and speech
    ___ Talking about language and speech development
    ___ Watching the speech-language pathologist demonstrate what to do at home
    ___ Reading handouts such as charts and "how to" guides given to us
    ___ Other (specify) _____

Additional comments (optional):

© 1990 by Communication Skill Builders, Inc. This form may be reproduced for instructional use.

Form 4
Home Visit Contact Record

Child's name _____ Date _____

Staff _____

Type of contact: ☐ Home visit ☐ School conference ☐ Other

Person/s involved in contact:

    (father) _____

    (mother) _____

    (sibling) _____

    (other) _____

Objectives of contact:

    ____ To explain initial assessments of the child and current status in language and speech

    ____ To review, plan, and discuss current instructional objectives

    ____ To explain the classroom language intervention activities

    ____ To foster awareness and understanding of speech development

    ____ To foster awareness and understanding of language development

    ____ To observe family interactions and styles of communication with the child

    ____ To recommend language enrichment activities and/or stimulation techniques for the family to use

    ____ Other (specify):

NOTES:

Results:
1. Were the objective/s met? ☐ yes ☐ no ☐ partially
   Comments:

2. Recommendations:

© 1990 by Communication Skill Builders, Inc. This form may be reproduced for instructional use.

Form 5
Suggestions for Language Enrichment Activities

For the parents of _____

From: _____ Date _____

    Suggestions following my visit of _____

© 1990 by Communication Skill Builders, Inc. This form may be reproduced for instructional use.

Form 6
Parent Workshop Evaluation Form
(Sample evaluation for a workshop on speech and language development and intervention)

Workshop title _____ Date _____

Please check the one that best answers each question or completes each statement:

1. In this workshop I received answers to my questions about language development in young children.

    ☐ Agree   ☐ Partially agree   ☐ Disagree

2. As a result of this workshop, I have a better understanding of articulation (pronunciation) skills and how they develop in young children.

    ☐ Agree   ☐ Partially agree   ☐ Disagree

3. As a result of this workshop, I have a better understanding of language enrichment techniques that I can use with my child at home.

    ☐ Agree   ☐ Partially agree   ☐ Disagree

    I have been present during home visits: ☐ Yes   ☐ No

4. The handouts and practical demonstrations given at this workshop were helpful.

    ☐ Agree   ☐ Partially agree   ☐ Disagree

5. Please check all below that apply.
   The most useful aspect/s of this workshop was/were:

    ____ Having my questions discussed

    ____ Hearing the concerns of the other parents

    ____ Watching the practical demonstrations

    ____ Reviewing the handouts

    ____ Other (please specify): _____
    _____
    _____

Thank you.

© 1990 by Communication Skill Builders, Inc. This form may be reproduced for instructional use.

Form 7
Preschool Parent Questionnaire—Year-End Survey
(Sample for a parent's year-end evaluation form)

Dear Parents,

This questionnaire is designed to gain information about the quality of the services provided for you and your child. Please contribute any comments that you wish. We are looking for your thoughts and ideas on how to best meet your needs and those of your child.

Part I

For each item, check the appropriate response.

1. Were you satisfied with the activities provided for your child in the classroom this year?
    ☐ Yes   ☐ No

If not, why? _____

2. Do you feel that your child's needs in the areas of speech/language therapy and socialization were met?
    ☐ Yes   ☐ No

What did your child need that was not provided?

3. How much progress do you feel your child has made in the following areas while in the program *this* year? Please indicate by number the appropriate degree.

    1 = very outstanding progress
    2 = good progress
    3 = adequate progress
    4 = very limited progress
    5 = no progress

Area	*Rating*
Speech and language	_____
Social (playing with other children, helping, sharing, etc.)	_____
Self-help (toileting, feeding, dressing, etc.)	_____
Fine motor (drawing, working puzzles, cutting, etc.)	_____
Gross motor (walking, running, balancing, climbing, etc.)	_____

4. What has your child learned this year that has been most helpful to him/her?

5. What do you wish your child had learned this year that he/she has not?

© 1990 by Communication Skill Builders, Inc. This form may be reproduced for instructional use.

Form 7 *(continued)*

Part II

1. Below is a list of activities offered to parents during the year. Please indicate the activities in which you took part, and describe by number your feelings about each of the activities in which you participated.

       1 = very useful
       2 = somewhat useful
       3 = waste of time

Activity	*Attended*	*Rating*
Workshop #1: Open house	_____	_____
Workshop #2: Advocacy	_____	_____
Workshop #3: Language activity	_____	_____
Observing child in class	_____	_____
Parent-teacher conferences at home	_____	_____
Parent-teacher conferences at school	_____	_____
Receiving a weekly newsletter	_____	_____
Parent-social worker conference in school	_____	_____
Parent-social worker conference at home	_____	_____
Parent group discussion meetings	_____	_____
Other (specify) _____	_____	_____

2. Would other activities have been more useful for you? ☐ Yes ☐ No

   If yes, please name these activities.

3. Of the activities you attended, how effective were they in the following areas? Please indicate by number as follows:

       1 = very effective
       2 = fairly effective
       3 = somewhat effective
       4 = hardly effective
       5 = not at all effective

Area	*Rating*
Helping you understand the preschool program	_____
Helping you understand your child's speech/language problem	_____
Changing the way you deal with your child's speech/language problem	_____
Increasing your ability to work with your child	_____
Helping to understand child behavior and development	_____
Giving you support as a parent	_____

Form 7 *(continued)*

Part III

Read each statement and then indicate by number your feelings regarding your own ability in this area. Rate as follows:

    1 = I am strong in this area.
    2 = My ability is average.
    3 = This is a weaker area for me.

Statement	*Rating*	*Has program helped?*
1. I know and can recognize normal developmental progress.	_____	_____
2. I can use everyday activities as learning opportunities for my child.	_____	_____
3. I can set realistic goals for my child.	_____	_____
4. I can give the child a stable home life.	_____	_____
5. I can set rules and limits for my child's behavior and consistently enforce them.	_____	_____
6. I can build my child's self-esteem.	_____	_____
7. I can accept my child as a unique and valuable individual.	_____	_____
8. I can understand my child's speech and language needs.	_____	_____
9. I can get other family members involved in my child's care and education.	_____	_____
10. I can teach my child skills in daily living (such as dressing, eating, toilet training, etc.).	_____	_____
11. I am aware of my own feelings regarding my child and his/her speech and language problems.	_____	_____

© 1990 by Communication Skill Builders, Inc. This form may be reproduced for instructional use.

Form 7 *(continued)*

Has the program helped?

1. Have both parents been active in the program?   ☐ Yes   ☐ No
   If no, please state reason.

2. Do you have suggestions for enabling or encouraging the inactive parent to be more involved?

3. The morning parents' discussion group has been praised by those who attend. If you have not attended, please state why and under what circumstances you would attend.

4. What do you see as the major strengths of the program?

5. What do you see as the major weaknesses of the program?

6. What changes would you recommend in the program and why?

7. If the program has changed the manner in which you parent in any way not mentioned previously, please explain briefly.

8. When did your child enroll?

9. If your child will be attending kindergarten this coming fall, please state your general expectations and feelings for your child as related to or affected by the program.

Parent signature

Some questions adapted from *Speech parent questionnaire*, Champaign, IL; *Preschool Parent Questionnaire*, Yorktown Heights, NY; KIDS, Dallas, TX.

© 1990 by Communication Skill Builders, Inc. This form may be reproduced for instructional use.

References

Blodgett, E., V. Miller, and J. Nantau. 1979. Facilitative language modeling. Paper presented at the annual meeting of the American Speech-Language-Hearing Association, Atlanta, GA.

Cantwell, D. P., and L. Baker. 1980. Psychiatric and behavioral characteristics of children with communication disorders. *Journal of Pediatric Psychology* 5(2):161-178.

Cardoso-Martins, C., and C. Mervis. 1981. *Maternal speech to prelinguistic Down's syndrome children.* Paper presented at the Gatling Conference for Research in Mental Retardation/Developmental Disabilities, March 1981, Gatlingburg, TN.

Cazden, C. B. 1981. Language development and the preschool environment. In *Language in early childhood education,* edited by C. B. Cazden, 3-16. Washington, DC: National Association for the Education of Young Children.

Cole, P. R. 1982. *Language disorders in preschool children.* Englewood Cliffs, NJ: Prentice Hall.

Corsaro, W. 1981. The development of social cognition in preschool children: Implications for language learning. *Topics in Language Disorders* 1:77-95.

Craig, H. 1983. Applications of pragmatic language models for intervention. In *Pragmatic assessment and intervention issues in language,* edited by T. M. Gallagher and C. A. Prutting. San Diego, CA: College Hill Press.

Cross, T. 1978. Mother's speech and its association with rate of linguistic development in young children. In *The development of communication,* edited by N. Waternson and C. Snow. Chichester, England: Wiley.

_____. 1984. Habilitating the language-impaired child: Ideas from studies of parent-child interaction. *Topics in Language Disorders* 4:1-14.

Culatta, B. 1984. A discourse-based approach to training grammatical rules. *Seminars in Speech and Language* 5:253-262.

Fey, M. 1986. *Language intervention with young children.* San Diego, CA: College Hill Press.

Fey, M., M. Newhoff, and B. Cole. 1978. Language intervention: Effecting changes in mother-child interactions. Paper presented at the meeting of the American Speech-Language-Hearing Association, San Francisco, CA.

Friel-Patti, S., and J. Lougeay-Mottinger. 1985. Preschool language intervention: Some key concerns. *Topics in Language Disorders* 5:40-57.

Grossfeld, C., and E. Heller. 1980. Follow the leader: Why a language impaired child can't be "it." *Working papers in experimental speech pathology and audiology* 9. New York: Department of Communication, Arts, and Sciences, Queens College of the City of New York.

Guess, D., W. Sailor, and D. Baer. 1978. Children with limited language. In *Language intervention strategies,* edited by R. Schiefelbusch. Baltimore, MD: University Park Press.

Hart, B. 1982. Language skills in young children and the management of common problems. In *Early childhood education: Special problems, special solutions,* edited by K. E. Allen and E. M. Goetz, 173-199. Aspen Systems Corporation.

Hetznecker, W., L. E. Arnold, and A. Phillips. 1978. Teachers, principals, and parents: Guidance by educators. In *Helping parents help their children*, edited by E. Arnold. New York: Bruner/Mazel.

Kaczmarek, L. 1985. Integrating language communication objectives into the total preschool curriculum. *Teaching Exceptional Children* 17:183-189.

Mattison, R. E., D. P. Cantwell, and L. Baker. 1980. Behavior problems in children with speech and language retardation. *Child Psychiatry and Human Development* 10(4):246-257.

McCartney, K. 1984. Effect of quality of day care environment on children's language development. *Developmental Psychology* 20:244-260.

McLean, M., and L. Vincent. 1984. The use of expansions as language intervention techniques in the natural environment. *Journal for the Division for Early Childhood* 9(1):57-66.

Nelson, K., G. Carskaddon, and J. Bonvillian. 1983. Syntax acquisition: Impact of experimental variation in adult verbal interaction with the child. *Child Development* 44:497-504.

Newhoff, M., and J. Browning. 1983. Interactional variation: A view from the language-disordered child's world. *Topics in Language Disorders* 4(1):49-60.

Ruopp, R. 1979. *Children at the center: Final report of the National Day Care study*. Washington, DC: U. S. Department of Health, Education and Welfare.

Russo, J. B., and R. B. Owens. 1982. The development of an objective observation tool for parent-child interaction. *Journal of Speech and Hearing Disorders* 47:165-173.

Sherer, N., and L. Olswang. 1984. Role of mothers' expansions in stimulating children's language production. *Journal of Speech and Hearing Research* 27:387-396.

Snow, C., and C. Ferguson, editors. 1978. *Talking to children: Language impact and acquisition*. New York: Cambridge University Press.

Tizard, B., and J. Rees. 1974. A comparison of the effects of adoption, restoration to the natural mother, and continued institutionalization on the cognitive development of four-year-old children. *Child Development* 45:92-99.

White, D., and G. Casto. 1985. An integrative review of early intervention efficacy studies with at-risk children: Implications for the handicapped. *Analysis and Intervention in Developmental Disabilities* 5:7-31.

Planning and Scheduling Language Intervention

Judith L. Bergman, M.S., CCC/SLP

This chapter will cover the elements of scheduling activities throughout the preschool day so that language intervention will most certainly occur during the varied activities provided for the children.

Scheduling to Guide Energy Flow

By scheduling structured learning activities as well as free-play times, a balanced, natural learning environment can be produced which is rich with possibilities for doing language intervention. The chapter on physical layout of the classroom discusses the importance of arranging the physical environment to cue talking. In the same manner, the consistency of schedule, characterized by routines and repetitions, allows for the development of expectancy on the child's part which, in turn, is important to language learning.

Figure 1 is a sample schedule for a half-day program that utilizes the cycles in children's energy levels, with activities that vary in the amount of structure and teacher control. The day begins at 9:00 a.m. with parallel or interactive play, which is moderately structured in that the activities are teacher-selected and all the children at a table engage in the same activity. This encourages topic maintenance in informal, spontaneous conversations.

After a transition activity, the children participate in very structured, teacher-directed Circle activities. Afterward, they are divided into groups of three or four that then disperse around the room for 10-minute "formal" structured language lessons that are completely teacher-directed, even though the lessons resemble games and seem like playtime to the children.

After returning to the Circle for weather, calendar, and helper chart routines, the children select places to play and from then until snack, the activities are progressively less structured and more child-directed. Noise and activity levels gradually increase to their peak during gross motor play outside or in an indoor playroom. By 11 a.m., the children are ready to quiet down for their snack and the quieter, more structured activities that follow.

In this schedule, the most structured activities occur during the first hour in the classroom. The second hour is divided between free play in designated play areas (home play, book nook, arts and crafts, painting, theme area, etc.) and gross motor play. The last half hour is a quieter time. Children easily adapt to this routine and are able to tolerate the structured activities very well once they learn that there is ample time for "real fun" and "play."

PLANNING AND SCHEDULING / 81

Figure 1
Sample Schedule for a Half-Day Program

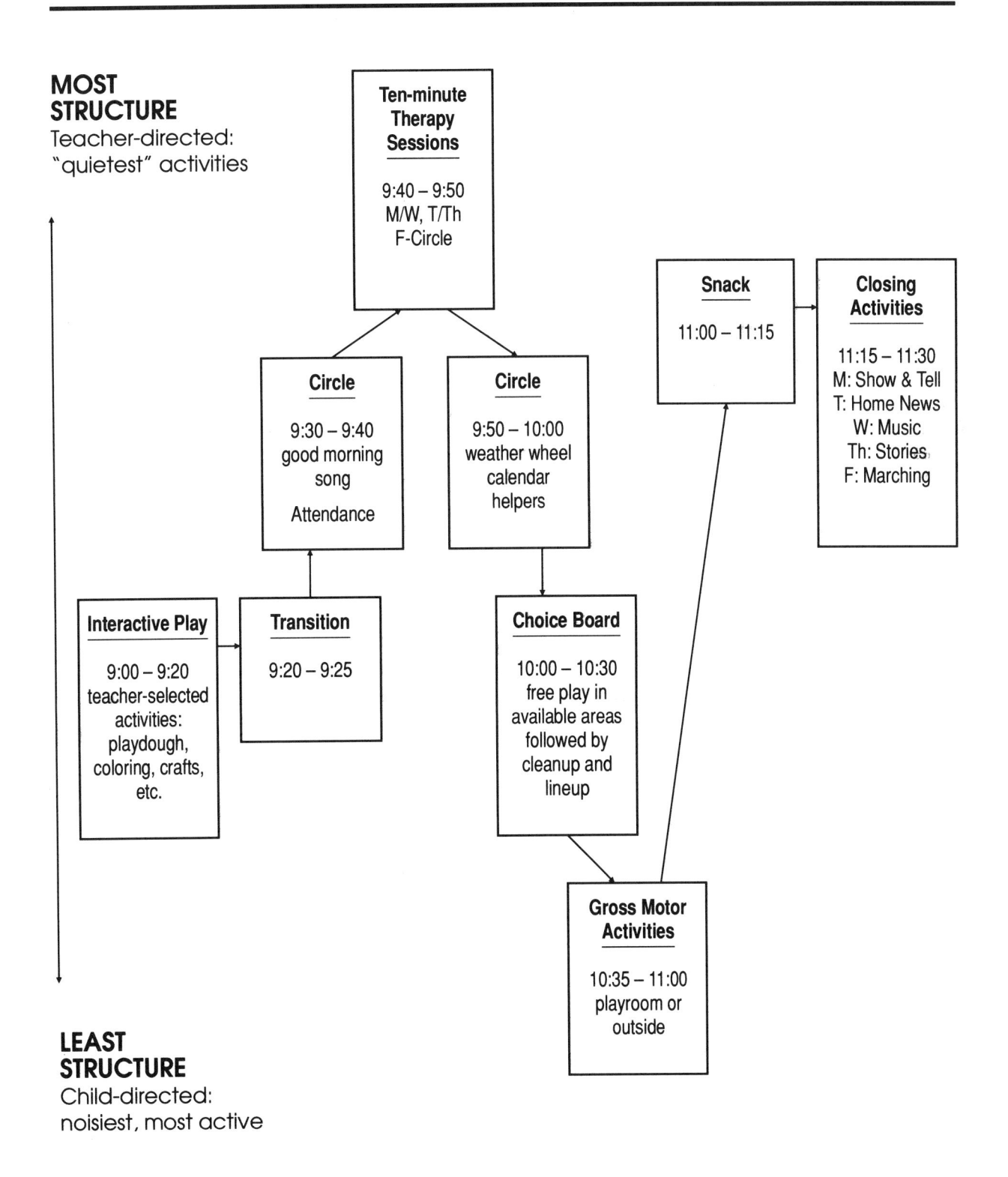

MOST STRUCTURE
Teacher-directed: "quietest" activities

Ten-minute Therapy Sessions
9:40 – 9:50
M/W, T/Th
F-Circle

Circle
9:30 – 9:40
good morning song
Attendance

Circle
9:50 – 10:00
weather wheel
calendar
helpers

Snack
11:00 – 11:15

Closing Activities
11:15 – 11:30
M: Show & Tell
T: Home News
W: Music
Th: Stories
F: Marching

Interactive Play
9:00 – 9:20
teacher-selected activities: playdough, coloring, crafts, etc.

Transition
9:20 – 9:25

Choice Board
10:00 – 10:30
free play in available areas followed by cleanup and lineup

Gross Motor Activities
10:35 – 11:00
playroom or outside

LEAST STRUCTURE
Child-directed: noisiest, most active

82 / PLANNING AND SCHEDULING

Components of the Daily Schedule

The discussion below follows the sample schedule in Figure 1, describing the individual segments in greater detail. Elements of the two-and-a-half-hour schedule can be expanded or curtailed to fit your individual scheduling requirements. Full-day programs may incorporate a supervised lunch period, a time for rest, and additional periods for gross motor activities.

Arrival. As children enter the classroom each morning, there are multiple opportunities for promoting social greeting skills. Other pragmatic functions, such as informing and commenting, are fostered naturally as a classroom adult takes the time to listen to and interact with each child as coats are hung up, lunches are stored, items and notes from home are shared, and so on.

Interactive, directed play provides a rich source of language exchange. As children complete their "arrival" routines and move into the classroom, they join other children at one of several tables set up with table top play materials (see list below), each staffed by a classroom adult. Placing materials in such a way that they are visible but inaccessible will promote requesting from the children. Additionally, children who are already seated at the table can give latecomers directions about obtaining the materials. As the children work with the materials, adults can easily incorporate modeling, expansion, and requests for clarification into the interactions that take place.

The following list suggests materials that are attractive and appealing to children, adapt easily to table top play, and foster creativity in their use:

    Bristle blocks
    Legos®
    Finger painting
    Puzzles
    Picture lotto
    Playdough (with accompanying tools: cookie cutters, rolling pins, sculpting implements, containers for "cookies" and "meatballs," etc.)
    Beads (small and large sets) with laces for stringing
    Dominoes
    Cutting and pasting pictures from magazines and catalogs (also provide paper, scissors, and glue)
    Drawing and coloring (use a variety of media)
    Watercolor paints
    Simple arts and crafts projects
    Pegs and pegboards
    Group collage (perhaps related to the season or the week's theme)
    Small blocks
    Computer games

The period of interactive play is a good time to work with children individually or two at a time, perhaps in an adjoining room, on articulation/phonological process therapy. Evaluations, such as criterion testing or specific evaluation for progress reports, could also be done during this period.

Transitions are very important to plan, especially as class size increases, to reduce aimless wandering and confusion. In the transition between Interactive Play and Circle Time, encourage children to select a book from the Book Nook, to sit on a mat (already arranged in a semicircle in the Circle area), and to "read" the book to themselves or to each other, or to ask an aide or teacher to read to them. Bathroom trips might also be scheduled during this period, especially for younger children who are still mastering potty training.

Circle time activities, scheduled several times throughout the day, are structured activities in that all children are listening to the teacher and only one child may respond at a time. Circle routines provide opportunities for children to gain skills in turn-taking and turn-waiting during such activities as attendance ("Here I am" or "I'm here today"), weather report (the "weatherman" for the day or week looks out the window and turns the pointer to the appropriate picture on the weather wheel), calendar, assignment of class helpers, and a general review of the previous day's events and the upcoming school day. Circle or group activities also allow for group language intervention through interactive stories which contain key linguistic targets or for listening to story books. The traditional "show and tell" assumes importance as a method for encouraging personal narratives, requests for information through questioning, and pragmatic functions of informing and explaining. During a weekly "home news" show-and-tell time, children bring in notebooks in which parents have written about recent activities and home events. Classroom adults can use the notebooks to prompt and model for children who then tell everyone about their "news."

The small-group *structured language therapy lessons* are the most structured and teacher-directed activities of the day. These lessons are usually tailored for treating phonological disorders and fluency or voice deviations, and for specific language features. Structured lessons can be scheduled during interactive play periods, or they can be conducted while some of the other children are engaged in preacademic activities directed by another classroom adult. For children who are attempting to change aspects of speech motor skills, it is sometimes helpful to schedule two lesson periods within one day. When treating language in these structured lessons, be sure to take advantage of opportunities throughout the day to facilitate generalization of these targets.

During *free play,* it is the children who create the agenda of activity and talk. Not all areas are open, to ensure that most children will be clustered in small groups and will have many opportunities for interaction with each other. Children who need a quiet refuge may select the Book Nook, the Science Area, or the Listening Center, easily created from a large, decorated carton and furnished with an uncomplicated (and sturdy) record or tape player with headphones, and appropriate records or tapes.

Children can select the interest center they want to play in from a "choice board," a flannel board at eye level on which laminated catalog pictures illustrate the various centers that will be open on a given day. Laminate and post identical pictures (from a second catalog or magazine) in the various play areas. Special theme areas can be designated with familiar logos or items (for example, a place mat from the local fast-food restaurant, a display of cancelled stamps to designate the Post Office Center, a red cross for the hospital). The picture for each area has a numeral and the corresponding number of stick figures drawn on it to indicate the number of children allowed in the center at one time. Very young children or those who are new to the program cannot be expected to understand or observe this refinement, but nearly all children three-and-a-half and older are able to count the number of children in an area and compare it to the number of stick figures. This has the added benefit of developing the concepts of "too many," "room for one more," "too crowded," etc.

Assign staff members to the different areas on a rotating basis. Studies have shown that conversations among children and between children and staff are more extended and richer in content if there is a "stationary" adult in the interest center (Cazden 1981). Spontaneous, role-played joint action routines often arise in these free-play areas and the teacher, speech-language pathologist, parent, or aide participates on an equal basis in role playing with the children. (See the section below on Theme Areas for further discussion of joint action routines.)

Announcement of *cleanup time* at the end of free play can be an assigned "helper's job," with a helper ringing a bell when cued by a staff member. Children should help clean up in the areas where they played, then line up for gross motor activities, either outside or in a playroom.

Gross motor play involves climbing, swinging, sliding, running, jumping, catching and throwing balls, or joining a dodge ball game, beanbag toss, or other game organized by an adult. If activities become too noisy or rowdy for some children, encourage them to retire, alone or with a buddy, to private corners and nooks of the playground or playroom.

Setting up for snack is an assigned helper job and is accomplished in the empty classroom (while the other children are engaged in gross motor activities) by two children and the speech-language pathologist or early childhood educator. This activity offers many opportunities to model targeted language skills.

The end of the gross motor play period is announced by the two snack helpers ("Snack is ready!"), who have been preparing a snack for the class. As the children line up for the walk back into the classroom, engage them in a guessing game about the identity of the snack food. Give clues about the food's appearance, taste, or category ("It's crunchy, yellow, salty, and shaped like a triangle" or "It's a fruit with red skin"), then ask, "What is it?" Children guess, "Is it corn chips?" "Is it apples?"

Snack time is perhaps the most powerful context of the day for practicing use of language for requesting. During snack time, the classroom adults should sit with small groups of children and control natural consequences for use of language. Feigned misunderstanding and requests for clarification may prompt expanded language form. If a child uses a single word in requesting "milk" or "juice," for example, you may confirm the naming function ("Yes, that's milk") while prompting for a specific language function ("What about the milk?"). This kind of reaction encourages the child to code the key request ("Want milk"). Children's needs (for straws, napkins, second servings, etc.) should never be anticipated, thus encouraging them to ask.

Snack time is also a good time to encourage conversations *between* children, as opposed to more formal, structured, "school" activities where children talk to the teacher. Adults can encourage children to direct remarks to other children by not always looking at the child who is speaking, unless the child is speaking directly to the adult or requesting assistance.

Group children at several small tables, with one adult per table. As children enter the room, they find their own place mats, marked with the child's name and specific symbol (a colored shape unique to that child). Intersperse normal-language peers at the different tables.

After-snack activities to end the morning can be conducted in several different formats. As indicated on the sample schedule in Figure 1, a different activity is planned for each day. Children can be divided into small groups for all but the music and marching activities, with the groups scattering to different corners of the room. Music, songs, movement activities, dances, and rhythm-band marching activities can be done as a large-group activity.

Departure. Preparing to leave at the end of class time can be a potent language lesson as events of the day are reviewed while children are getting coats on and collecting notes and other items. You can keep the level of confusion down somewhat by having the children leave the room in small groups (rather than a mass exodus) to meet their parents in the hallway. Add novelty to the departure routine by having the children crawl through a tunnel (under a teacher's desk or through a large box in the doorway) and tell the speech-language pathologist or other classroom adult about what they did in class that day. The clinician can use this interchange for expansion of language and for providing general feedback regarding the child's behavior and communication performance. As with the "opening" activities, a natural context for using future reference in language occurs as the children inform the clinician of activities they will engage in later that day.

Planning for Language Intervention

Lesson planning is a highly individualized activity, dependent upon such factors as the nature of each child's language disorder, the scope of the curriculum in areas other than speech and language, and whether the class is team taught or managed solely by the speech-language pathologist. The importance of planning and the time that effective planning requires should not be minimized. "Programming language/communication skills across the preschool day is not an easy task; it takes careful planning of objectives, analysis of existing curriculum, coordination of classroom staff, and an effective data collection system" (Kaczmarek 1985, p. 183).

Before beginning the planning process, you will need to develop individualized objectives for each child that are tailored to the priority needs for improving communication and that comply with your program's requirements for accountability (for example, Individual Education Plan format, Individual Family Plans, etc.). These objectives will have been determined through analysis of classroom language samples and data from initial and progress testing.

Write these objectives on large charts, one poster per child, and post the charts on a wall, so that all classroom adults can easily make reference to these during the interactions and activities of the preschool day. Another way to make these objectives visible is to fashion a name tag for each child in which the key targets are listed. Such labels ("target tags") can be designed and crafted by children during a crafts activity. Most children accept these readily and seem to take pride in their individual signs.

The components of the planning process include (1) the daily schedule, (2) lesson plans for arts and crafts, music, cooking, stories, circle activities, and special theme days and weeks, (3) lesson plans for the short, structured language therapy sessions, and (4) planning for theme areas (this includes assembling materials, creating posters to list roles and possible dialogue sequences, and planning related field trips).

In planning the *daily schedule,* you and your staff will select the activities for interactive play, decide which classroom areas will be open during free play, and determine which of the classroom adults will staff which centers. (While some of the interest areas will be available only on a rotating basis, certain centers such as the Home Area, the Building Blocks Center, the special Theme Area, and the Arts and Crafts Center, should always be available to the children.) The early childhood educator can print the day's schedule on a blackboard near the entrance and usually will be the person to make the decisions involved in this component of the planning.

Lesson plans are developed to guarantee that language intervention will occur during the activities that typically take place in the preschool classroom. The second half of this manual, the Sample Lesson Plans section, provides numerous examples of lessons and activities for the different interest centers and theme areas in the classroom. All of the classroom staff can be involved in generating these lesson plans, either choosing subject areas of interest (music, cooking, science, arts and crafts, etc.), or working with the different areas on a rotating basis.

The "specific language target" portion of the plans for each of the selected activities should be developed by the speech-language pathologist (and the graduate student speech-language pathology intern, if available). Each lesson plan in the second half of this manual includes a list of suggested "specific language targets" for that activity, and several of the sections also include a list of "generic" language targets that apply to most of the activities for that interest area.

The lesson plans for the *10-minute structured language therapy* sessions are written by the speech-language pathologist, working from the language targets back to the activity, as opposed to the other lesson plans in which the SLP selects targets needed by many of the children which are appropriate for and intrinsic to the particular activity. A set of sample lesson plans for this structured language therapy is presented in the second half of this manual.

There are a variety of ways to structure a preschool group for participation in these individual or small-group sessions. Children can be divided into groups based on language abilities and age or social/emotional status, with one normal-language peer and two or three high-risk children per group. In the schedule shown on the next page, each group of children has the same lesson on Monday and Wednesday and another lesson on Tuesday and Thursday, with Friday left open for special circle activities. The same staff member presents the same lesson all four days, so that each group of children meets with two staff members per week for structured language therapy. The chart below presents this type of scheduling in a graphic format.

Targets for each group may remain the same from week to week, but the lessons should be changed, to encourage generalization and keep interest high. (Popular lessons, however, may be repeated at three- or four-week intervals, as appropriate.)

Data can be collected during the structured language therapy sessions; see the chapter on Data Collection for a sample form that requires a minimum of writing and that can be individualized for each group and lesson.

Theme areas are a vital element in the preschool language classroom. A theme area is a special setting that duplicates a place of real interest to young children, such as a fire department, a hospital, or a favorite fast-food restaurant. Theme areas can be maintained for at least a month without children losing interest, and can easily be coordinated with field trips, related arts and crafts, music, and story books containing the same theme. These special interest centers provide rich opportunities for language intervention as

Sample Schedule
for Structured Language Intervention Sessions

Group	Monday/Wednesday	Tuesday/Thursday

Group A
  Samantha
  Alyson
  Emily Ann
  Richie*
	4. Mixed-up shoes**
	   possessive nouns
	   [NORMA]
		14. Animal capers
		   I('m) + verb + -ing
		   [PAT]

Group B
  Alyssa
  Henry
  Brett
  Beth*
	14. Animal capers
	   I('m) + verb + -ing
	   [PAT]
		4. Mixed-up shoes
		   possessive nouns
		   [NORMA]

Group C
  Sarah
  Joey
  Danielle*
	17. What's wrong?
	   negatives, contracted copula
	   [MARY ANN]
		27. What happened in between?
		   regular and irregular past tense
		   [JUDITH]

Group D
  Michelle
  Jessica
  Ryan
  Melissa*
	27. What happened in between?
	   regular and irregular past tense
	   [JUDITH]
		17. What's wrong?
		   negatives, contracted copula
		   [MARY ANN]

*Peer model

**The numbers refer to the specific lesson plan in the Structured Language Therapy portion of this manual's Lesson Plans section.

---

children engage in joint action routines, which provide the eight critical elements identified as promoting measurable language gains in language (Snyder-McLean et al. 1984):

1. *An obvious unifying theme or purpose.* The Lesson Plans section of this manual includes suggestions for fast-food restaurant, beauty salon/barber shop, department store, hospital, post office, fire station, and supermarket activities. Selection of theme areas will be influenced by regional preferences and the children's personal experiences.

2. *Joint focus and interaction* must occur, not just parallel activity.

3. *Limited number of clearly delineated roles* (defined by the SLP who writes the plans or "script guides"). The roles are determined by the setting of the theme area. The sample lesson plans specify between two and five roles for each activity.

4. *These roles are exchangeable,* and the classroom adult directing the activity may assume any role in order to model the associated communication or other behaviors.

5. The theme suggests a *logical, nonarbitrary "script" sequence* or "scenario" which provides the "scaffold for the language impaired child to practice targeted communication responses in a naturally sequenced discourse context" (Snyder-McLean et al. 1984, p. 217).

6. *Turn-taking* is structured.

7. *Planned repetition* occurs by keeping the theme area open every day for at least a month, allowing small groups of children to select it during free play. The theme areas tend to be very popular with children, and it is wise to maintain a list of who has participated, to allow equal access to the area.

   Note: Although children are allowed to select the theme area during their free-play periods, the purpose of the theme area is not for children to engage in unstructured play, but rather to be guided by a classroom adult into directed discourse that addresses specific language targets.

8. *Controlled variation* in the activity is planned. For example, the doctor may make house calls, the milk purchased in the supermarket is sour, the postal worker is told that someone has moved.

Children are very receptive to any language structures or discourse routines modeled for them while they are role playing. It is as easy as feeding actors their lines, which in fact is what may occur.

Other joint action routines which often occur spontaneously during free play include giving a baby doll a bath in home play, baking a cake or making dinner for a "family" group in home play, building an airport and having the airplanes land in the building area, and making muffins for "company" in the sandbox.

Theme days and weeks coordinate several different types of lessons. For example, arts and crafts, music, the circle time story, and a related snack may all focus on the theme of patriotism on "Red, White, and Blue Day" (timed to coincide with Presidents' Day in February). The sample lesson plans for Theme Days and Weeks in the Lesson Plans section of the manual offer several suggestions for coordinating the different activities.

Conclusion

Much time and work will be involved in choreographing the "free-style" and apparently loosely structured activities so that language therapy will occur. Intervention in the preschool classroom makes considerable demands of the speech-language pathologist and early childhood educator.

Any clinician who has struggled to keep the interest, attention, and motivation of a squirming preschool child in a sterile therapy cubicle, and has wondered how performance in therapy can be generalized to other contexts, will appreciate the experience of seeing a group of young children bounding into a language intervention classroom just as bright-eyed and eager for adventure in June as they were in September—and demonstrating significant gains on such measures as MLU and standardized tests.

It is also true that a speech-language pathologist attempting to accomplish language intervention in a classroom setting will have moments in the midst of the bustle of free play, on the playground, or cleaning up a spill during snack, when thoughts of "What am I doing here?" and "Is anything really happening?" will intrude. Most traditional training has not been geared toward experientially based therapy with groups of children who are not "under control" at all times.

What is most reassuring are the data already collected and analyzed by preschool SLPs, particularly the data derived from extended classroom language samples. Language training does generalize to natural discourse contexts, especially when it occurs in these contexts or in settings arranged to resemble them. The task of the SLP working with a preschool teacher and aides, when possible, is to make *intentional* teaching of preschool children—intervention on preselected targets—look like or incorporate the features of *incidental teaching* and not sacrifice the data base on which accountability must rest.

References

Cazden, C. B. 1981. Language development and the preschool environment. In *Language in early childhood education,* edited by C. B. Cazden, 3-16. Washington, DC: National Association for the Education of Young Children.

Kaczmarek, L. S. 1985. Integrating language/communication objectives into the total preschool curriculum. *Teaching Exceptional Children* March: 183-189.

Snyder-McLean, L. K., B. Solomson, J. McLean, and S. Sack. 1984. Structuring joint action routines: A strategy for facilitating communication and language development in the classroom. *Seminars in Speech and Language* 5:213-228.

Classroom Management: Guidelines for Understanding and Managing Behavior

Mary Ann Gianni, B.S.E.

Facilitating Young Children's Total Growth in a Preschool Setting

The National Academy of Early Childhood Programs defines a high-quality early childhood program as one which meets the needs and promotes the physical, social, emotional, and cognitive development of the children and adults—parents, staff, and administration—who are involved in the program. Each day of a child's life contributes to the growth and development of a healthy, intelligent, and contributing member of society.

Planning a program for young children should include the following areas: mental development, physical development, emotional development, social development, and creativity (Hildebrand 1976). These areas are not independent in either adults or children. They are all interrelated, and a deficiency in one area may create inadequacies in the others. In planning for children to reach their fullest potential, then, one must plan for the totality of experience for the whole child.

Because these areas of early childhood development are all integrated, it is very important that preschool teachers be reminded of the important ways they can provide opportunities for children to develop them. Optimal development in all these areas derives from positive, supportive, individualized relationships with adults.

The following material is taken from the Program Standards developed by the National Association for Education of Young Children (1984) which are useful to review when planning any preschool program, especially a program for children with mild to mildly moderate language impairment. (Additionally, the appendix at the end of this chapter provides a profile of the social and emotional development of preschoolers and gives some suggestions for integrating your teaching approach to meet the needs of a broad range of developmental levels.)

Be responsive and warm. Adults in the classroom should interact with children frequently. Express respect for and affection toward children by smiling, touching, holding, and speaking to children *at their eye level* throughout the day, particularly on arrival and departure and also when diapering young children. Interaction with adults contributes to all areas of growth and development. Both verbal and nonverbal contact should be frequent.

Be available and responsive to children, encouraging them to share experiences, ideas, and feelings, and listening to them with attention and respect. It is inevitable the children will have to wait for a response at times, but such waiting should be minimized as much as possible, particularly for very young children who need to experience a responsive environment to develop a sense of trust and security.

Converse with children. Speak with children in a friendly, positive, courteous manner. Converse frequently with individual children, asking open-ended questions. Children's communication skills develop from verbal interactions with adults, and open-ended questions prompt more elaborated responses. Expansion techniques should be used as well.

Treat children of all races, religion, and cultures with respect and consideration. Both sexes should be provided with equal opportunities to take part in all activities. Because cultural diversity is an American norm, recognition of and respect for a child's unique heritage is essential.

Encourage independence as developmentally appropriate. Develop independence in routine activities such as picking up toys, wiping spills, personal grooming (toileting, hand washing), obtaining and caring for materials, and other self-help skills. Because independent functioning is a very important part of a young child's growth, give the child as many opportunities for successful practice as possible, even if it means that your schedule might not run as smoothly as planned.

Remember that independent functioning in children will vary with the developmental level of the child. In a classroom setting where the age span might be more than two years, it is essential to keep in mind the developmental levels of each child. An assessment tool such as the *Brigance Diagnostic Inventory of Early Development* (1978) can help define each child's developmental profile.

Help children learn to use resources other than the teacher to answer questions. If a child asks you about something another classmate knows, redirect the child to that classmate. If a question occurs in a group setting, open the question up to all children. The answer might be found in a book or on a sign; point out these resources as the situation arises. The ability of a child to realize that the classroom adults are not the only source of information will help foster independent functioning when you are working with other students. Rehearsal of such resourcefulness will ease problems when children do not have access to the "teacher." Whenever possible, model situations that might arise (for example, "I don't know what to do next." "Where can I get a pencil?" "I have to go to the bathroom." "Can I get a drink?"). Children should know from day to day how to access the bathroom and when they can get a drink. These should be independent of teacher permission. If the bathrooms are outside the classroom, walk children to this area several times until they are familiar with the route.

Use consistent positive guidelines. Use positive techniques of guidance, including redirection, anticipation of and elimination of potential problems, positive reinforcement, and encouragement, rather than competition, comparison, or criticism. Abstain from corporal punishment or other humiliating or frightening discipline techniques. It is extremely important that a classroom be run with consistent, clear rules and that these rules be explained to children and understood by all adults who work in the classroom.

Guidance techniques should be nonpunitive and accompanied by rational explanations of expectations. Limits should be set, but the environment should be arranged so that a minimal number of "no's" are necessary.

Maintain pleasant sound levels. The sound of the preschool environment should be characterized by pleasant conversation, spontaneous laughter, and exclamations of excitement. Harsh or stressful noise should not be tolerated. Likewise, "enforced" quiet is not desirable. The sound of the classroom environment is an indicator of the quality of the adult-child interaction. Since the children in any class, especially one for language-impaired children, are constantly practicing language, conversation is of course to be encouraged. Children's voices, not adults', should predominate.

Help develop appropriate social behavior. Always assist children to be comfortable, relaxed, happy, and involved in play and other activities. Again, the level of involvement will vary, depending on the age of the children, the time of day, type of activity, and other factors. Many times children will display strong emotions such as anger, frustration, and sadness, and adults must keep in mind that these emotions are permissible.

One goal of quality early childhood education is the development of prosocial behavior such as cooperating, helping, taking turns, and talking to solve problems. These behaviors can be fostered through modeling and encouragement rather than through punitive measures.

Classroom adults should have expectations of children's social behavior that are developmentally appropriate. Most social skills develop through interaction with peers and adults and may vary greatly, depending on developmental age and experience. While development of socially appropriate behavior is an important curriculum goal, it is equally important that staff members recognize the developmental differences of young children and adjust their expectations accordingly.

Encourage creativity and cognitive growth. Help children develop individual creativity, the ability to see new relationships, push boundaries beyond present knowledge, and organize ideas aesthetically.

Encourage all children to verbalize feelings and ideas as much as possible. While preverbal children will naturally communicate physically, classroom adults should redirect their actions constructively and encourage verbal expression when possible.

Techniques for Guiding Young Children

Use a *positive suggestion* when dealing with young children. Tell the child what to do instead of what not to do. "We walk in the halls," instead of "Don't run." Speak with a pleasant and encouraging voice and always use "please" and "thank you." Avoid bossy commands in a preschool classroom.

Use *alternative suggestions* rather than negative commands. Suggest an alternative activity, instead of "Don't do that" when a child is exhibiting negative behavior. If a child takes a toy away from another child, suggest a way to share or choose another toy to play with. Children cannot stop doing, but they can do something different.

Always praise and emphasize aspects of behavior that are desirable. Let children know that you have confidence in their ability to use desired behaviors. "Tashelle knows about scissors." "Henry is remembering to keep water in the sink." "Li is very thoughtful to help Richie pick up the crayons." Try to comment on good aspects of a child's behavior, especially a child who often exhibits negative behavior.

Always use "positive strokes." This develops a sense of security, trust, and self-worth in the shy and withdrawn child as well as the normal child. Give quiet children an opportunity for success in social situations by asking them to help the teacher or another child, helping others notice their achievements, giving them praise and encouragement, or noticing a new shirt or belt or a pretty color they are wearing.

Use a soft, calm voice. Speaking softly maintains calmness in the classroom. Firm but soft voices are more effective than harsh, loud voices.

Avoid anger in the children's presence. Adults and children alike have limits of endurance, and punishing and scolding are seldom effective when one is angry. Simply stating that you "feel angry today because . . . " lets the children know how you feel without losing control.

Avoid public confrontations with children. Handle difficult children individually outside the classroom, without calling attention to their negative behavior. When dealing with a child who needs to be removed, give the child a choice of places to go so the child makes the decision and the situation doesn't turn into a confrontation and resistance. "Do you choose to have your cooldown/timeout/thinking time in the yellow chair or the blue chair?" If the child cannot calm down in a chair in the room, then present the choice of trying the chair by the door or outside the room.

Observe a child's behavior to better understand that child's behavior. A push by a young child may indicate a desire for social contact, or it may indicate fatigue or illness. Before attempting to change a behavior, find out the reason behind the behavior.

Facilitate a transition to self-control. Be judicious in your response to undesired behavior. A preschooler or kindergartner should be able to respond to a request for behavioral change but still may need a cushion before the final consequence. A name chart with cards containing yellow "warning" dots and the final "red light" dot helps show the child the progression of occurrences of behavior which needs to change. Set up such a system with the child who is repeatedly in need of discipline. This will help that child chart and remedy a given behavior which is causing repeated reminders. Children need to realize that their behavior is controlled from within themselves, not by adults and others.

Be consistent in your requests and restrictions. Have rules and enforce them. Always let the child know what is expected.

Explain the reasons behind the rules. Whenever possible, add explanations to your verbal directives. "Put the toys in the box. If you throw them, they might break and we might get hurt." This helps the child learn cause/effect relationships.

Do not back down on the rules you have made. Avoid idle threats, and follow through on the rules that you have set. This helps the child learn that you mean what you say.

Give children choices whenever possible. This tends to give children a feeling of freedom in determining their own plans and develops decision-making ability. Make the choice simple, to avoid confusing the child: "Would you like to color or play with blocks?"

Avoid general statements. Preschool children respond better to specific requests. "Put your clothes on" is a general request which makes the task seem complicated for a three- or four-year-old. "Put on your socks" and "Now put on your sneakers" are specific requests that tell the child what you expect.

Avoid asking a question unless you really want to give children a choice. Instead of asking, "Do you want to read a story?" state, "It is time to read a story." With a classroom full of children, avoid asking, "Who would like to be the first to ___"; say, rather, "Jane, you can be first to ___."

Avoid "hurrying" comments. Use unhurried statements, such as, "You can do it quickly" instead of "Hurry up, hurry up." Hurrying a child often tends to slow things down and often produces dislike and confusion for a task.

Isolate overactive children from the group whenever possible, not as a punishment but to decrease the stimulation the child is receiving. Helping the child understand the reasons for isolation is very important. Help the child to comprehend that this is not a punishment, just a calming-down time.

Avoid asking children "What is it?" when commenting on art work or any object they may show you. Encourage children to tell you about the picture or toy, or just comment on how pretty it is or what nice colors they used in a drawing or painting.

Help children to understand and accept their feelings as normal. Children, like everyone else, have feelings of happiness, sadness, anger, loneliness, etc., and should never be made to feel guilty about how they feel.

Creating a Healthy and Positive Social/Emotional Environment

Adults in a preschool classroom should strive to create an atmosphere that is conducive to preventing behavioral and emotional problems. A classroom that prevents these problems also helps resolve conflicts that develop between young children and their environment. The following characteristics are considered essential to optimal growth during the early childhood years: consistency, routines, limits (rules must be definable, reasonable, and enforceable), constructive consequences, logical connections, variety, avoidance of frustration, encouragement of desirable expression of feelings, and promotion of appropriate behavior modeling (Cook and Armbruster 1983).

The following guidelines, taken from Cook and Armbruster (1983), may help to facilitate the development of positive behavior in the classroom.

Group children for playful interaction who are functioning at a similar developmental level. Include children with higher skills if imitation is desired. Group children who are socially compatible. If imitation is definitely a goal, group children by gender. (Researchers believe the tendency to model is high with children of the same sex.) Keep the groups relatively small (two to four) when structured learning activities are involved.

Provide materials appropriate to the skills or interactions desired. Children must learn to use play materials before they can be expected to play with them in cooperative situations. For example, simple games with specific rules (such as Lotto or Candyland®) may be more conducive to cooperative play than less structured play materials such as sand. Observe carefully to determine which materials are most conducive to the behavior desired.

Make sufficient materials available to promote cooperation and imitation. When children outnumber materials available, cooperative play obviously is dependent upon children's willingness to share. If sharing is not a priority, then more materials should be available to the children.

Plan definite activities. Remember that some children must be taught how to imitate or to model the behavior of others.

Quickly reinforce specific desired behaviors. The role of positive reinforcement or reward in guiding and directing children's behavior is well documented. Be prepared to reinforce the behavior of those children modeling a desired behavior, whether it be spontaneous or prompted by the teacher. Merely being in the presence of a good model does not ensure imitation.

When children exhibit desired behaviors, act quickly to say or do something that makes the children feel better about themselves. This reward must be bestowed as soon as possible and should include a verbal statement. Words should clearly state the behavior you wish to see repeated. The statement, "Yang, you may be the first to choose a free-play area because you cleaned up and then sat still and waited so nicely," is more exact and to the point than "Yang, you may be the first to choose your free-play area because you were so helpful." Yang and the other children may not be certain about what is considered helpful.

Identify potential reinforcers. Observe the children carefully to determine their interests, desires, and dislikes. Most young children thoroughly enjoy physical reinforcement such as a hug or pat on the shoulder, but some find this aversive. Children usually respond to smiles and words of praise.

The following list gives some examples of effective reinforcers for young children, along with useful specific rewarding statements (Cook and Armbruster 1983):

Social activity
Verbal praise
Physical praise (hug, pat, smile)
Showing and telling
Helping with task or errand
Applause from others in the class
Going to the head of the line
Displaying art work or photo
Choosing songs for music or play
Phoning parents
Inviting parents to the class

Concrete activity
Food or special treats
Toys
Stamping smiling face on hand
Giving gold stars
Playing with special puppet or game
Giving special hat or cloak to wear
Going on a special field trip
Giving parties
Sending a happy note to parents
Playing records

Rewarding statements
"You are really trying hard. I like that!"
"Thank you very much!"

"Wow!"
"That's right. Good for you!"
"You should be proud of your good work today."
"I appreciate your help."
"Give yourself a smiling face for being so helpful."
"Thank you for using an inside voice."
"I like the way Johnny is sitting."

When children enter a preschool classroom with behaviors and attitudes that interfere with learning, it is very important to help them overcome their overactivity or shyness, their lack of self-discipline, or their over-dependency on adults. Positive reinforcement and appropriate modeling of behavior should always be used to help promote social and emotional development, but most importantly, enhancing young children's self-esteem should be an ever-present goal.

Respecting the Value of Play

The value of play for the younger child is being publicized more and more. Newspapers and magazines are advising parents on how to select toys for their children according to their interests and level of development. It is also becoming easier for teachers to convince parents that although children look as if they are "just playing," they are actually "working" (Cook and Armbruster 1983). The idea that painting, coloring, and pasting develop fine motor skills, that puppet play and housekeeping activities as well as all learning-center activities foster language skills, and that cooperation can be taught in the puzzles and games area and block center is becoming more widely accepted. All learning areas set up in the classroom can and should help develop language skills if teachers and aides are aware of the children's individual language needs.

It is extremely important to create an environment that promotes spontaneous and appropriately directed play (Cook and Armbruster 1983). Early childhood educators have long realized the need for play activities within all preschool curricula, but the issue of accountability has jeopardized the role of spontaneous play in some classrooms. The challenge now is to create a three-way balance among less structured creative activities, freedom of choice, and directed tasks designed to remedy developmental deficits (Cook and Armbruster 1983). The following guidelines should aid in setting the stage for productive free-play time (Cook and Armbruster 1983).

Establishing rules and guidelines

1. Keep rules simple and limited in number.

2. Telling children rules is important but not very effective. They will need to learn guidelines by observation and experience, and all classroom adults should have the rules firmly in mind.

3. Rules should be designed to establish thoughtful, kind, and courteous behavior.

    a. The child who chooses a toy first may decide to play alone or with others. The child's decision should be respected.

b. Sharing is not required, especially if the item to be shared belongs to a particular child. However, sharing **is** encouraged. Providing duplicate items of very popular toys helps to solve this problem of sharing.

c. Children wanting to join in an established group must be invited to join. The newcomers may ask to play, but should not move in without a welcome.

d. Just as child newcomers should not barge into an established group, so adult newcomers (teachers or parents) should ask permission and be accepted.

e. Good manners are modeled and expected. All classroom adults should routinely use "May I," "please," and "thank you." Children absorb these courtesies quickly.

f. When a child or group is finished with an item, the item must be returned to its proper place before a different toy or game is chosen.

g. Respect a child's wish to just watch for a while.

Play areas

1. Provide adequate space both indoors and out. Avoid crowding.
2. Arrange small play spaces, separated by shelves or other dividers.
3. Prepare larger spaces for cooperative play with blocks and other building materials.
4. Maintain the same basic room arrangement over time, but vary the play materials available. Have a storage area where toys may be withdrawn from active circulation for a while.
5. Include clay and easels but monitor their use.
6. Puppets, dolls and doll houses, barns, and animals should be regularly available. These imagination stimulators require set-up space, whether used by a single child or with a group.
7. Remove toys that appear to encourage an activity or noise level incompatible with the best interests of all the children. In a small area, larger cars and trucks usually generate too high an activity level for safety.
8. Plan to alternate indoor and outdoor play whenever possible. Outdoor areas should provide safe climbing and running spaces, as well as tricycles and structures for crawling in, over, and under.
9. Be alert for special needs.

Free play

1. Respect children's abilities to choose activities suited to their present learning needs. By providing a range of materials and possible activities, you are allowing the self-knowledge of each child to function.
2. Trust each child to use good judgment. Interfere only if real danger or unkindness is imminent. *Anticipate* and *prevent* trouble rather than punish it after the fact.
3. Be aware of what is happening throughout the room. Even when attending to one individual child, the teacher must be alert. Evidence of this awareness from the beginning leads children to follow the rules consistently.

4. Avoid overprotecting the child who lacks assertiveness. When more aggressive children are forced to share, the unassertive child is rewarded for a lack of assertiveness. Rather, suggest to quiet ones that they ask for a turn. If they fuss, remove the object in question for a time. Explain that they will have to resolve the problem themselves.

5. If an unacceptable behavior persists, reevaluate the whole situation. For example, if objects are being thrown in the wrong place, move the throwers to a place where it is appropriate to throw.

6. Avoid making children self-conscious. Calling everyone's attention to a mistake or a mess is very unkind.

7. Avoid comparisons. Respect uniqueness consistently.

Appendix
Social and Emotional Development of the Preschool Child
Barbara Zellan, M.S.W., A.C.S.W.

The purpose of this appendix is to provide an overview of the classroom behaviors that can be expected of the preschool child, as well as the developmental basis of such behavior. For a classroom to function smoothly, it is imperative that the teacher be aware of major differences in all areas of development. A 2½-year-old is a far different child in all ways—physically, motorically, cognitively, socially, and, of course, linguistically—from the 5-year-old in the same classroom. This overview provides practical understanding and guidelines; you may also wish to consult the individual references for a fuller grasp of specific concepts.

For purposes of delineation, development will be discussed at 6-month stages, from 2½ to 5 years of age. Since all stages overlap, it is important to remember that each child operates on an individual timetable, based on many different factors. In addition, the child with a mild to moderate speech-language delay may vary from the norms in some areas more significantly than in others.

The world of the very young child is an unstable one, peopled with dangers that lead to behaviors puzzling to adults. Because adults cannot remember this time of life, they are unaware that "many of the problems presented by a child in these early years are, quite simply, disorders created by a primitive mental system that has not yet been subdued and put into its place by rational thought processes" (Fraiberg 1959, p. x).

There are formidable tasks to be accomplished for the primitive mental system to be replaced by orderly, logical, secondary thought processing, particularly during the first five years of life.

The 2½-Year-Old

Each stage of development presents a major task that the child must master prior to moving on to the next stage. The major task for the 2½-year-old is separation. "The ability to trust that mother will indeed return when she leaves becomes an important step in the mastery of the environment and is a necessary prelude to entering nursery school" (Kestenbaum 1980, p. 112). Most children are not able to take this step comfortably until age 3 or 3½. Therefore, the younger child, placed in a preschool setting, can reasonably be expected to have some difficulty separating from the primary caretaker. As part of this process, the 2½-year-old child develops behaviors that can be quite difficult to manage, if one loses sight of the underlying internal struggle.

The struggle for autonomy (that is, separation from mother) begins at about 18 months and continues to 3 or 3½ years. During this same period, toddlers are struggling with control over their own bodies and over their impulses. Reality and the requirements of socialization are thrust more and more on the toddler. Children of this age are presented with their first opportunity to control parents by not performing during efforts at toilet training. With all of these internal and external struggles occurring simultaneously, it is not surprising that the 2½-year-old is often difficult to manage on a one-to-one basis, and can present quite a challenge in a classroom setting.

The child at this age may be characterized by rigidity, assertiveness, negativity, and temper tantrums when thwarted. The 2½-year-old is not ready to interact with peers. This child may look at other children and, if encouraged, play momentarily, but genuine interaction is lacking. The ability to recognize the feelings of others and the impact of their actions is still six months to a year away. Clearly, this age child and the 5-year-old will have little in common. More individualized attention as well as additional patience and understanding will be necessary. Offering choices to a child at this age will only produce more frustration because the child is unable to cope with decision making. Distraction and substitution are more useful and mutually satisfactory methods for gaining cooperation. Structuring and streamlining routines and schedules helps to alleviate some of the internal anxiety and will enable the child to feel in better control.

The 3-Year-Old

The 3-year-old is quieter, more conforming and cooperative, and wishes to please. "Their desire and ability to imitate their elders and to conform make 3-year-olds quite obedient. Due to their enlarged usable vocabulary, most 3-year-olds can be managed by reasoning and distraction" (Caplan and Caplan 1983, p. 157). People are very important, especially mother, and the child wants to please and is willing to share. This child may continue to have temper tantrums but is more manageable, and use of language can help when the tantrum is over. The 3-year-old knows that when mother is out of sight, she continues to exist and will be there when needed. Therefore, the child can better deal with separation than the 2½-year-old and can more easily adjust to preschool. Imagination is entering play situations, and there is increasing interest in playing with other children. Improved motor abilities allow the 3-year-old to perform tasks that were previously difficult and frustrating. Excessive ritualization is not needed and the child has, in general, a relaxed attitude toward other people and toward life in general.

The 3½-Year-Old

In contrast to the contented 3-year-old, the 3½-year-old appears "anxious, unsure, and self-willed. Feelings of insecurity can be seen in physical ways—stuttering, stumbling, even trembling on occasion . . . They may appear excessively shy at one time and unbearably aggressive the next" (Caplan and Caplan 1983, p. 177). The underlying causes are related to the change in psychological orientation. Between 3½ and 5, the focus is on sexuality (Lidzt

1968; Lieberman 1979; Mahler et al. 1975). The child "courts" the parent of the opposite sex but realizes, however, that the parent cannot be won and fears losing the nurturing of the same-sex parent. Simultaneously, the child loves this parent and wants to please, to be good, and to be loved. To young children, loss of love and protection are the natural consequences of "bad" thoughts. Reality and fantasy are not yet fully differentiated. The child resolves the conflict by "forgetting" it for the present. Repression is not a selective defense, and, therefore, all memories prior to the age of four are also erased. At this stage, the conscience or superego is developing out of a desire to keep parents' love and avoid their anger. The conscience is becoming internalized, a part of the child's own personality. Ultimately, as the conflict is resolved, the child chooses to identify with the parent of the same sex and thereby enjoy the relationship with the parent of the other sex vicariously. This presents the first solution of the oedipal crisis. It appears again in adolescence for a final working through, with resolution of sexual identity. This stage, 3½ to 5, presents major internal conflicts for the child, reflected in changes in behavior. Once again, if one can identify the underlying causes of behavior, one can cope more intelligently with the child.

The emotional insecurities related to the psychological processes may appear in the 3½-year-old as difficulties with peers and parents, incessant and annoying whining, frequent complaints and questions, and emotional extremes. Adults need to realize that the instability of this age is a normal part of development and provide the patience and understanding necessary for the child to grow through this stage. At the same time, it is necessary to have rules to ensure the well-being of the entire group. To that end, it is useful to have the fewest rules necessary to maintain order and safety, but to enforce those rules with firmness, kindness, and consistency. Providing individual attention during periods of weepiness and obvious feelings of insecurity will help the child recover quickly and return to classroom activities.

The 4-Year-Old

The key words describing the 4-year-old are "out of bounds." The 4-year-old is out of bounds in just about everything. When angry or frustrated, the child may kick, spit, and throw things to the point where physical restraint is necessary. Profanity is a favorite, as is the use of imaginative storytelling and fabrication. The line between fact and fiction remains very thin, and children may find their way of telling a story much more interesting than reality.

The 4-year-old child is on an emotional roller coaster. Loud, silly laughter alternates with wild rage. They enjoy other children and are often distressed when playmates are not available. Children need to be monitored carefully, however, since at this age, two children often will "gang up" on a third, and fighting is frequently accompanied by yelling and/or hitting. There is a determination to be self-sufficient, self-reliant, and domineering. Perhaps due to the increased imagination, fear—of monsters, of the dark, and things unusual or not easily understood—is prevalent. This child loves and hates equally strongly and can be alternately charming and totally obnoxious.

The adults managing this child must be pleasant, patient, and firm. Boundaries must be established, for the child's sake as well as for the rest of the class. But whenever possible, safety factors and other issues permitting, it is helpful for 4-year-old children to test out their abilities and to be permitted expanding limits. If permitted some leeway, the 4-year-old can be surprisingly responsive to other requirements.

The 4½-Year-Old

By 4½ the child is beginning to demonstrate more control, on the way to a more focused five when life becomes more balanced and inner conflicts have settled down for the moment. The 4½-year-old is working at sorting out reality from fantasy and sometimes can become confused by what is real, what is pretend, and what is happening on television. The child is absorbing more and more from the environment and can accumulate a surprising amount of information. Self-control and motor control are improving, and a decided interest in drawing takes place. Attending skills are increasing, as demonstrated by the ability to maintain interest in activities for longer periods. Language and cognitive abilities usually enable the child to respond to reasoning in matters of behavior such as taking turns, sharing, and complying with rules.

The 5-Year-Old

"Five years of age marks, in many children, a time of extreme and delightful equilibrium... Gone is the out-of-bounds exuberance of the 4-year-old. Gone is the uncertainty and unpredictability of 4½. The 5-year-old tends to be reliable, stable, well adjusted" (Ilg and Ames 1966, p. 33). This child enjoys pleasing parents and teachers and is learning the social skills necessary for successful interpersonal relationships. Language and learning capacities have grown considerably along with all motor skills. Inventiveness and creativity are apparent in play, and the 5-year-old is fascinated by the world around. This child generally desires to please, and usually does. Others are pleased with the child, and life for the 5-year-old is satisfying.

Integrating these Ages

The contrast in a classroom of, for example, 16 children, between the rigid, demanding 2½-year-old and the flexible, adaptable 5-year-old is clearly enormous, presenting a considerable challenge to the teacher's resources. In addition to the techniques for communicating with children described earlier in this chapter, special attention to grouping within the preschool setting can provide some answers. Planning group activities appropriate for each age level is an obvious technique. One can intermix ages on occasion as well. The teacher can use the 5-year-old's abilities and desire to please to interest a recalcitrant 2½-year-old in complying. The creative teacher who is aware of the differences in maturational levels can develop many ways of encouraging constructive interaction.

The key to dealing with these polarities in behavior lies in understanding that the children are doing what children are supposed to do—grow, discover, learn, act, react, develop. Task mastery is the key to moving on developmentally and to developing a positive self-image. Children observe, imitate, and interpret the world. Sometimes these processes are hard on both adults and children. If the adults understand that difficult behaviors are a necessary part of growth at particular ages, they can help the children in positive, affectionate, and understanding ways.

References

Brigance, A. H. 1978. *Diagnostic inventory of early development.* North Billerica, MA: Curriculum Association, Inc.

Caplan, T., and F. Caplan. 1983. *The early childhood years.* New York: Putnam Publishing Group.

Cook, R. E., and V. B. Armbruster. 1983. *Adapting early childhood curricula: Suggestions for meeting special needs.* St. Louis, MO: M. V. Mosby.

Fraiberg, S. 1959. *The magic years.* New York: Charles Scribner's Sons.

Hildebrand, V. 1976. *Introduction of early childhood education.* 2nd ed. New York: MacMillan Publishing Company, Inc.

Ilg, F., and L. B. Ames. 1966. *Child behavior.* New York: Harper and Row.

Kestenbaum, C. 1980. Early childhood: The toddler years. In *Child development in normality and psychopathology,* by Jules R. Bemporad. New York: Brunner/Mazel.

Lidzt, T. 1968. *The person.* New York: Basic Books, Inc.

Lieberman, F. 1979. *Social work with children.* New York: Human Sciences Press.

Mahler, M. S., F. Pine, and A. Bergman. 1975. *The psychological birth of the human infant.* New York: Basic Books, Inc.

National Association for Education of Young Children. 1984. *Program standards written for criteria for high quality early childhood programs with interpretations.* Washington, DC: NAEYC.

Data Collection

Judith L. Bergman, M.S., CCC/SLP

In the self-contained language classroom, the children are available on a daily basis for collection of data. This affords the opportunity for periodic sampling of communication behavior, which increases the reliability of measures based on spontaneous language samples. Due to the variety of contexts within which language can be sampled throughout the day and the fact that the clinician does not need to elicit language in only one situation, it is likely that a more representative (hence, valid) sample can be gathered. Furthermore, the clinician is not constrained by the need to gather the entire sample within one sitting. A 50- to 100-word corpus, for example, might be constructed from three consecutive days of sampling. Likewise, the collection of child-child samples and samples based on interaction with a variety of adults is facilitated within the classroom environment.

The challenge, then, is to organize data collection to track the children's progress accurately. There are several charting and tallying techniques described in the literature (Friel-Patti and Lougeay-Mottinger 1985; Snyder-McLean et al. 1984; Strong 1983). The methods outlined below provide some suggestions and guidelines on how to fit data collection into the different activities described in the chapter on scheduling and planning.

Classroom Contexts for Data Collection

Free play. Wall charts posted in each interest center can be used by classroom adults for on-line data collection (see Form 1 in the appendix at the end of this chapter). These charts allow you to see which children are playing in which areas during free play, and what language intervention is occurring for them at these times. This type of charting is useful in determining which language targets are not being addressed, and for which more structured intervention will need to be planned.

Structured language therapy sessions. Collect data during the 10-minute structured language sessions on the second day of each lesson (this produces two sets of data per week for each child). Form 2 in the appendix shows a sample format that could be used for data collection in this context, and Form 3 is a sample of a completed chart. This type of chart requires a minimum of writing and is individualized for each lesson and group prior to the session. Data is then transferred onto summary forms for each child by language target, so that progress can be tracked readily.

Criterion testing may be desirable to measure a child's progress on specific linguistic, semantic, or pragmatic objectives. Conduct criterion testing twice yearly, on a one-to-one basis with each child, in a game-like, interactive, and informal atmosphere. Tests should cover all possible targets for the child, but should not include anything that is not on that child's specific educational plan. The sample test forms for nouns, pronouns, verbs, question forms, and negatives (Forms 4, 5, 6, and 7 in the appendix at the end of the chapter) use materials commonly available in the classroom, along with specific picture cards.

Extensive language sampling can be done during regular classroom activities in which spontaneous conversation is most likely to occur. It is a good idea to train your aide/s in live transcription, emphasizing the coding of nonlinguistic context and transcribing utterances that precede or follow the individual child's response. Trained graduate students and aides are ideal as recorders, since the speech-language pathologist is often identified by the children as the "tester," and children's behavior and language become less spontaneous whenever the SLP is present with a clipboard, pen, and/or tape recorder.

This language sample is taken once per child (and only one child should be recorded per day with notations of dialogue, etc.) at the beginning of school, mid-year, and at the end of the school year. Measures to be derived are MLU, analysis of Brown's fourteen grammatical morphemes, and analysis of structural complexity (Stage Level of Yes/No and WH questions, negatives, and percentage of complex sentences) using guidelines in Miller (1981). Also, it may be helpful to derive a Developmental Sentence Score or look at Developmental Sentence Types (Lee 1974). A "Language Developmental Checklist by Brown's MLU Stages" (Khan and James 1980) may be consulted to see which linguistic forms should be targeted, given the child's MLU. In addition, the language sample can be analyzed for types of communicative intentions comprehended and expressed (based on the Speech Act Coding System of Dore et al. [1978]) (see Form 8).

Additional Testing

The SPELT (*Structured Photographic Expressive Language Test—Preschool*) (Werner and Kresheck 1983) is a brief, high-interest measure of syntactical and morphological skill which utilizes a set of colored photographs of appealing toys and children and the "cloze" sentence completion technique in which the child supplies the target word. Cut-off scores for normal development and means and standard deviations are provided.

If the school setting requires standardized testing in addition to those measures provided by an analysis of the language sample, the SPELT would be useful. If a more detailed analysis of oral expressive language is desired (perhaps as a child is tested prior to entering kindergarten, or if data to verify your program's effectiveness is desired), the TEEM (*Test for Examining Expressive Morphology*) (Shipley et al. 1983) is useful. It also uses a cloze technique with black and white line drawings, and it has an excellent table for analysis of results.

The tests mentioned above relate to oral expressive language and this area appears to be the one most disordered in the high-risk child. Excellent receptive language instruments are readily available. The *Test of Pragmatic Skills* (Shulman 1986) is useful for analyzing expression of intentions in a structured play/conversational situation. Many assessment tools exist for assessing articulation/phonological process and are not detailed here.

Some children may also require specific assessment for behavioral, motor, and other disorders, to determine whether referral to other specialists would be appropriate. An early childhood educator, occupational therapist, and psychologist (if your staff includes such personnel) will be excellent resources for assistance in determining whether evaluation in these areas is appropriate, and which tools would best serve this purpose. Forms 9 and 10 can be used as screening tools in the classroom to assess for motor and behavior disorders; they are furnished as guides only, to determine whether further assessment and/or referral to appropriate specialists is recommended.

Appendix Forms

The forms included in this section are intended to serve as guidelines and suggestions, to be altered and tailored as necessary to fit your specific requirements.

- Form 1. Data Collection in Free-Play Areas
- Form 2. Data Collection during Structured Therapy Sessions
- Form 3. Completed Sample Chart for Structured Therapy Sessions
- Form 4. Criterion Test for Noun Forms
- Form 5. Criterion Test for Pronoun Forms
- Form 6. Criterion Test for Verb Forms
- Form 7. Criterion Test for Negative Forms
- Form 8. Assessment of Pragmatic Abilities: Communicative Intentions
- Form 9. Motor Skills Assessment
- Form 10. Preschool Behavioral Checklist

Form 1
Data Collection in Free-Play Areas

Area _____ Date _____

Forms	Name of child						
Noun plurals and possessives							
Pronouns							
Verb form: Irregular past							
Verb form: ED (regular past)							
Verb form: IS MAIN*							
Verb form: Can/Will							
Verb form: Contraction**							
Verb form: Other***							
A The							
Preposition							
Yes/No question							
WH question							
Negatives							
Comparative adjectives							

*is, are, was, were   **I'm, he's, we're   ***could, would, does, has

© 1990 by Communication Skill Builders, Inc. This form may be reproduced for administrative use.

Form 2
Data Collection for Structured Language Therapy

Teacher _____ Date _____

Check one: ☐ Monday/Wednesday (data on Wednesday)
                ☐ Tuesday/Thursday (data on Thursday)

Key:

M = Model
I = Independently

  + and circle M: child repeats target correctly after you

  0 and circle M: child does not repeat correctly after you

  + and circle I: child correctly uses target form with NO direct model from you, although you may cue by showing a picture, asking a question, etc.

  NR and circle M: child refuses to attempt to repeat your model (no response)

Instructions for eliciting responses: Question or cue to give the child a chance to respond independently unless you are sure a model is needed. If child is incorrect in an independent attempt, do NOT mark "0" but instead give a model and mark the child's attempt to repeat the model.

Children	Language target forms or behaviors			
	_____ M I _____ M I _____ M I _____ M I _____ M I	_____ M I _____ M I _____ M I _____ M I _____ M I	_____ M I _____ M I _____ M I _____ M I _____ M I	_____ M I _____ M I _____ M I _____ M I _____ M I
	_____ M I _____ M I _____ M I _____ M I _____ M I	_____ M I _____ M I _____ M I _____ M I _____ M I	_____ M I _____ M I _____ M I _____ M I _____ M I	_____ M I _____ M I _____ M I _____ M I _____ M I
	_____ M I _____ M I _____ M I _____ M I _____ M I	_____ M I _____ M I _____ M I _____ M I _____ M I	_____ M I _____ M I _____ M I _____ M I _____ M I	_____ M I _____ M I _____ M I _____ M I _____ M I
	_____ M I _____ M I _____ M I _____ M I _____ M I	_____ M I _____ M I _____ M I _____ M I _____ M I	_____ M I _____ M I _____ M I _____ M I _____ M I	_____ M I _____ M I _____ M I _____ M I _____ M I

© 1990 by Communication Skill Builders, Inc. This form may be reproduced for administrative use.

108 / DATA COLLECTION

Form 3
Sample Data Collection for Structured Language Therapy

Teacher __J. B.__   Date __10-1__

Check one: ☐ Monday/Wednesday (data on Wednesday)
☒ Tuesday/Thursday (data on Thursday)

Key:

M = Model
I = Independently

+ and circle M: child repeats target correctly after you

0 and circle M: child does not repeat correctly after you

+ and circle I: child correctly uses target form with NO direct model from you, although you may cue by showing a picture, asking a question, etc.

NR and circle M: child refuses to attempt to repeat your model (no response)

Instructions for eliciting responses: Question or cue to give the child a chance to respond independently unless you are sure a model is needed. If child is incorrect in an independent attempt, do NOT mark "0" but instead give a model and mark the child's attempt to repeat the model.

Children	*Language target forms or behaviors*			
	Possessive proper nouns ("Henry's")	It's...	Two-step directions	Comprehends "behind"
Samantha	+ Ⓜ I + Ⓜ I + M Ⓘ + M Ⓘ + M Ⓘ	0 Ⓜ I 0 Ⓜ I + Ⓜ I ___ M I ___ M I	+ M Ⓘ + Ⓜ I ___ M I ___ M I ___ M I	+ M Ⓘ ___ M I ___ M I ___ M I ___ M I
Emily Ann	+ M Ⓘ + Ⓜ Ⓘ ___ M I ___ M I ___ M I	0 Ⓜ I 0 Ⓜ I 0 Ⓜ I ___ M I ___ M I	+ M Ⓘ + Ⓜ Ⓘ ___ M I ___ M I ___ M I	+ M Ⓘ ___ M I ___ M I ___ M I ___ M I
Alyson	+ Ⓜ I + Ⓜ Ⓘ + M Ⓘ ___ M I ___ M I	0 Ⓜ I 0 Ⓜ I + Ⓜ I ___ M I ___ M I	+ M Ⓘ ___ M I ___ M I ___ M I ___ M I	+ M Ⓘ ___ M I ___ M I ___ M I ___ M I
	___ M I ___ M I ___ M I ___ M I ___ M I	___ M I ___ M I ___ M I ___ M I ___ M I	___ M I ___ M I ___ M I ___ M I ___ M I	___ M I ___ M I ___ M I ___ M I ___ M I

Form 4
Criterion Test for Noun Forms

Check items to be given to _____

Date tested_____ by _____

> **Key:**
>
> M = Model
> I = Independently
>
> + and circle M: child repeats target correctly after you
>
> 0 and circle M: child does not repeat correctly after you
>
> + and circle I: child correctly uses target form with NO direct model from you, although you may cue by showing a picture, asking a question, etc.
>
> NR and circle M: child refuses to attempt to repeat your model (no response)

____ **Possessive Nouns**

   Materials: pictures of the children

   Whose picture is this?

   _____ M I   _____ M I   _____ M I

____ **Plural Nouns**

   Materials: doubles of common objects or pictures of common objects

/z/	airplane	_____ M I	/s/	bat	_____ M I
	apple	_____ M I		boat	_____ M I
	car	_____ M I		cake	_____ M I
	_____	_____ M I		_____	_____ M I
	_____	_____ M I		_____	_____ M I
/z/	blouse	_____ M I	Other	_____	_____ M I
	bus	_____ M I		_____	_____ M I
	box	_____ M I		_____	_____ M I
	_____	_____ M I		_____	_____ M I
	_____	_____ M I		_____	_____ M I

© 1990 by Communication Skill Builders, Inc. This form may be reproduced for administrative use.

Form 5
Criterion Test for Pronoun Forms

Check items to be given to _____

Date tested _____ by _____

Key:

M = Model
I = Independently

+ and circle M: child repeats target correctly after you

0 and circle M: child does not repeat correctly after you

+ and circle I: child correctly uses target form with NO direct model from you, although you may cue by showing a picture, asking a question, etc.

NR and circle M: child refuses to attempt to repeat your model (no response)

____ **I**

Tell about something you are wearing. Model "I." Child takes turn.

_____ M I   _____ M I   _____ M I

____ **WE**

We tell about something we both are wearing.

_____ M I   _____ M I

____ **HE/SHE**

Materials: Photographs depicting occupations

You tell about what one person does. "HE delivers the mail." Child guesses who it is: HE is the ____. Child has turn.

HE   _____ M I   SHE   _____ M I

        _____ M I   _____ M I

© 1990 by Communication Skill Builders, Inc. This form may be reproduced for administrative use.

Form 5 (continued)

____ **HIM/HER/THEM**

Materials: boy and girl dolls; cloth to "hide" them.

Game: I CAN SEE HIM/HER. Partially hide one of the dolls. Model: "Can you see him?" Say, "I can't see him," or "Yes, I can see him." Repeat game with both together for THEM.

HIM	_____ M I	HER	_____ M I	THEM	_____ M I
	_____ M I		_____ M I		_____ M I

____ **YOU**

Child tells you what to do. "YOU have to ____."

_____ M I

_____ M I

____ **THEY vs. HE OR SHE**

Materials: Two people puppets, one animal puppet

"Here are two people and one dog. I will make the people do something and the dog do something. Guess what the people are doing and what the dog is doing."

THEY	_____ M I	HE/SHE	_____ M I
	_____ M I		_____ M I

____ **OTHER**

© 1990 by Communication Skill Builders, Inc. This form may be reproduced for administrative use.

Form 6
Criterion Test for Verb Forms

Check items to be given to _____

Date tested _____ by _____

Key:

M = Model
I = Independently

+ and circle M: child repeats target correctly after you

0 and circle M: child does not repeat correctly after you

+ and circle I: child correctly uses target form with NO direct model from you, although you may cue by showing a picture, asking a question, etc.

NR and circle M: child refuses to attempt to repeat your model (no response)

_____ **IS as main verb**

Materials: photographs or pictures of common objects

_____ **Y/N question:** IS IT A ___?

Child selects and gradually uncovers a picture. Teacher guesses, "Is it a ___?"

IT IS _____ M I   IT ISN'T _____ M I

Teacher takes a turn; child guesses.

IS IT A _____ M I   (can count also for Y/N question)

_____ **CAN** (also use for CAN'T and YES/NO question)

_____ **CAN'T, DON'T**

_____ **YES/NO question with Interrogative Reversals**

Materials: flannel board, small flannel board sets, category cards, nonsense pictures

Teacher shows item and asks, "Can you wear a banana?", "Can a chair talk?", etc., to elicit, "No, you CAN'T wear a banana," or "Yes, you CAN wear a hat." Then the child has a turn to be "teacher" and asks the Yes/No questions to the adult.

CAN _____ M I   CAN'T _____ M I
DON'T _____ M I   CAN YOU VERB A ___? _____ M I

© 1990 by Communication Skill Builders, Inc. This form may be reproduced for administrative use.

Form 6 (continued)

___ **I'M VERB + -ING**

___ **WHAT AM I DOING?**

Take turns playing a guessing game: act out an activity such as brushing teeth, then ask, "What am I doing?" You can also model the correct answer, "I'M brushing my teeth." Child has a turn (score Q form). Pretend not to understand, to elicit "I'M ___" from the child.

I'M verb + *-ing*   _____ M I   WHAT AM I DOING?   _____ M I

___ **THIRD PERSON SINGULAR ENDINGS**

Materials: dolls or puppets

"You can pick some cards to see what these children do every day" (cue: "Every day he ___"), or "Guess what this doll/puppet does every day."

/z/ _____ _____ M I   /s/ _____ _____ M I
     _____ _____ M I   _____ _____ M I
     _____ _____ M I   _____ _____ M I
     _____ _____ M I   /z/ _____ _____ M I
     _____ _____ M I   _____ _____ M I

___ **IT'S . . . contractible copular verb**

Materials: touch box or bag

Child and teacher take turns, each telling what the item might be. "I think IT'S a ___."

IT'S   _____ M I
            _____ M I
            _____ M I

___ **COULD and WOULD . . . modal verbs**

Materials: doll family (boy/girl and adult)

Pantomime and model parent asking child to do helpful chores, then switch roles so child can manipulate the adult puppet and ask:

COULD you pick up your toys?   _____ M I
WOULD you turn off the TV?   _____ M I
         COULD   _____ M I
                               _____ M I
         WOULD   _____ M I
                               _____ M I

© 1990 by Communication Skill Builders, Inc. This form may be reproduced for administrative use.

Form 6 (continued)

____ **DOES, THIRD PERSON SINGULAR IRREGULAR**

____ **DOESN'T, NEGATIVE FORM**

____ **YES/NO QUESTIONS**

Materials: nonsense pictures

Help the child find items and ask, "Does a boat fly? Does a man ride a cat?", etc. Child answers, "Yes, it/he DOES," or "NO, it/he DOESN'T."

DOES	_____	M I
	_____	M I
DOESN'T	_____	M I
	_____	M I
DOES A	_____	M I
	_____	M I

WH QUESTIONS:

____ **WHAT**

____ **WHO**

____ **WHERE**

Materials: pictures of people depicting occupations, pictures of places (beach, movies, etc.), pictures of common objects

Teacher guesses after child asks "What is it?" or "Who is this?"

WHAT	_____	M I
	_____	M I
WHO	_____	M I
	_____	M I
WHERE	_____	M I
	_____	M I

© 1990 by Communication Skill Builders, Inc. This form may be reproduced for administrative use.

Form 7
Criterion Test for Negative Forms

Check items to be given to _____

Date tested _____ by _____

Key:

M = Model
I = Independently

+ and circle M: child repeats target correctly after you

0 and circle M: child does not repeat correctly after you

+ and circle I: child correctly uses target form with NO direct model from you, although you may cue by showing a picture, asking a question, etc.

NR and circle M: child refuses to attempt to repeat your model (no response)

Materials: puppets, nonsense pictures

Puppet scenario is of a naughty girl (tester) and the mommy, who is denying permission (child).

Request:	Elicits:		
____ 1. Can I go out?	CAN'T	_____	M I
____ 2. Do I get cookies?	DON'T	_____	M I
____ 3. Will we go to the movies soon?	WON'T	_____	M I
____ 4. Did you buy me a treat?	DIDN'T	_____	M I
____ 5. Does the TV show start soon?	DOESN'T	_____	M I
____ 6. Were my toys neat?	WEREN'T	_____	M I

Using nonsense pictures, ask ridiculous questions.

Question:	Elicits:		
____ 1. Are socks for your hands?	AREN'T	_____	M I
____ 2. Does a car fly?	DOESN'T	_____	M I

© 1990 by Communication Skill Builders, Inc. This form may be reproduced for administrative use.

Form 8
Assessment of Pragmatic Abilities: Communicative Intentions

Name: _____

Dates of language samples: _____

Total number of utterances obtained: _____

> **Code:** T = Teacher
> C = Child
> P = Playmate

Intention	Comprehension	Expression	Actual utterance and/or nonverbal component
REQUESTS that solicit information			
1. Direct requests for action, for items, or for factual information			1a. 1b. 1c. 1d.
2. Indirect requests for action, items, factual information			2a. 2b. 2c. 2d.
3. Requests permission			3a. 3b.
4. Requests clarification ("What did you say?", etc.)			4a. 4b.
5. Other requests (specify)			5a. 5b.
RESPONSES that provide information directly complement prior requests			
6. Yes/No answers			6a. 6b.
7. Answers to WH questions			7a. 7b.
8. Other answers (specify)			8a. 8b.

© 1990 by Communication Skill Builders, Inc. This form may be reproduced for administrative use.

Intention	Comprehension	Expression	Actual utterance and/or nonverbal component
DESCRIPTIONS			
9. Describes activities			9a. 9b. 9c.
10. Identifications that label objects, events, properties, or locations of objects			10a. 10b. 10c. 10d.
STATEMENTS that express facts, rules, attitudes			
11. States "rules," gives orders			11a. 11b.
12. Evaluations of self and others			12a. 12b.
13. Internal reports expressing emotions, sensations			13a. 13b.
14. Explanations and predictions			14a. 14b.
ACKNOWLEDGMENTS			
15. Recognizes and evaluates responses: approvals, disapprovals			15a. 15b.
16. "Returns" acknowledging rhetorical questions, etc. ("What, really?")			16a. 16b.
17. OTHER statements or acknowledgments (specify)			17a. 17b. 17c. 17d.
ORGANIZATIONAL DEVICES regulating contact and conversation			
18. Boundary markers indicating openings, closings, changes in topic ("Hi," "Bye," "By the way")			18a. 18b. 18c. 18d.

© 1990 by Communication Skill Builders, Inc. This form may be reproduced for administrative use.

Intention	Comprehension	Expression	Actual utterance and/or nonverbal component
19. Solicit attention ("Hey," "John," "Look")			19a. 19b.
20. Speaker selections			20a. 20b.
21. Politeness markers ("Thanks," "Sorry")			21a. 21b.
22. PERFORMATIVES accomplish facts by being said			22a. 22b.
23. Jokes display nonbelief			23a. 23b.
24. Claims to establish rights ("That's mine," "I'm fast")			24a. 24b.
25. Warnings ("Watch out")			25a. 25b.
26. Teases			26.

See *Speech act coding system* (Cole, Dore, Hall, and Dowley 1978), pp. 119-176.

Form 9
Motor Skills Assessment

Date tested_____ Name_____

Scoring key:
+ correct
− incorrect
NR no response

Total score:
+ _____
− _____
NR _____

Motor score interpretation: Locate total number of + responses on the chart below, regardless of age.
Fail — 4
High risk — 5
Pass — 6
A score of 4 or below indicates more thorough testing immediately. A child who receives a score of 5 should be given a more thorough motor skills survey within six months.

Directions: Allow two trials at the appropriate age range. For items 1-4, say, "Look at me. Now you do it." For items 5 and 6, say, "See it? Now you make one like it."

Activity	Ages 2-6 to 3-0		Ages 3-1 to 3-6		Ages 3-7 and above	
1. *Standing balance:* Child stands on one foot without holding on. Child's foot may not touch the other leg. Stop if foot moves.	attempts one foot		1 foot, 1 second		1 foot, 3 seconds	
2. *Jumping:* Child must jump with feet together without falling.	jumps in place		broad jump, 9"		broad jump, 12"	
3. *Catching:* Child must bounce/drop and catch ball with both hands. If child is to catch a bounced or thrown ball, it must be with arms and body, from a distance of two meters.	drop and catch		catch bounced		catch thrown	
4. *Throwing:* Child stands at the designated distance from you. Give a "correct" response if you can catch the ball without changing position.	throw 3 meters		throw 4 meters		throw 5 meters	
5. *Block towers:* Child needs good opposition (pad to pad/pincer). Child may be passed if switches hands (note this). Child does not pass if must stabilize tower with helping hand (note this).	tower of 8		tower of 9		tower of 10	
6. *Block construction: Train*—Demonstrate placing three blocks horizontally, adding fourth block on top of third. *Bridge*—Demonstrate placing three blocks resting on top edges of two separated blocks. For ages 3.6-4.0, shield model while building; no demonstration permitted.	chimney to train		imitate bridge		bridge from model	

Developed by Anne Milkowski, OTR

© 1990 by Communication Skill Builders, Inc. This form may be reproduced for administrative use.

Form 10
Preschool Behavioral Checklist

Child's full name _____ Birth date _____

The following are behaviors often seen in preschool children. Circle the entry in each question which you think applies best to your child *at the present time.*

1. a. Seems happy and pleased most of the time
    b. Sometimes has periods of sadness
    c. Reflects a presence of sadness and unhappiness

2. a. Easy to get to bed and to sleep
    b. Some difficulties in settling at bedtime
    c. Often takes a long time to settle at bedtime

3. a. Usually shows good appetite, not fussy about food
    b. Sometimes poor eater, picky about food
    c. Mealtimes often difficult and child won't eat many different foods

4. a. Generally maintains consistent mood for the day
    b. Some up and down days, but not a regular occurrence
    c. Shows mood changes frequently within the same day; depressed one moment, overactive the next

5. a. Socializes easily without apparent difficulties
    b. Sometimes has social difficulties, but manages with support
    c. Has no friends and tends to remain isolated

6. a. Generally not a worrier
    b. Occasionally worries but can be reassured
    c. Has many worries, and appears bothered by things in the world

7. a. Generally confident about skills and abilities
    b. Lacks confidence and requires much reassurance about self
    c. Child is hypercritical of self

8. a. Acts the same as most children of similar age
    b. Sometimes acts younger when frightened, confused, or insecure
    c. Acts younger than chronological age in most situations

9. a. Usually succeeds at expected level with tasks attempted
    b. Must have approval for tasks attempted or completed
    c. Gives up easily and often expects failure

10. a. No problems noted in verbal, social, or motor skills for a child of this age
    b. Sometimes shows difficulties with verbal, social, and motor skills which others do not seem to have
    c. Shows marked limitations in verbal, social, and motor skills for someone of the child's age

© 1990 by Communication Skill Builders, Inc. This form may be reproduced for administrative use.

11. a. No problems with somatic complaints (aches or pains outside of actual illness)
    b. Child sometimes complains of aches or pains with no apparent physical cause
    c. Child often complains of aches or pains (may be employed to avoid responsibilities or to withdraw from unsatisfactory situations)

12. a. Easy to manage or control
    b. Sometimes difficult to manage or control
    c. Frequently very difficult to manage or control

13. a. Child has never been observed displaying unusual motor behavior
    b. Child occasionally displays unusual behavior when under stress
    c. Child displays unusual motor behaviors (spinning, hand flapping, gesturing, etc.)

14. a. Child displays good judgment about things and situations for this age
    b. Child's judgment is generally good but steady monitoring is required
    c. Child often displays poor judgment, needs much supervision

15. a. Child gets on well with other children
    b. Some difficulties playing with other children
    c. Finds it difficult to play with other children

16. a. Hardly ever wakes at night
    b. Sometimes wakes at night
    c. Frequently wakes at night and difficult to settle

17. a. Activity level seems right for child's age and situation
    b. Not active enough
    c. Very active, won't sit for more than five minutes at a time

18. a. Easy to manage or discipline
    b. Sometimes difficult or out of control for short periods
    c. Does not conform to limits independently without control from others

19. a. Appears attentive and interactive with surroundings
    b. Sometimes stares blankly into space
    c. Repeats one idea, thought, or activity over and over

20. a. Maintains a caring attitude about most objects in the environment
    b. Sometimes destroys objects when upset
    c. Often destroys or takes objects apart

21. a. Independent, doesn't ask for a lot of attention
    b. Sometimes asks for a lot of attention
    c. Demands constant attention, follows mother around all day

22. a. Manages adversity with others in usual fashion for age
    b. Sometimes strikes back with angry behavior to teasing by other children
    c. Doesn't protest when others hurt, tease, or criticize

23. a. Few or no fears
    b. Has some fears which require reassurance
    c. Expresses concern about something terrible or horrible that might happen

© 1990 by Communication Skill Builders, Inc. This form may be reproduced for administrative use.

Form 10 (continued)

Scoring:

"a" response is scored as zero points

"b" response is scored as one point

"c" response is scored as two points

Behavior score interpretation:

Locate the total number score below:

Score	Intervention
0-10	No behavior problems
11-23	Demonstrates significant behavior problems; probably needs some intervention
24+	Demonstrates major behavior problems; intervention indicated.

Developed by Frank Wilson, Ph.D., Clinical Psychologist

© 1990 by Communication Skill Builders, Inc. This form may be reproduced for administrative use.

References

Cole, M., J. Dore, W. S. Hall, and G. Dowley. 1978. Speech act coding system: Situation and task in young children's talk. *Discourse Processes* I:119-176.

Dore, J., M. Gearhart, and D. Newman. 1978. The structure of nursery school conversation. In *Children's language,* Vol. 1, edited by K. Nelson, 371-372. New York: Gardner Press.

Friel-Patti, S., and J. Lougeay-Mottinger. 1985. Preschool language intervention: Some key concerns. *Topics in Language Disorders* 5:40-57.

Khan, L., and S. L. James. 1980. A method for assessing use of grammatical structures in language disordered children. *Language, Speech and Hearing Services in Schools* 11:188-197.

Lee, L. 1974. *Developmental sentence analysis.* Evanston, IL: Northwestern University Press.

Miller, J. F. 1981. *Assessing language production in children.* Baltimore, MD: University Park Press.

Shipley, K., T. Stone, and M. B. Sue. 1983. *Test for examining expressive morphology.* Tucson, AZ: Communication Skill Builders.

Shulman, B. B. 1986. *Test of pragmatic skills.* Tucson, AZ: Communication Skill Builders.

Snyder-McLean, L. K., B. Solomson, J. McLean, and S. Sack. 1984. Structuring joint action routines: A strategy for facilitating communication and language development in the classroom. *Seminars in Speech and Language* 5:213-228.

Strong, J. 1983. *Language facilitation.* Baltimore, MD: University Park Press.

Werner, E. G., and J. D. Kresheck. 1983. *Structured photographic expressive language test: Preschool.* Sandwich, IL: Janelle Publishers, Inc.

Part II

Structured Language Therapy: Sample Lesson Plans for 10-Minute Sessions

Mary Ann Gianni, Judith L. Bergman, Paul E. Quin

This section includes 33 sample lesson plans outlining brief, structured language sessions designed to target specific language needs. Tasks cover a wide range of activities, including arts and crafts, action and memory games, identifying absurdities, and listening skills. (The following index indicates the specific language targets for each lesson.)

The structured language therapy period represents the most structured portion of the preschool language classroom's schedule. The presentation of activities is highly structured to elicit desired responses from the children. The groups should be kept small, no more than four children for one adult. Children should be grouped by language ability and language target.

Because of the intensity of these sessions, it is profitable to follow this period with less-structured activities where the children either make something or can move around and unwind. (See Figure 1 in the chapter on scheduling and planning for a sample schedule of activities.)

The structured language lessons provide a good opportunity to record children's responses to the lessons. Record-keeping can be done by the therapist or, preferably, by a trained classroom aide or student intern, so that the process of recording does not interfere with the intent of the activity. These documented responses can serve as a criterion-referenced check on the students' progress. (See Forms 2 and 3 in the chapter on data collection for samples of data-recording forms that are easily used in this context.)

Index of Language Targets

Targets	*Lesson numbers*
A. General	
Color or shape matching	1
Color or shape naming	1
Concepts of *same/not same*	1
Concepts of summer/winter	26
Following two-step directions	1, 3, 4
Describing functions or use	8
Sentence repetition, auditory memory	19
Logical and analytical thinking skills	27, 28
B. Vocabulary	
Nouns	3, 5, 7, 14, 22, 25
Verbs	5, 7, 33

Targets	Lesson numbers
C. Noun forms	
Plural nouns	6, 8, 16, 25
Possessive nouns	3, 4
Noun expansions (articles *a* and *the*)	5, 7, 8, 9, 10, 11, 12, 13, 14
D. Verb forms	
Progressive *-ing*	5, 6, 7, 9, 13, 14, 33
Irregular past tense	6, 19, 24, 25, 26, 27
Regular past tense	6, 8, 19, 20, 21, 24, 25, 26, 27
Uncontractible copula (*is, are, was* as main verb)	10, 15, 19, 24, 26
Modal verb *will, 'll*	6, 28
Uncontractible and contractible auxiliary verbs (Is he going? He's going home. I'm going home.)	4, 6, 7, 9, 10, 11, 12, 13, 14, 17, 33
Third person singular regular	17
Third person singular irregular	8 (does)
Other (*had*)	26
E. Prepositions	
in, on, under	2, 5, 15
with, of, for, to	7
around, behind, beside, between, through	2, 3, 4
Prepositional phrases	2, 15
in front of, in back of, next to, near	2, 15
F. Pronoun forms	
Demonstratives *this* and *that*	8
I, you, me	5, 7, 9, 10
he, she	5, 6, 7, 17, 24, 27, 28
him, her	26
my, mine, hers, his	6
their, theirs	26
we, they, them	15, 16, 28
G. Interrogative forms	
Yes/No questions with inversions	8, 10, 16, 22
WH questions—comprehension	5, 7, 14
WH questions—expression	15, 16, 19, 21
H. Negative forms	17, 18, 19, 25
I. Adjectives	
Comparatives *-er, -est*	2
J. Pragmatic	
Turn taking	most lessons
Topic maintenance	most lessons
Narrative sequences	23, 24, 25

1. Musical Colors/Musical Shapes

Language targets
- Following two-step directions
- Color or shape matching and naming
- Concepts *same/not same*

Materials
1 small chair per child
a record or tape player
recording of music

For *Musical Colors*, you will need two 8" squares each of red, blue, green, or yellow paper per child. For *Musical Shapes*, you will need two shape cutouts per child (use black paper to cut out squares, circles, rectangles, half-circles, and triangles).

Preparation
Set up chairs in a circle, and lay on each chair one of the duplicate color squares or shapes.

Procedure
(Instructions are for Musical Colors; for Musical Shapes, substitute shape names.)

1. *Today we will play Musical Chairs. Every chair has a colored paper on it and I Have matching papers. See* (matching paper in your hand to the one on each chair): *Red—red; blue—blue; green—green; yellow—yellow.*

2. *Now I Will give each one of you one a colored paper.* (Give each child a color square.) *When the music plays, you march around. What will you do?* ("Play music, we march.")

3. *When the music stops, quick find a chair with a paper the same as your color and sit down. What will we do?* (Children retell the last two steps: music plays, march; music stops, find same color and sit down.)

4. Run through one trial with the children. After each trial: *Wow! You all sat down fast. Let's see if you sat down in the right chair. Are your colors the same?* (Children respond yes/no.)

5. *What color do you have?* (Children name the primary colors/shapes.)

2. Cube Game

Language targets
- Prepositions *in, out, through, behind, in front of, around*
- Comparative adjective *shortest*

Materials
large plastic interlocking cube (approximately 3' square) or sturdy cardboard box of similar dimensions, with open top

1 drinking straw per child and participating adult (cut one straw shorter than the others)

Preparation
Set the cube up in the middle of the play area.

Procedure
1. *This is a fun game. First everyone pick a straw.* Have all the children and participating adults select straws. *Who has the shortest straw?* Have the children compare the lengths of their straws with each other (include the adults) to find who has the shortest straw.

2. *You're (I'm) "IT."*

3. *We can each tell ["IT"] what to do with this cube.* (If necessary, whisper a sample direction to the children until they learn the prepositions.)

4. You or the child give a direction to "IT:" *Go in the cube.* "IT" follows the direction.

5. *Did ["IT"] Follow the direction? Did ["IT"] do what you said? Yes!* (etc.)

6. Other directions:
Come out of the cube.
Run around the cube.
Jump in front of the cube.
Crawl through the cube.

7. The final step is for the children giving directions to think of the preposition they wish to use all by themselves, and to give "IT" correct feedback as to whether the directions were followed.

3. Mixed-up Clothes (A Winter Game)

Language targets
- Possessive nouns
- Following two-step directions
- Naming outer clothing
- Comprehending preposition *behind*

Materials
large cardboard box

the children's hats, mittens, boots, jackets, scarves, etc.

Preparation
Plan this activity for a day when the children have worn their winter coats and other cold-weather clothing to school. Make sure all clothing articles are labeled.

Procedure
1. Introduce the activity: *Today we will play a fun game called "Mixed-Up Clothes."*

2. *Listen carefully. Everyone go out to your cubbies. Wait and listen some more. When you get to your cubby, put your boots, hat, mittens, scarf, and coat in this big box. I will carry out this big box.* After the children have followed the directions, tell them to return to their classroom space. Have them sit on the floor in a circle around the box.

3. *Now let's sit around this box. I will close my eyes and pick out one thing from this box.* (Alternately, hold the box behind the children and have them reach around without peeking. Otherwise, children will select their own items.)

4. Ask, *What is it?* The child names the item. *Whose _____ is it?* "Henry's" or "Mine." *Okay, put it behind [the owner].*

5. Continue with children taking turns responding.

4. Mixed-Up Shoes

Language targets
- Possessive proper nouns
- Following two-step directions
- Comprehension of *behind*
- *it's* contracted auxiliary and copula

Materials a large box or bag

Procedure
1. *Today we will play a fun game called "Mixed-Up Shoes." Look at everyone's shoes.*
2. *Listen carefully. Take off your shoes and put them in this box.* (Remove your shoes and add them to the box also.)
3. *Now let's sit in a circle around this box. I will close my eyes and pick out something from this box. Ashley, you can guess first. Whose shoe is it?* The child names the owner: Henry's shoe/Henry's/It's Henry's shoe, or It's my shoe.
4. *Good! Put it behind Henry.*
5. Continue with children taking turns. Model "It's, noun's" if necessary.

5. In the Park

Language targets
- Noun and verb vocabulary
- He/She verb + *-ing* or *is* verb + *-ing*
- Prepositions *in, on, under, in front of, in back of*
- WHat and WHere question comprehension

Materials a large picture or a picture book with large, clear pictures, depicting children engaged in readily identifiable activities

Possible sources: *Folding Picture* and *Name and Know Books* (Bank Street College of Education, 1968); *In the Park* (Early Childhood Discovery Materials, New York: Macmillan)

Procedure
1. Have children sit in front of a picture. Engage the children in discussion of what the picture depicts. The following is an example using the large picture from *In the Park*.
2. *This is a big picture. What is this picture about?* or *Where are the children in this picture?* Children respond, "In the park."
3. *Let's take turns telling what we see. I see a girl.* (Point to the girl in the swing.) *She is swinging.*
4. Call on one of the children, or ask for volunteers: *What do you see? Who do you see?* The child responds, "I see a ____."
5. *What is he/she doing?* "He/She is [verb + *-ing*]" or "He/She [verb + *-ing*]."

6. *Where is the _____?* Child responds with the appropriate preposition: "in the _____," "on the _____."

7. *Can you find the _____ in front of the _____? Can you find the _____ in back of the _____?* The child points to the appropriate item in the picture.

6. Playing in the Park

Language targets
- Plural nouns
- He/She/Noun verb + *-ing* or *is* verb + *-ing*
- WHat/WHere/WHo question comprehension
- Past tense (*-ed* and irregular)
- Contractible *'ll*
- Pronouns *he, she, my, mine*

Materials — children's picture books that have sequentially arranged illustrations (no words) depicting boys and girls in various group and individual activities

Possible sources: *Folding Picture* and *Name and Know Books* (Bank Street College of Education, 1968); *In the Park, Give Me the Pail* (Early Childhood Discovery Materials, New York: Macmillan)

Procedure
1. Become familiar with the story before you show it to the class.
2. Show the book to the children and tell the story to the group, incorporating and verbally emphasizing the language targets noted above.
3. *Let's look at this story. Who wants to help me tell the story?* Children can tell the story, cued by your questions or modeled responses. One child can tell one page and then the second child the next (start with the peer model). Each child reads or repeats along with the teacher.
4. Ask WH questions relative to the story, and elicit the following types of answers:
   Noun verb + *-ing*: "The boys (were/are) fighting."
   Noun *is* verb + *-ing*: "Mommy is running."
   He/Me/My: "He says, *I want my pail / Give me my pail.*"
   She: "She says, *Stop fighting!*"
   Plural nouns: "Mommy picks up and takes the pails and shovels."

7. At the Supermarket, Part 1

Language targets
- Noun and verb vocabulary
- Food categories
- He/She is verb + *-ing*
- Prepositions *to, with, for*
- Comprehension of WHere, WHat questions

Materials
: a large picture of people buying food in a supermarket (or engaged in any other identifiable activity) (possible source: *At the Supermarket;* Early Childhood Discovery Materials, New York: Macmillan)

puzzles and sequence puzzles (Bank Street College of Education, 1968)

Procedure
1. Have children sit in front of the picture.
2. *This is a big picture. Where are the people in this picture?* Children respond, "At the supermarket." *What are they doing?* "Shopping/buying food."

    Let's take turns telling what we see. I see a girl (point). *She is buying _____.*

    What do you see? Who do you see? Children respond, "I see a _____." *What is she/he doing?* He/She (is) [verb + -ing].

    Who is with _____? "The baby is with the Mommy."

    What is the [object] *for?* "The _____ is for _____."

    What is she doing? (Handing food to a cashier: elicit *to.*) Child responds, "She is giving it *to* the cashier."

3. If there is time during second exposure to the lesson, allow the children to pick a puzzle or a sequence puzzle and talk about the pieces or the depicted sequence, to elicit the same targets.

8. At the Supermarket, Part 2

Language targets
- Describing functions or use contexts of items
- Demonstratives *this* and *that*
- Regular past tense
- Yes/No questions with *do* and *does*

Materials
: a poster of a supermarket

picture books of situations (such as "I'm lost" or "What's for lunch?")

pictures of specific food items

picture sequences of shopping (for example, selecting food from shelves, checking out at the register, bagging groceries, putting bags in car)

Possible sources: *Name and Know* and *Look and Listen* (Bank Street College of Education, 1968); *At the Supermarket* (Early Childhood Discovery Materials, New York: MacMillan).

Procedure
1. *I have some special story books for you to read. Some are picture stories. You can look at the pictures and tell the stories.* Have each child select a book such as the *Name and Know* books.
2. *Let's look at this story.* Guide the children to name items and produce extended narratives that describe the functions and contexts of the pictured objects: *What is this? Tell about this picture. What is this for? What is he/she doing with this?* Children might respond, "This is an apple. The man is picking apples. Then people will eat them." "The shopping cart is FOR

shopping in a supermarket. You put your food in it. Then you take the food to the cashier and you pay for it."

3. If you have time, add another book (for example, *Look and Listen*). Read the story to the children and, when possible, have them finish sentences for you using the language targets.

9. Touch Box Teasers

Language target
- Contractible auxiliary: I*'m* touching a _____.

Materials
a Touch Box filled with common objects: small tea cup, ball, comb, crayon, pencil, belt, hat, sock, penny, children's scissors, etc. (See the Science Unit for construction of a Touch Box.)

Procedure
1. *Today we will play another touch box game. But today, I won't show you what is in here.*
2. *We will take turns.* Select a child to start.
3. *Put your hands in the holes. Don't look. Don't take it out. Tell us what you're touching.* Have the child follow your or a normal-language peer's model: I*'mmmmmm* touching a _____.
4. *Okay, now take it out. You're right!!* Say to the others, *He/She's right!*
5. Children who correctly guess an object's identity by touch are allowed to keep the object for the duration of the game. Keep playing until the box is empty, then refill it with the same objects, or use a different collection of objects.

10. Touch Box: What Do You Think It Is?

Language targets
- WH questions
- *is* as main verb or contracted copula: *it's*

Materials
a Touch Box

a tray or bag of familiar objects (ball, comb, crayon, pencil, belt, hat, sock, penny, raw carrot, small tea cup, etc.) (See the Science Unit for construction of a Touch Box.)

Procedure
1. *I will put all these things in the Touch Box.* Display the items.
2. *Let's take turns.* Select one child to reach in the box and touch an object. *Don't take it out. Feel it. Tell us: What do you think it is?* Model the desired response: "I think it is a _____," or "I think it's a _____," and have the child follow your instructions.

11. Playdough Surprises

Language targets
- Auxiliary and copula forms contracted: I'm, he's, she's, they're, it's a _____

Materials
playdough
plastic knives
molds or cookie cutters

Procedure
1. *Today we're going to make playdough surprises. Let's all make something. Let's see, I'm making a _____.* Select a child: *Tell us what you're making.* The child responds, "I'm making a _____."

2. Alternately, have the other children guess: *Let's guess. What is it? Who knows?* Model the response: "It's a _____;" "He's making a _____." Have the children guess before the object is completed.

12. Watercoloring Spring Creations

Language targets
- I'm, She's, He's

Materials
yellow or pink construction paper (one 8½" x 11" sheet per child)
watercolor sets (one per child)
water in paper cups
You should also have your own materials and paint along with the children.

Procedure
1. *Today we will paint some spring pictures. We will use watercolors and we can tell what we are painting.* Engage the children in a discussion of "spring" things (sunshine, grass, flowers, birds, etc.).

2. As you paint along with the children, announce *I'm painting too.* Comment on what you are painting, modeling use of I'm: *I'm painting a _____.* Comment on others' paintings: *He's painting a _____; She's using green paint.*

3. Either let the children paint for about 5 minutes, then stop and talk about what they are doing, or ask them *while* they are in motion, which is more conducive to producing the target form.

13. Let's Dress Up

Language targets
- 'm auxiliary and copula: I'm a [noun]; I'm [verb + -ing].

Materials
an assortment of pocketbooks, hats, blouses, belts, jewelry, shoes, ties, scarves
standing mirror of reflecting safety material

Procedure
1. *This game is "Let's Dress Up." Let's all find some things to put on. Then we will take turns showing them.*

2. After the children have dressed themselves up, say to the first child, *You can walk up and down. You can look in the mirror.*

3. *Tell us who you are. Say, "I'm a [lady/princess/big man/movie star/etc.]."* The child responds with "I'm a [noun]."

4. *Now tell us what you are wearing. Say, "I'm wearing a ____."* Have the children name each item in a separate sentence.

14. Animal Capers

Language targets
- Contracted copula: I'*m* a [animal name]
- Contracted auxiliary: I'*m* [verb + *-ing*]
- Basic level: I + verb + *-ing*
- Vocabulary; WHo/WHat question comprehension

Materials
large plastic animals (jungle set, farm set)
pictures of animals
plastic bag (optional)

Procedure
1. If desired, place the animals or pictures in the "grab bag" and have each child reach in to select an animal.

2. *Today we will play an animal game. We will pick an animal. We will make believe we are the animal.*

3. Have an adult or peer model go first. *I will show you our animals. What is this? What can it do?* Have a child name the animal, and name the typical noise or action associated with the animal:

   Lion—roars

   Fish—swims

   Horse—gallops, neighs

   Giraffe—runs, eats

   Monkey—swings from trees, eats bananas

4. *Now, [name], pick an animal. Make believe you are the animal. Who are you?* The child responds, "I'm a lion." *What are you doing?* "I'm roaring."

15. Where Are We? Blindfolded Travel Quiz

Language targets
- WH questions
- Yes/No questions (Are we in ____?)
- Prepositions *next to, in, near*
- Copula *are*
- Pronoun *we*

Materials   a scarf to use as a blindfold

Procedure	1. You will be blindfolding one child and taking that child by the hand, while the others come along too, to a preselected spot in the classroom or school grounds. The blindfolded child may touch walls and other features, as well as listen, to guess the location. Possible locations include the painting easel, hallway water fountain, cubbies, teacher's desk, sandbox.
	2. *We are going to play "Where Are We?" I will blindfold one child. I will hold your hand, so don't be scared. We will turn you around two times, then we all will help you walk someplace. When we get there, we will all take turns asking you, "Where are we?" You have to guess where we are. The other children will tell you if you are right. Then we will take off your blindfold and go back to our classroom doorway and pick someone else.*
	3. Select a child to be "IT." Lead the child to the destination, then select another child to ask IT, "Where are we?" The blindfolded child answers, "Are we at the water fountain?" Let the other children answer the blindfolded child's question.

16. What Animal Are We?

Language targets	- Pronouns *we, they*
	- WH questions
	- Yes/No questions
	- Plural nouns
Materials	animal photographs (select pictures of easily mimicked animals such as snakes, lions, cats, dogs, birds, etc.)
Procedure	1. This is an activity for a group of three children—two high-risk children and one normal-language peer.
	2. *This is a special guessing game called "What Animal Are We?" We will have two teams.* You and one high-risk child will be on one team, with a normal-language peer and one high-risk child on the other team.
	3. *One person on my team will pick an animal picture. Don't show it to the other team. Just show it to me. The other team can't see it.* The child on your team follows your directions.
	4. *Now we won't say it. We will pretend to be the animal.* Have your team member join you in acting out the animal behavior and noises (for example, fish swim, birds fly, horses say "neigh," etc.), then have the child ask the other team, "What animal are we?" (If desired, you may use a selection of animal pictures with which the children are familiar, to limit the range of possibilities.)
	5. *Now the other team has to talk about it and decide. Ask each other, "Are they lions? Are they fish?" Then ask us.*
	6. The other team will first ask each other, "Are they fish?" then ask your team, "Are you fish?"
	7. *Let's tell them: Yes we are / No we aren't.*

17. What's Wrong?

Language targets
- Negatives
- He's/She's
- Third person singular verbs

Materials pictures of scenes with absurdities, such as the "What's Wrong" pages found in *Highlights for Children.*

Procedure
1. The children can all have their own pictures and tell what's wrong with them, or one picture can be passed from child to child until everything wrong has been discovered. Children will respond with statements such as, "She's wearing two different shoes. Her shoes don't match." "Grass can't grow inside." "She's wearing one flipper," etc.

2. It is helpful to discuss the general context and content of the pictures (for example, *What are the children doing? They're decorating pumpkins for Halloween. What's wrong with this picture?* or *It's fall on the farm. What's wrong here?*).

18. What's Wrong? Memory Game

Language targets
- *wasn't, weren't, didn't, don't, can't*

Materials pictures of scenes with absurdities, such as the "What's Wrong" pages found in *Highlights for Children*

(Make one copy of the picture for each child.) The suggested dialogue below uses "Let's Go Skating" (D'Amato, J. P. February, 1986. *Highlights for Children.* Columbus, OH.)

Procedure
1. Distribute a copy of the absurdities picture to each child and explain, *This is a What's Wrong memory game. Everyone gets a picture called "Let's Go Skating." Let's look at it. This girl is going skating. She is carrying her ice skates. It is winter. She calls to this boy, "Let's go skating." He says, "As soon as I finish making this snowman."*

2. *There are lots of things wrong with this picture. Don't say them yet. Look at your picture until I say "Stop."* (Allow 30 seconds for the children to examine their pictures.) *Now you turn over your picture. Can you remember one thing that was wrong?* (The memory technique is used to elicit past-tense verbs.) Children's responses might include such sentences as, "Her mittens *weren't* the same." "Her other boot *wasn't* on." "Flowers *don't* grow on trees in winter," etc.

19. Animal Story: "You Don't Look Like Your Mother"

Language targets
- Negative *don't*
- Past tense verbs (regular and irregular)
- WH questions
- Copula *is, are*
- Sentence repetition and auditory memory
- Vocabulary

Materials Book: Fisher, A. 1973. *You Don't Look Like Your Mother, Said the Robin to the Fawn.* Glendale, CA: Bowmar Publishing Co.

Procedure
1. *I will read this animal story with you. First I will read a page and then you can take turns saying what I said.* Have one child "read" each page. Some pages are very long; the child can repeat sentence by sentence, or even phrase by phrase. Have everyone join in on the repeated phrase, *You don't look like your mother!*
2. Do not correct any repetition, but stress the *-ed* endings, is, are, etc.
3. You might want to discuss or explain the following vocabulary items: perched, aspens, ferns, fawn, dapples, aslant, milkweed, brink, knothole, ambled, squat, darting, slit, gauzy, occurred. Develop the concept that baby animals don't look like their mothers until they grow up.

20. Memory Game: What Happened Yesterday?

Language targets
- Past tense verbs (regular) with final /d/ or /t/

Materials pictures showing people engaged in various activities (suggested source: Shipley, K. G., and C. J. Banis. 1981. *Teaching Morphology Developmentally* [past tense /d/ cards]. Tucson, AZ: Communication Skill Builders)

Procedure
1. *This is a memory game. This is "What Happened Yesterday?" I am putting down four cards* (lay them face up). *Let's all look at them and say them so we can remember them.* Have the children state the actions depicted on the cards: "Yesterday he/she/they [verbed]."
2. *Now I am turning them over.*
3. Ask one child, *Pick one. Don't turn it over. What happened yesterday in this card? Can you remember?* Encourage the child to answer, "He/She/They [verbed] the ____."

140 / STRUCTURED LANGUAGE THERAPY

21. Mail Carrier

Language targets
- Past tense (regular)
- WH questions in complex sentence structure

Materials
pictures of familiar locations (possible source: Kerr, J. Y. K. 1979. *Photo Cue Cards*. Published 1985 by Communication Skill Builders, Tucson, AZ)

mail carrier's hat (optional)
envelopes
mail carrier's bag
long table

Procedure
1. *Today we will play "Mail Carrier." Our mail carrier will deliver letters to four places. Here are pictures of four places.* (Show the pictures to the children and identify them together.) *I will put them at each corner of this table.*

2. Select a child to be the mail carrier, and instruct, *Mail Carrier, you deliver this mail to these places.* Give the mailbag containing the letters to the designated mail carrier, and have the child deliver a letter to each picture.

3. *Now I will turn over the pictures so you can't see them. Let's ask our Mail Carrier, "Tell us where you delivered mail today."* Have children who did not deliver the mail repeat the question for the mail carrier (children may ask the question as a group, or you may ask individual children to question the mail carrier).

4. Then instruct the mail carrier, *"Mail Carrier, you tell us, 'Today I delivered mail to [the four locations],'"* and encourage the child to follow your model.

5. Suggestion: Select the normal-language peer model to be the mail carrier the first time, to model the *-ed* form.

6. Select new pictures for each new mail carrier.

22. Twenty Questions

Language targets
- Yes/No questions
- Vocabulary

Materials
pictures of common household objects (possible source: Kerr, J. Y. K. 1979. *Photo Cue Cards*. Published 1985 by Communication Skill Builders, Tucson, AZ)

bell or cymbals
small block or wooden spoon for microphone
paper money (optional)
puppet (optional)
paper to record number of questions

Procedure	1. *Today we are playing a TV quiz show game called "Twenty Questions."*
	2. *You are the contestants. I am the Master of Ceremonies.*
	Hello, Ladies and Gentlemen. Our friendly puppet here (operated by an adult) *will pick a picture of something in your house* (you may want to give a few clues here). *You can ask twenty questions to find out what it is. Let's see who wins the first prize: one thousand dollars and a trip to Hawaii.*
	3. Help the children ask questions of the puppet: "Is it a _____?" "Do you _____ with it?" "Is it big/small/other attributes?"

23. Mixed-Up Stories

Language targets	• Past tense verbs (regular and irregular)
	• Picture sequencing
	• Telling a narrative
Materials	4- or 6-card sequential picture stories
	slotted board to display the cards in a sequence
Procedure	1. Mix up the cards depicting the sequence of a familiar activity (building a snowman, going shopping, getting up and ready for school, etc.). *This story is all mixed up. Let's fix it. Let's tell what happened.*
	2. All the children can work on one story, or each one can sequence a story while the other children "help."
	3. *Which one goes first?* The child selects the first card.
	4. *What happened first?* The child can either imitate your model or independently describe the action in the first card, using past tense verbs.
	5. Continue until the story is finished. If time permits, encourage volunteers to tell their stories again.

24. Little Red Riding Hood (Flannel Board Story)

Language targets	• Past tense forms
	• She/He
	• Auxiliary *was*
	• Narrative sequencing
Materials	flannel board
	flannel board figures for "Little Red Riding Hood"
Procedure	1. Arrange flannel board pieces in a left-to-right sequence. Tell the story as suggested, pausing to give the children a chance to ask questions, to repeat part of the story, or to tell what happened next. You may want to leave some of the flannel board pieces on the floor or table for individual children to

place on the board if they take roles or take turns telling the narrative during a repeat telling of the story. During the retelling of the story, pause and let the children fill in.

Once upon a time, a little girl lived with her mother. She lived in a cottage near the forest. (Ask the children to tell you what a forest is.) *She had a lovely red cape and hood that her mother made for her. She loved it and she wore it all the time, so everyone called her "Little Red Riding Hood."*

(Place basket on Red Riding Hood's arm.) *One day Red Riding Hood's mother said to her, "Please take this basket of goodies to your grandma. She is sick." So Red Riding Hood started out with the basket of goodies. She was going to her grandmother's house in the woods.*

(Place Grandma's cottage and woods background scene to the right of Red Riding Hood; move her to the beginning of the path.) *As she was walking along, suddenly a big wolf appeared.* (Place figure of wolf to the left of Red Riding Hood.) Continue story with appropriate flannel board figures.

2. Emphasize *she* and past tense models and simplify most complex sentence constructions.

25. Three Little Pigs (Flannel Board Story)

Language targets
- Past tense (regular and irregular)
- Negatives
- Telling a narrative sequence
- Vocabulary: straw, twigs, bricks, wagon, sheepskin covering, fireplace, chimney, boiling pot

Materials
flannel board
flannel board characters for "The Three Little Pigs"

Procedure
1. Arrange the flannel board pieces (follow a left-right sequence).
2. Tell the story, pausing to give the children a chance to ask questions or to tell the next step. On the second telling, encourage the children to fill in the verbs when you pause or to tell what happened next. You may also have the children assume the roles and dramatize the story.

Once upon a time there were three pigs. The first pig was playing, but he needed to build a house. He met a man with a wagon. He said, "Can I buy some straw for my house?" The man said okay. The straw house was easy to build but it wasn't very strong. The first pig played near his house.

The second pig said, "I need to build a house." The man loaded twigs on his wagon and he came along . . . (same for bricks).

Then the Big Bad Wolf came along.

The first pig saw the Big Bad Wolf and he ran into his house. (Remove pigs and place head only in door of house.)

The wolf said, "Let me in, let me in." "No, No," said the pig, "Not by the hair of my chinny chin chin. I won't let you in." "I'll huff and I'll puff and I'll blow your house down . . ." (each pig runs to the next house).

The twig house was stronger . . .

. . . but the brick house was the strongest. The wolf couldn't blow it down. He said, "I'll come down the chimney," etc.

26. Book: The Fourteen Bears Summer and Winter

Language targets
- Concepts of summer vs. winter activities
- Past tense (regular and irregular)
- Copula or irregular verb *was, had*

Materials Book: Scott, E. 1973. *The Fourteen Bears Summer and Winter.* New York: Golden Press.

Procedure
1. *Today we will read stories about The Fourteen Bears in Summer and Winter.*
2. Read the stories and talk about the pictures. Elicit the target forms, using the cloze technique, in which children can complete a sentence you start once they have learned what to expect through repetition (example: This one had a modern couch. This one had a braided rug. This one ____. Response: "Had a ____.") Also use informal questioning to elicit the targets.
3. Talk about winter activities and summer activities: what you do and why, what you wear, etc.

27. What Happened In Between?

Language targets
- Past tense (regular and irregular)
- He/She
- Logical and analytical thinking skills (advanced levels)

Materials interpolation cards (such as those from Zachman, L., C. Jorgensen, M. Barrett, R. Huising, and M. K. Snedden. 1982. *Manual of Exercises for Expressive Reasoning—Interpolative thinking.* Moline, IL: LinguiSystems.)
- Candyland-type game or toys that fit together or add on, such as bristle blocks or parquetry pieces (optional)

Procedure
1. *This game is "What Happened In Between?" I (or peer) will go first.*
2. Pick a card. Have the child look at it while you read the material on the back. Example: *You see your friend in the morning and he looks fine. You see him after school and he has a cast on his arm. What happened in between?* (He broke his arm. He went to the doctor/hospital and they put a cast on it.)

3. You may liven this up by giving the children turns at playing Candyland, or pieces of a bristle block or parquetry set after they talk about the cards. Or you may lay the cards face down in a pile and have the children draw cards, imitating a card game.

28. What Will Happen If . . .

Language targets
- *Will*
- Comprehension of complex sentences beginning with *if, when, after,* with picture cues
- Ability to predict possible outcomes
- Pronouns *he, she, they*

Materials MEER Cards: Predicting Possible Outcomes (Zachman, L., C. Jorgensen, M. Barrett, R. Huising, and M. K. Snedden. 1982. *Manual of Exercises for Expressive Reasoning—Predicting Possible Outcomes.* Moline, IL: LinguiSystems.)

Procedure
1. *I am going to show you some pictures. You have to guess what will happen next.*
2. *Look and listen.* Show the picture and read the material on the back of the card. If possible, select those cards which will cue use of *will*. Alter the wording if necessary. (Example: After she eats breakfast, what will she do?)

29. Find the Honey Pot (Teddy Bear Week)

Language targets
- Prepositions *in, on, under, in front of, behind, next to*

Materials 4 yellow paper honey pots

Procedure Set this up in the theme area during Teddy Bear Week, or play in a larger play area. Each child may bring one teddy bear to play.

VERSION I:

Teddy bears like to eat honey in honey pots in some stories. There are four honey pots hidden right around here.

You and your teddy bears can look around and find the honey pots when I say "Go." Let the children search for and find the honey pots.

Now let's tell where we found the honey pots. Cue preposition phrases describing where the honey pots were found: "Was it *on* the shelf? *In* the _____?" etc.

VERSION II

One child leaves the area. You and the remaining children decide where to hide one honey pot. After the child returns, tell where the honey pot was hidden. For subsequent turns, have other children describe the hiding place, using the correct prepositions.

30. Teddy Bear Following Directions Game (Teddy Bear Week)

Language targets
- Variety of verbs, prepositions, body parts (such as *turn around, move your legs,* etc.)
- Following one-step directions

Materials *Look 'n' Do: Following Directions Activity Cards.* 1975. Trend Enterprises.

Procedure VERSION I:

Today we will play Teddy Bear "Look, Listen, and Do." I will pick someone to be first.

You and your teddy bear will pick one card. I will help you tell the other children what to do. You will tell them and show them the picture. Start with the normal-language peer, and have the remaining children follow the directions.

VERSION II:

I will show your teddy bears a picture and tell them what to do. You help them to do it.

31. Teddy Bear Stories (Teddy Bear Week)

Language targets
- Past tense (regular and irregular)
- Yes/No and WH questions
- Negatives

Materials books about bears (the following are suggestions):

Freeman, D. 1978. *A Pocket for Corduroy.* New York: Viking Press for Scholastic Book Services.

Disney, W. 1979. *Winnie the Pooh and the Honey Tree.* Buena Vista, CA: Walt Disney Productions, Inc.

Asch, F. 1978. *Sand Cake.* New York: Parents Magazine Press.

Procedure
1. Read the stories and show the pictures. On the second reading, use the "cloze" technique where you start a sentence and the children try to finish it using the correct target forms.
2. Alternately, ask the children to help you tell the story and cue them by modeling phrases and sentences containing target forms.

32. Teddy Bear Tall Tales (Teddy Bear Week)

Language targets
- don't, can't, won't

Materials teddy bears   bells or clackers

Procedure

1. *Today I am going to tell you and your teddy bears a tall tale. A tall tale is a story that has some BIG mistakes in it. When you and your teddy bear hear a mistake, ring your bell/shake your clacker.* (If these are unavailable, have the children clap their hands.)

   Once upon a time there lived a Teddy Bear family. There was a mommy and a daddy and one hundred children [clackers]. Ask one child, *What's wrong?* Response: You *can't* have one hundred children.

   Every morning they woke up, brushed their noses [clackers]. *What's wrong?* You *don't* brush your noses!

   Then they got dressed. Daddy Bear put on his dress [clackers]. Daddies *don't* wear dresses.

   Mommy Bear put on her diapers [clackers]. Mommies *don't* wear diapers.

   The children, Tommy and Sally, put on their bathing suits to get ready for school [clackers]. You *don't* wear bathing suits to school.

   If we hurry, we will be late [clackers]. They *won't* be late.

2. Continue to use absurdities to elicit the targets.

33. Guess What I'm Doing

Language targets
- I'm [verb + -ing]
- you're [verb + -ing]
- Verb vocabulary

Materials everyday action cards (use verbs that are easy to act out). Possible source: Courtman-Davies, M. 1980. *Everyday Actions* (cards). Wisbech, England: Bemrose UK, Ltd.

Procedure

1. *This is a card game and a "let's pretend" game and a guessing game!*

2. *I will show you three cards. Look at them. Now I will pretend to do one of the things on one of the cards. Guess what I'm doing.*

3. Select one child to guess what you are doing and to describe your actions using the "You're [verb + -ing]" form.

4. *Right, I'm [verb + -ing].*

5. *Now who wants to be the teacher?* Select one child who will select three more cards and act out one of them. Cue the child to say, "Guess what I'm doing?"

6. You can guess (to model *you're*) or you can prompt others by whispering in their ears.

… / 147

Arts and Crafts

The arts and crafts activities are grouped according to seasonal and/or holiday themes, and include suggestions of language targets to work on while the children are engaged in these tasks.

Introduction

List of Language Targets

Activities

September
- Making a Face
- Painting a Mailbox
- Cutting Family Pictures

October
- Leaf Prints
- Matching Shapes of Leaves
- Fall Collage
- Leaf Creature
- Tissue Ghosts
- Stand-Up Halloween Cat
- Playdough Pumpkins
- Sponge Pumpkins

November
- Finger Painting
- Making Playdough
- Coloring a Turkey Body
- Turkey Feathers
- Turkey Handprints
- Indian Headdress
- Indian Hand Tracing

December
- Making Christmas Stockings
- Foil Paintings
- Santa Claus Face (sectioned paper plates)
- Yarn Holiday Bells
- Tissue Wreaths
- Lollipop Holiday Ornaments (take-home gifts)
- Gift-Wrapping Paper (to wrap lollipop ornaments)
- Holiday Cards (to give to parents)
- Rudolph the Red-Nosed Reindeer (paper-bag puppets)

January
- Snowflakes
- Popcorn Snowman
- Painting with White (on black paper)
- Macaroni Jewelry
- Shape and Object Rubbings

February
- Heart Collage
- Coloring and Cutting Hearts
- Valentine's Day Cards and Envelopes
- Favorite Things Collage

March
- March Bulletin Board
- Painting a Fire Engine
- Tracing Shapes with Stencils
- Paper Plate Bunnies
- Making Kites
- Easter Chicks
- Easter Basket (bag)
- Pussy Willows

April
- Butterfly, Butterfly Fly Away (picture)
- Ladybugs
- Daffodils (three-dimensional pictures with egg-carton cups)

May
- Cupcake Flower Vase for Mother's Day
- Caterpillars
- Paper Plate Fish

Introduction

Arts and crafts activities with preschool children provide one of the best opportunities for language remediation. These types of activities provide concrete tactile and visual materials to use in a naturalistic presentation and/or discussion. Objects can be labelled, spatial concepts (such as *on, under, next to,* etc.) can be modelled, pre-academic skills (such as rote counting, matching, shape and color identification) can be developed, and fine motor control can be emphasized as part of the activity.

To facilitate language objectives during arts and crafts, it is best for the teacher to have most of the materials collected in one spot, with a few of the items in their designated spots throughout the classroom. That is, materials should not be presented to each student individually before the project is started. The students then will have to help identify the necessary materials, find them, and distribute them. This teaches vocabulary, direction following, and sequencing of activities.

With preschool children, it is generally a good idea to have a sample of the finished work. At times, you may want to create the item as the students observe, but for the most part, it is a good idea to have the finished product to present as a model.

During art activities involving more than simple pencil/crayon-and-paper activities, the ratio of children to adults should not exceed three to one. If there are more than three children working with one adult, an atmosphere of behavioral supervision is created, rather than a pleasant art experience. Additionally, because preschool children's abilities vary greatly, the adult-child ratio should depend on the complexity of the task and the amount of assistance the children will need in activities involving water, paint, and especially cutting. If too much attention is required by one child, the other children will quickly lose interest in any activity.

When using any liquid substance or anything that may damage tables or floors, be sure to cover the table and/or floor with paper or plastic. All children and adults should have plastic or heavy cloth paint shirts to wear during messy art activities. Most preschoolers will need assistance with multimedia materials such as paint and glue. It is generally easier to have each child work from individual containers of such materials, rather than having a community pot. Having the children involved in distributing the containers provides the opportunity for counting, naming, sequencing, and development of quantity concepts. (Make sure the containers are stable and do not tip easily. Baby food jars are excellent for paint, and the lids work well for small amounts of glue, which can be applied easily with cotton swabs or toothpicks.)

Remember to emphasize the *process* rather than the *product*. Self-esteem is greatly enhanced when preschoolers are allowed to produce products based on their abilities, with little or no correction in the process.

List of Language Targets

The following is a sample list of language targets to model, prompt, and elicit during the art and craft activities.

Basic Level

Nouns
- circle (and other shapes)
- crayon
- easel
- paint
- paper
- pencil
- paintbrush
- scissors (singular)
- shape
- smock
- sponge

Noun plurals
- circles
- crayons
- lines
- pencils
- pieces
- shapes

Noun possessives
- possessives of children's names (John's, Katie's)

Verb + -ing
- counting
- cutting
- gluing
- holding
- painting
- picking
- pressing
- standing

"I'm [verbing] the [object]."
Prompt: "What are you doing?" or "Tell ___ what you are doing."
- I'm cutting the paper.
- I'm drawing a ___.

Advanced Level

Regular past tense verbs
- colored
- counted
- crayoned
- glued
- painted
- pasted
- picked
- pressed
- traced

Irregular past tense verbs
- chose
- cut
- did
- drew
- found
- held
- made

"I [verbed] the object" (regular and irregular past tense):
Prompt: "What did you do?" or "Tell ___ what you did."
- I crayoned the picture.
- I cut the pattern.
- I made a snowman.
- I painted a picture.
- I made a snowstorm.

Prepositions
- around
- beside
- between
- for
- in
- on
- to
- under
- with

Pronouns
- he
- her
- hers
- him
- his
- it
- she
- you
- yours
- etc.

Making a Face

Language targets
- Lower-level model:
  I want ___ (part).
  Eyes go here.
  Mouth goes here.
  Also model: put *on* face, *two* eyes, gluing, pressing

- Higher-level children: Irregular past tense—describe to the children what they just finished doing (you *found* a nose; you *drew* the smile; you *made* _____).

- Regular past tense: Describe what they just finished doing, then ask them to tell another child (you glued on the ___, you colored the ___).

- Colors

- Prepositions *under, in the middle*

- Location words: *on the side, above, below*

- You can also model the yes/no and WH question forms: Is the girl/boy smiling? Is she sad? Where are the girl's/boy's eyebrows? (Note the possessive forms to model.) Where is the nose?

Materials
a paper plate per child (preferably the divided kind with three sections)
glue
scissors
markers or crayons
colored construction paper
mirrors

Preparation
Cut out shapes for ears, eyes (be sure to include eye colors of all the children involved in the project), nose, and hair (use white paper to cut appropriate numbers of boys' haircuts and girls' haircuts). Place all materials on the work table.

Procedure
Have the children look in mirrors to determine colors for their eye shapes and hair. Help them select appropriate colors for the eyes, and guide them to use crayons to color the appropriate "hair piece." Glue the hair and eyes onto the plates, then discuss and draw in eyebrows and eye pupils. Glue on the noses, and have the children draw happy smiles with a marker.

Painting a Mailbox

Language targets
- Colors

- Following one- and two-step directions

- Concepts: top, bottom, sides, inside, outside, wet, dry

- Possessive nouns (commenting on another's mailbox): "Jessica's"

Materials	shoebox and cover (one per child) paints brushes newspapers or plastic tablecloths paint smocks
Procedure	Cover the tables where the children will be painting, and set out paints, brushes, shoeboxes, and lids. Let the children paint their shoeboxes. Remind the children of the different parts to paint: top, bottom, sides, inside, outside.

Cutting Family Pictures

Language targets	• Modeling of WH questions (Encourage children to ask questions of each other.) • Conversational turn taking and topic maintenance • Responding to WH questions • Presuppositions: Learning to identify family members named (for example, my brother, sibling's name) • Correct use of verb tenses to describe family activities
Materials	magazines glue scissors white construction paper
Procedure	Have children find pictures of whole families and of individuals in magazines, cut them out, and paste them on white paper. Encourage discussions about the students' own families and about the families in the pictures: Who is this? What is this family doing? Who is in your family? What do you do with your ___?

Leaf Prints

Language targets	• Following one-, two-, and three-step directions • Color identification • Verb tenses: *will:* Tell the children what they *will* do. *is + verb + -ing*: Comment on or ask them to tell what they are doing. Ask the children to tell one another what they *did* (using such past-tense verbs as *painted, pressed, made, rolled*). • Vocabulary: tissue paper, print, rolling pin
Materials	leaves of different shapes gathered while on a walk red, yellow, and orange paint brushes newspaper tissue paper rolling pins

152 / ARTS AND CRAFTS

Preparation | Cut tissue paper to desired size (slightly larger than a single leaf, or large enough for composite leaf prints). Put a sheet of newspaper in front of each child.

Procedure | Have the children arrange their leaves on the newspaper. (Leaves can be arranged either for single prints, or as a "collection" of three or four leaves to be printed on one sheet of paper.) Guide the children to paint their leaves, using a separate color for each leaf. Show them how to lay a piece of paper *carefully* over the painted leaves and to use their hands or rolling pins to press the paper down on the leaves. Carefully remove the tissue papers, label each with the child's name and/or symbol, and lay them out to dry.

Matching Shapes of Leaves

Language targets
- Following a complex one-step direction
- Concepts of *same, doesn't match*
- Vocabulary: connect

Materials | crayons

a reproducible worksheet of leaf outlines with two matching pairs and one different leaf

Preparation | Make one photocopy of the leaf worksheet per child.

Procedure | Have children draw lines to connect the leaves that match, and have them circle the one leaf that doesn't belong.

Fall Collage

Language targets
- Vocabulary and plural nouns: leaves, acorns, chestnuts, pine cones, pine needles, branches, tree trunk, sky, ground, grass, dirt
- Prepositions: *on, through*
- Concepts:
  Colors (orange, green, brown, yellow)
  Textures (smooth, pointy [pine needles])
  Shapes (same/different—compare leaves)

Materials | items found on fall walk (leaves, acorns, branches, chestnut shells, pine cones, etc.)

sheets of large white construction paper (one for every three or four children)

glue

crayons

Preparation | Plan for three or four children to work at each table or work station. Draw a tree trunk and branches on each sheet of white construction paper. Lay out the tree drawings on the tables, and either place collections of the gathered materials on each table or keep the collection of materials with you, so that the children have to ask for them.

Procedure	1. Guide children into groups of three or four to each table. Give suggestions as to where they glue their leaves and other materials: Some green leaves and some colored leaves can go *on* the branches *of* the tree; some leaves are falling *through* the air, and some leaves fell *on* the ground.
2. Also ask the children, "Do you want to color brown dirt or green grass on the ground?"
3. Show the other objects to the children, naming them as you hold them up. Ask, "Do you want a leaf OR a pine cone?" "What do you want?" "What color leaf do you want?" etc.

Leaf Creature

Language targets	• Following directions
• Body parts: body, head, eyes, arms, legs
Materials	leaves (look for leaves that are at least 2" to 3" in diameter)
paper plates (one per child)
glue
markers
Preparation	Gather leaves that have either just recently fallen or are still on the tree. Avoid dry leaves that will crumble if flattened (the leaves need to be fairly flat, or supple and pliable for this activity).
Procedure	1. Distribute paper plates and allow children to select (or distribute) a leaf.
2. Have the children glue the leaves to the paper plates, and then let them use markers to add a face, arms, and legs to make a person, or add "feelers," eyes, and lots of little legs to make a "creepy crawler."

Tissue Ghosts

Language targets	• Verbs: future tense *will*
• Vocabulary: names of the materials (tissue, cotton balls, yarn, marking pen, face, head, body)
• Concepts: open up, in the middle, three, white, same color

Source	Warren, J. 1983. *Crafts: Early Learning Activities*. Palo Alto, CA: Monday Morning Books.
Materials	white facial tissues cotton balls (three per child) white thread or yarn (cut in 18" lengths) markers
Preparation	Explain the activity to the children, but do not distribute the materials. Instead, keep the materials with you and pass them out as the children request them.
Summary of activity	Lay out a tissue and place three cotton balls in the middle of it. Bring the corners of the tissue together, then wrap the yarn around the tissue at the base of the cotton balls to form a head, leaving a long tail of yarn for a hanger. Draw eyes and/or mouth with a marker.
Procedure	1. Tell the children, "This is what we will do. We will make ghosts. What will we make them with?" Cue or tell the children as necessary as they name the materials, and give one tissue, three cotton balls, and a length of string to each child. 2. Describe the process for making the ghost, then repeat these directions one step at a time as the children follow the instructions and construct their ghosts: "First we will open up the tissue. Then we will put three cotton balls right in the middle," etc. 3. Give assistance as needed in helping the children wrap the yarn around the ghost's neck and tie it.

Stand-Up Halloween Cat

Language targets	• Following one- and two-step directions • Vocabulary comprehension: half-circle, fold, eyes, ears, tail, nose, mouth, whiskers, paws • Colors: black, orange • Possessive nouns: cat's body, head, tail, etc.
Source	Doan, R.L. 1979. *Arts and Crafts Achievement Activities*. West Nyack, NY: The Center for Applied Research in Education, Inc.
Materials	black construction paper (9" x 12", one sheet per child) chalk orange paper scraps scissors paper clips (optional) paste or glue

Preparation
1. For each child, center a 6" semicircle along the 9" side of a piece of black construction paper and trace with chalk (see diagram A).

2. Draw two eyes, a nose and mouth, two ears, and a tail on orange construction paper for each child to cut out. (See diagrams B and C for assembly layout.)

Procedure
1. Give each child a sheet of the prepared black construction paper. Have them fold it in half crossways (demonstrate if necessary). Show them where to cut out the half-circle. (If necessary, paper clip the edges of the folded paper together to make cutting of the two thicknesses easier.)

2. Instruct the children to cut out the eyes, ears, etc., and glue them onto one of their black half-circles for the cat's head. Be ready to give assistance to children who need help with cutting.

3. Glue on completed head and tail to finish the cat, and fold out "paws" to help it stand up, if necessary.

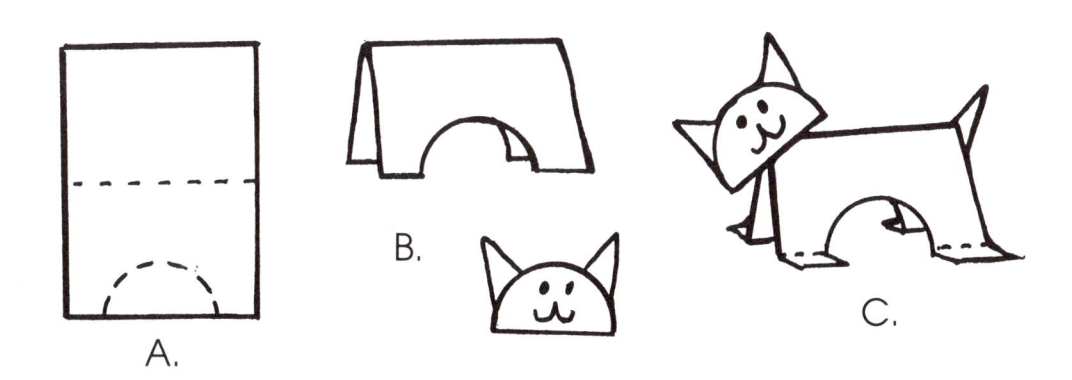

Playdough Pumpkins

Language targets
- Vocabulary and basic concepts to discuss while working:
  A pumpkin with a face is called a "jack-o'-lantern."
  The popcorn seed is *not* popped; *can't* eat it.
  What is a face? (See if children can define a "face.")
  Right now, playdough is soft. What *will* happen when it dries?
   It will get hard.

Source
Warren, J. 1983. *Crafts: Early Learning Activities.* Palo Alto, CA: Monday Morning Books.

Materials
orange playdough
unpopped popcorn kernels
round plastic lids (3" to 4" diameter, one per child)

Note: the playdough recipe below does not use vegetable oil, and produces a clay that dries completely.

Preparation
Keep all the materials while you are explaining the activity to the children.

Procedure	1. Today we will make playdough pumpkins. *What will we need?* (Hold up the materials and see if the children can name them and guess what the popcorn seeds are for.) *This is what we will need:* lids, orange playdough, popcorn seeds.
	2. Give each child approximately ¼ cup of playdough. Have them press the orange playdough into the lids, then let them press popcorn kernels into the dough to make jack-o'-lantern faces. Allow the playdough to dry. Children may leave the face in the lid or remove it.

Cornstarch and baking soda playdough

Recipe	1 C cornstarch
	2 C baking soda (one-pound box)
	1¼ C water
	yellow and red food coloring
Preparation	Mix dry ingredients; add water and food coloring. Cook in a microwave on high power for 3 to 5 minutes, stirring after each minute of cooking, until the mixture is thickened; or cook over a medium heat burner, stirring constantly until the mixture thickens. Cover and allow to cool, then turn out onto a flat surface and knead lightly. Store in an airtight container. After it has dried, the surface of this dough has a sparkly, shiny look, excellent for ornaments and decorations. One recipe makes 2½ cups of dough.

Sponge Pumpkins

Language targets	• Verbs: future tense *will*
	• Vocabulary: sponge, dip, paint, orange, black, clothespin
	• Optional ideas for "pumpkin" conversation:
	Pumpkins are food. You can cut them up and cook them. You can boil them in water. You can bake them. You can make pumpkin bread or pumpkin pie. Pumpkins grow from a seed. You plant the seed in the ground, etc.
Source	Warren, J. 1983. *Crafts: Early Learning Activities.* Palo Alto, CA: Monday Morning Books.
Materials	small sponge pieces (one or two per child)
	spring clothespins (one per child—optional)
	orange and black paint
	paper plates (one per child)
	newspapers
	paint smocks

Preparation	Attach a clothespin to each small sponge for easier handling. Cover work surfaces with newspaper.
Procedure	1. Before distributing the materials, tell the children what they *will* do, and see if they can name the materials and the colors you show them. 2. Have children put on their paint smocks, and give each child a paper plate and a sponge piece. Have children dip sponges in orange paint and sponge-paint the front of a paper plate. Have the children help in washing out the sponges as the orange paint dries. The children then can dip the sponges into black paint to make eyes, nose, and mouth on the orange faces. 3. If you do this activity in small groups, you might ask one child who has just finished to explain to another child what to do.

Finger Painting: Making a Picture with Shapes

Language targets	• WH and yes/no questions (teacher models): What colors do you want? What did you make? Do you want _____? Child: May I have _____? • Concepts: shapes (circle, square, triangle, rectangle) • Prepositions: *for, with* • Verbs (irregular and *-ed* past tense: I made a _____, I drew a _____, I painted a _____) • Vocabulary: zigzags, circles, lines across and down, loops
Materials	finger paints (selected colors) finger-paint paper wet sponges newspaper painting smocks small cups or cans
Preparation	Cover tables with newspaper and have children put on their painting smocks.
Procedure	1. Ask children, "What color do you want?" Put a small amount of paint in a cup. 2. If desired, ask the children, "Can you make a picture with different shapes?" man: circle for head, triangle for body house: square for building, triangle for roof horse: rectangle for body, triangle at one end for head, sticks for legs 3. Other options: free style (loops, zigzags, circles, lines across and down)

Making Playdough

Language targets
- Future tense: We *will* make ___. We *will* add ___.
- Copula: It *is* hot (sticky, lumpy, soft, etc.)
- Auxiliary: Henry *is* stirring.
- Vocabulary: flour, salt, oil, water, cream of tartar, colors

Materials
heavy saucepan
large spoon
measuring cup
measuring teaspoon and tablespoon
waxed paper

Recipe
2 C flour

1 C salt

4 Tbsp oil

4 tsp cream of tartar

2 C water

Food coloring

Mix ingredients in the order given.

Preparation
Set out ingredients, saucepan, and measuring cups and spoons. Print the recipe on large paper so the children can help "read" it.

Procedure
1. *We will make playdough. First we need two cups of flour* (fill cup twice). *Then we will add one cup of salt; then cream of tartar and oil. Add food coloring to water and mix.* Children can participate in the measuring and initial stirring. Adults should handle the stirring as the mixture heats and thickens.

2. Cook on low-medium heat, stirring constantly, until the mixture is the consistency of mashed potatoes. It will "ball up" off the bottom of the pan. (To cook in the microwave, mix the ingredients in a glass or plastic bowl and cook for three to five minutes on high power, stirring after each minute of cooking.)

3. Turn onto waxed paper and, after dough has cooled, divide it among the children and have them knead out the lumps.

Coloring a Turkey Body

Language targets
- Vocabulary: parts of turkey (head, body, wattle, feet)
- Concept of Thanksgiving turkey:
  A turkey is a bird.
  Gobbles.
  Lives on a farm.
  Has big feathers.

- Concepts: colors (red, brown, yellow, orange)
- Following directions, relaying them to others (latecomers)

Materials
a large turkey body (body, head, wattle, feet)

crayons (red, brown, yellow, orange)

Preparation
Draw a large turkey body (without tail feathers) on a sheet of paper (18" x 24" or larger).

Procedure
Children will color all parts of turkey body together. Talk about parts. Tell them we will put our turkey and his feathers (see the activity below) on the door for everyone to see.

Turkey Feathers
(for the turkey body from the activity above)

Language targets
- Concept of Thanksgiving turkey:
  A turkey is a bird.
  Gobbles.
  Lives on a farm.
  Has big feathers.

- Colors

- Following directions: Each child will trace a feather, choose favorite color, then color feather, and cut it out. Each child will tape picture to feather and put feather on turkey.

- Verbs: future and past tense
  will trace, traced
  will cut, cut
  will choose, chose
  will color, colored
  will tape, taped

Materials
feather patterns (approximately 4" x 9", for the turkey dimensions listed in the activity above)

pencils
white paper (one or more sheets per child)
crayons
scissors
tape
picture of each child

Preparation
1. Do this activity after the turkey body from the above activity is completed.
2. Trace and precut several turkey feather tracing patterns for the children to use.

Procedure — Distribute feather patterns to the children and have them trace a feather on the white paper. Have each child select one crayon to color the feathers. Have children cut out their feathers. (You may need to retrace the outline if they have colored heavily over it.) Then they will tape their picture to the feather, and tape the feathers to the turkey on the door.

Turkey Handprints

Language targets
- Colors: recognition of red, brown, orange, blue, green, yellow
- Following directions
- Parts of the hand and parts of a turkey:
  thumb—head
  palm—body
  fingers—feathers
  legs and feet
- Vocabulary: print, press

Materials — paints (red, brown, orange, blue, green, yellow)

brushes

paper (single sheets for individual prints, or a large sheet of shelf paper for a collage)

newspapers

paint smocks

wet paper towels

markers or crayons

Preparation — Cover work surfaces with newspapers; have children put on paint smocks. Have wet paper towels available at all work areas for children to wipe their hands. Set out paints and brushes.

Procedure
1. Have children paint the palmar surfaces of their nondominant hands: thumbs *red,* palms *brown,* and fingers assorted colors for feathers. Have the children spread their fingers and make prints of their painted hands on the paper. Children may each make their own turkey prints, or the entire group can work together to make a turkey-print collage on a large sheet of paper. You may need to help the children press their hands to the paper, to make sure that the paint on the entire hand transfers to the paper.

2. After the children have finished pressing their hands onto the paper, help them wipe the excess paint off their hands. They may then use crayons or markers to add legs to each turkey.

Indian Headdress

Language targets
- Plural nouns: feathers, pieces of paper
- Colors
- Vocabulary: Indian, headdress
- Concept: Indians were the first Americans or Native Americans. They already lived here when the Pilgrims came.

Materials
black construction paper (12" x 18") cut into 1½" strips (you will probably need two strips per child, stapled together)

small strips of colored construction paper (to fit the feather pattern)

one feather pattern (approximately 2" x 8") per child

pencils
glue
scissors
stapler

Preparation
Photocopy or trace a feather pattern onto heavy paper or card stock, making one pattern for each child.

Procedure
1. Give each child a black headband. Have the children select five pieces of colored paper and one feather pattern. (Note: not all children may want to make five feathers.) Have the children trace the feather pattern on their pieces of construction paper and cut them out. As the children work, tell them about Indians.

2. Have the children glue the feathers onto the headband. Allow the glue to dry, then adjust the headband to fit the child's head and staple the headband together in the back.

Indian Hand Tracing

Language targets
- Following directions and demonstration
- Vocabulary:
  face, palm, feathers, fingers

  Indians: first people to live in this country (Native Americans)

  Explain Thanksgiving (Indians already here; people came from far away in boats to live here, met the Indians)
- Verbs (regular and irregular past tense: traced, colored, drew)

Materials
light-colored paper (one sheet per child)
crayons
markers

Procedure
1. Using your recessive hand as a pattern, demonstrate how to trace around your hand and fingers (fold thumb under your palm) to make the Indian outline. Draw face, feathers, and war paint.

2. Have the children trace their recessive hands in the same manner. They can then use markers and crayons to add the facial features and head band, and to color in the feathers.

Making Christmas Stockings

Language targets
- Vocabulary: stocking, cuff, cotton balls
- Verbs:
  past tense regular: colored, decorated, glued
  past tense irregular: cut, made
- Discourse: Telling latecomers what we *will* make, *are* making, or *made*; explaining the sequential steps in completing the project
- Colors

Materials
white construction paper (9" x 12", one sheet per child)
crayons
markers
glue
cotton balls

Preparation
1. Make a stocking pattern that will fit onto the construction paper, trace onto the white construction paper, and cut out a stocking shape for each child.

2. Lay out precut stockings, crayons, markers, glue, and cotton balls.

Procedure
Let each child color a stocking, leaving the upper portion (cuff) plain. The children can then glue cotton balls to the cuff.

Foil Paintings

Language targets
- WH question: What color do you want?
- Verbs:
  future tense: will
  past tense: picked, painted, stapled, dipped
  past irregular: made

- Vocabulary and concepts: foil, cotton swabs, paper, stapler, shiny
- Colors (red, green, white)
- Sequential narratives describing the project to latecomers

Materials aluminum foil (12"-wide roll)

cotton swabs

tempera paints (green, red, white)

small cups for paint

red, green, and white construction paper (12" x 18")

stapler

Preparation 1. Tear off 16" lengths of foil; cut off a 2" strip to make 10" x 16" rectangles. You may staple the foil to the construction paper backing, or you may choose to let the children select the backing colors for themselves.

2. Pour paint into small cups. Make one set of paints for each pair of children.

3. Lay out cotton swabs to use in applying the paint to the foil.

Procedure 1. Show the children the foil stapled to the construction paper and say, "Today we *will* make shiny, pretty pictures."

"This is what we need *to make* the pictures." Show materials; have children name them and tell late arrivals about them.

"I *will* pick a helper to pass out the colored paper" (pick helper). "You can tell him/her *what color* you want." (Children tell what colors they want.)

"Next we *will* staple this foil *to* the colored paper."

"Now you can *dip* your cotton swab into this paint and make a design or Christmas picture."

2. Have the children explain the activity to latecomers and show their finished products to others.

Santa Claus Face

Language targets
- Verbs:
  will (Guess what we WILL make today. How WILL we make it?)
  past (regular): glued
  past (irregular): made
- Vocabulary: Santa Claus, mustache, beard, hat, eyes, nose, mouth
- Prepositions: mustache is *above* the mouth; beard is *below* the mouth

164 / ARTS AND CRAFTS

Materials
paper plates (preferably the three-sectioned type, one per child)
red and black paper
glue
cotton balls

Preparation
1. Cut out one set of the following for each child: black eyes, red nose, red mouth, red triangular hat
2. Lay out all the materials on the table.

Procedure
1. Ask the children to identify the materials needed and guess what might be made out of them.
2. Explain what the Santa Claus face will look like, and have the children glue eyes, nose, and mouth on the paper plates, gluing on the hat above the eyes. Then have the children glue cotton balls along the lower rim and the tip of the hat, and above the mouth to make a mustache. The last step is to glue cotton balls around the edge of the paper plate to make sideburns and a beard.

Yarn Holiday Bells

Language targets
- Interactive language:
  Children try to guess how the project was constructed.
  Children name materials and explain process to latecomers.
  Children ask for help (Can you help me? yes/no questions).
- Size concepts: small, bigger
- Number concepts: two, three
- Locatives: around, through, next to
- Vocabulary: yarn
- Encourage the child who finishes early to help a latecomer.

Materials
small and medium paper cups (two small and one medium per child)

glue (in cups or small jars)

craft sticks or cotton swabs (to apply glue)

green and red yarn

construction paper or seasonal gift-wrapping paper

stapler

scissors

Preparation
1. Punch very small holes in the bottom of each cup. Cut bows out of construction paper or seasonal gift-wrapping paper (one per child). Cut yarn into 3' to 4' lengths.

2. Make a sample bell: Coat the outside surface of a paper cup with glue, then wind yarn around the cup, covering the entire surface. Use different colors of yarn, if desired. Cut a 12" length of yarn and insert one end through the small hole in the bottom of the paper cup. Make a large knot, and pull the knot up against the bottom of the cup. (Three of these bells will be tied together and stapled to a bow for the finished product.)

Procedure
1. Today we *will* make paper bells. Look at mine. Who can guess *how* I made this one? (See if children can reconstruct the process, then explain how to make the bells, showing your model cup and the materials.)

2. You can pick out two small cups and one bigger cup.

3. We have to put glue all around the cup. Why?

4. Now we will wind the yarn all around. Can you wind the yarn with the rows *right next* to each other?

5. Can you push the yarn *through* the hole? (Encourage them to ask for help.)

6. You can pick out a bow. Let's *attach* all three yarns together and staple them to your bow.

Tissue Wreaths

Language targets
- Ideas for interactive language: Put children in charge of tissue paper, berries, and glitter distribution if they finish early. These children can then explain the project and help latecomers. Children must ask for the materials they need, either from you or from the children designated to distribute them.

- Yes/No questions: *May I have ___, please?* or *Do you want ___?*

- Vocabulary: names of materials

- Verbs:
  future: will
  past (regular): glued, pasted, sprinkled, crunched, ripped, dotted
  past (irregular): tore, cut

Materials
green construction paper (one 9" x 12" sheet per child)

red construction paper scraps (for berries)

scraps of colored construction paper and/or seasonal gift wrap (for bows)

glitter
glue
cotton-tipped swabs (glue applicators)
small paper or plastic cups (glue containers)
green tissue paper
newspaper (for covering tables)
If possible, provide a real wreath for comparison.

166 / ARTS AND CRAFTS

Preparation
1. Cut 9" wreaths from the green construction paper. Cut bows from the colored construction paper and/or wrapping paper (one per child); cut small circles (holly berries) from the red construction paper.
2. Make a sample: tear off small pieces of tissue paper, crumple them, and glue them to the paper wreath. Glue on small red circles for holly berries. If desired, sprinkle glitter on the wreath while the glue is still tacky; shake off excess. Glue on a bow.
3. Cover tables with newspaper; pour glue and glitter into small containers.

Procedure
1. Today we *will* decorate paper wreaths (show finished model).
2. Here is what we need to *make* them. (Have children name materials.)
3. First I will do this (demonstrate ripping and crunching up the tissue paper). Who can tell [latecomer] what I did? (Elicit *ripped/tore/crunched/crinkled*.) Now you can do it.
4. Now we'll glue our tissue onto the wreath.
5. Now we'll dot the glue all around the wreath and glue on these paper berries.
6. Do you want to sprinkle on the glitter? Do you want a bow?

Lollipop Holiday Ornaments (Take-Home Gifts)

Language targets
- Verbs:
  future: we *will*
  past (regular): threaded, pushed, glued, tied, wrapped
  past (irregular): held, cut
- Concepts: straight line, "pinked" line from pinking shears
- Vocabulary: styrofoam, ornaments
- Question forms (Can you help me?)

Materials
styrofoam balls (1" to 1½" diameter)

small dowels (no larger than ¼" diameter, cut 5"-6" in length)

Christmas fabric

pinking shears

glue

needle and thick thread

colored yarn (8" to 12" lengths)

Preparation
Use pinking shears to cut the fabric into 6" squares. (Note: the children may be able to do the fabric cutting; measure and mark dark lines on the wrong side of the fabric.)

| Procedure | 1. Work with two or three children at a time.
| | 2. Give each child a styrofoam ball and a stick; instruct them to push the stick into the ball, then pull it out, dot glue on the end of the stick, and push it back into the ball.
| | 3. Have children cover the balls with the fabric, and help them tie yarn around the fabric to hold it.
| | 4. Help children use the needle and thread to make a very small loop on the top of the ornament, so an ornament hanger can be inserted into it for hanging.

Gift-Wrapping Paper
(To Wrap Lollipop Ornaments)

| Language targets | • Vocabulary: wrapping paper, prints, names of cookie shapes or designs
| | • Verbs:
| | future: *will* dip, *will* dry, *will* wrap, *will* give
| | past (regular): dipped, dried
| | • Colors

| Materials | Christmas cookie cutters
| | roll of white shelf paper or newsprint
| | tempera paints (red, blue, green, orange)
| | paper plates, pie pans, or other shallow containers (for paints)
| | newspapers to cover the work area

| Preparation | Cover tables with newspapers. Pour a small amount of paint into the shallow pans. Cut 20" squares of paper (one per child).

| Procedure | 1. Have the children make prints on their sheets of paper with the cookie cutters dipped in paint.
| | 2. Explain that this paper will be used to wrap presents for parents *after* the paint dries.

Holiday Cards
(To Give to Parents)

| Language targets | • WH questions: *What* color paper do you want? *Where* do you want to glue your picture? (You may pick a helper to ask other children these questions.)
| | • Verbs:
| | future: *will*
| | past (regular): glued, picked, folded
| | past (irregular): wrote, made

Materials	colored Christmas or seasonal pictures that will fit on the 9" x 12" card (old holiday greeting cards work well)
	colored construction paper (12" x 18")
	markers
	scissors
	glue
Preparation	Collect the fronts of old holiday greeting cards or have children color an appropriate picture.
Procedure	1. Have each child select a piece of colored paper and fold it in half. Let them glue their pictures on the front of the card or inside (allow them to choose).
	2. Tell them this *will* be for Mom and/or Dad and have them think of something appropriate for you (or a helper) to write inside (*You are the best Mom and Dad. Merry Christmas. I love you very much,* etc.)
	3. Have children write their names or help the children to trace their names.

Rudolph the Red-Nosed Reindeer

Language targets	• Verb tenses: future: *will* (in telling children what we *will* do) past (regular): glued, folded past (irregular): cut
	• Noun vocabulary: reindeer, head, antlers, eyes, nose, breast
	• Colors: red, black, white, brown
	• Shapes: round, circle, triangle
Materials	white construction paper (for antlers and breast)
	lunch bags (one per child)
	red and black construction paper (scraps)
	chalk (for tracing on black paper)
	scissors
	glue
	stapler (optional)
	crumpled newspaper
Preparation	1. With the lunch bags still flat, round off the open end as shown in diagram A.
	2. Cut antlers out of white construction paper (one per child; see diagram B).
	3. Draw circles on red and black construction paper (one red, two black per child) for eyes and noses. On the white scraps left over from the antlers, trace triangles for the children to cut out the breast piece.
	4. Prepare a sample: Open up the paper bag and fold out the bottom (as if you were going to put something in it). If desired, push a little crumpled newspaper into the bottom of the bag to fill it out. Then hold the top edges together and fold them down approximately 3½" from the top edge, to make the face. Glue eyes and nose on the folded flap; open flap up to glue in the

antler piece, then glue (or staple) the face flap down. Glue on the white breast piece below the face.

Procedure
1. Display the sample, and show children how to fold the top of the bag to make the face area.

2. Have the children cut out two black eyes, one red nose, and the white triangular breast piece, and give each child an antler piece.

3. Have them glue the eyes and nose in the appropriate places on the face, and glue the antlers to the bag underneath the folded flap.

4. Help them glue down the face fold (or staple right below the nose, to save time and frustration); let them glue on the breast piece.

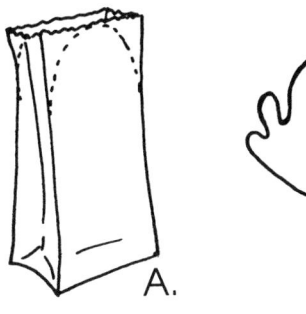

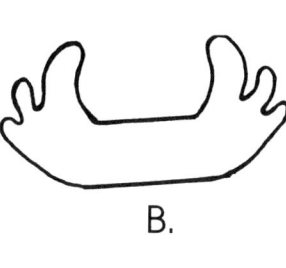

A.   B.

Snowflakes

Language targets
- Verbs:
  future: *will* (in giving instructions)
  past (regular): folded, unfolded, taped
  past (irregular): drew, cut, made, hung

- Vocabulary: snowflakes, designs, lacy, every one is different, fold, unfold

- Optional: Talk about what real snowflakes are like. Using a magnifying glass to make something bigger, explain how snowflakes look like lace when they are magnified, and every snowflake is different. Snowflakes are cold and wet. They pile up and make snow. They melt into water.

Materials
light-weight white paper
scissors
pencils
optional: tape, thread, coat hangers

Preparation   Cut paper into 8½" or 9" squares.

Procedure
1. Have children fold the paper diagonally in half (into triangles) three times.

2. You may either guide the children to cut randomly into the sides of the folded triangles, or have them draw shapes along the folded edges that they will cut out of the folded paper. (Note: encourage them not to cut on the folds excessively, or the snowflake will fall apart.)

3. Mount the snowflakes on a window or a bulletin board, or have the children tape lengths of thread to their snowflakes, and hang them from the ceiling or coat-hanger mobiles.

Popcorn Snowman

Language targets
- Vocabulary: scarf, head, body, black hat, buttons, face
- Colors: blue, white, black
- Negative: *don't* eat, *not* for eating
- Past tense: Telling latecomers what they did; glued, didn't eat
- Future tense: *will* (as teacher explains what they *will* do)
- Pronouns: He/She (telling someone what another child did: She made ___, He made ___.)

Materials
blue construction paper (9" x 12", one sheet per child)
popped popcorn (two cups per child)
paper plates or other containers
glue
small cups (for glue)
cotton-tipped swabs or craft sticks (for glue applicators)
black tempera paint powder
paper bag
chalk

Preparation
1. Shake several cups of popcorn in a bag with black tempera paint powder to make black popcorn.
2. Use chalk to trace a two-circled snowman on each sheet of blue construction paper.
3. Place white popcorn on paper plates or other containers.

Procedure
1. Instruct children to glue white popcorn in the circles on the blue paper to make snowmen. They are NOT to eat the popcorn (you may choose to have fresh popcorn for them to eat at snack time).
2. Distribute ½ to ¾ cup black popcorn to each child.
3. Instruct them to glue on the black popcorn to make a scarf, a black hat, buttons, and a face for the snowman.

Painting with White

Language targets
- Vocabulary: black/white, sponge
- Noun plurals: fences, houses
- Verbs: irregular past (snow *fell* on)

Source   Doan, R. L. 1979. *Arts and Crafts Achievement Activities.* West Nyack, NY: The Center for Applied Research in Education, Inc.

Materials	white tempera paint black construction paper (9" x 12" or larger, one sheet per child) brushes small sponges felt-tip markers (optional)
Procedure	Assist children in painting a snow scene using brushes and/or sponges. Suggest snowmen, falling snow, snow on houses, fences, ground, etc. Encourage the children to use both sponges and brushes and to compare the different results each produces.

Macaroni Jewelry

Language targets	• Verbs:
	  future: will pick, will string
	  past (irregular): made
	• Vocabulary and noun plurals: necklaces, bracelets, macaroni, colors, shape names
	• Yes/No questions: Will you please tie my necklace?

Source	Warren, J. 1983. *Crafts: Early Learning Activities.* Palo Alto, CA: Monday Morning Books.
Materials	small stringable macaroni (different shapes) rubbing alcohol food coloring (red, green, blue; make purple and orange if desired) pint jar strainer paper towels yarn tape
Preparation	1. Cut yarn to 24"-28" lengths; tape the ends to make a sturdy "needle" for stringing the macaroni. 2. Measure ¼ cup rubbing alcohol into a pint jar with a tight-fitting lid; add an ample amount of food coloring. Pour 1 cup of macaroni into the jar and shake. Strain the macaroni and lay out on paper towels to dry. Repeat for the other colors. 3. Make a sample necklace and a bracelet.
Procedure	1. Introduce activity: Today we *will* make necklaces and bracelets. 2. What do we need to make these? (Children name materials displayed: yarn, macaroni.) 3. Discuss the shapes and colors of the macaroni pieces. 4. Encourage the children to ask for help in tying their finished necklaces and bracelets.

Shape and Object Rubbings

Language targets
- Vocabulary and concepts: names of shapes and objects, sideways, firmly, across, rubbings
- Following two- and three-step directions
- Ask children to tell latecomers what they *did*.
- Verbs:
  past (regular): placed (on/under paper), rubbed, peeled (crayons)
  past (irregular): laid (paper over), held (crayon)
- WH questions: What is it? Why did we peel this crayon?
- Yes/No questions: Can you guess what is under this?

Materials
shapes (cut out of cardboard or sandpaper)

objects for rubbing (need to be relatively flat: keys, paper clips, coins, rickrack, etc.)

paper

peeled crayons

Preparation
Cut various shapes out of thin cardboard and/or sandpaper; collect flat objects that will give interesting shapes and textures when rubbed.

Procedure
1. Have children arrange shapes or objects as desired, then lay paper over them. (Optional: have one child arrange shapes or objects for another child, who then will identify the shapes and objects as their images appear during rubbing.)
2. Demonstrate how to rub: hold a crayon sideways and rub firmly across the paper several times.

Heart Collage

Language targets
- Vocabulary and descriptive terms: big, small, plain, with a design, colors, with a center cut out, etc.
- Yes/No questions: May I have the heart that is ___?
- Concept: overlap
- Verbs:
  past (regular): overlapped, pasted, glued, picked, designed
  past (irregular): chose, made, cut

Materials
white construction paper (12" x 18", one sheet per child)
red construction paper
papers and fabrics of different textures, colors, and patterns
glue
scissors

Preparation Cut out many different types of hearts (large, small, solid-colored, patterned, hearts with centers cut out, etc.). Trace some hearts for older children to cut out by themselves. Trace one large heart on red construction paper for each child.

Procedure
1. Give each child a large sheet of white construction paper and a large red heart.
2. Let them make a heart collage by selecting whichever hearts they prefer and gluing them on the white construction paper.
3. Encourage experimenting with overlapping.
4. Optional: If you are working with a small group of children, keep a display of hearts on a tray in front of you and have the children describe which hearts they want. Alternately, have them talk about the hearts they glued on their collages.

Coloring and Cutting Hearts

Language targets
- Vocabulary and concepts: heart, valentine, shape, color
- Ideas for "Valentine" conversation: ask the children to tell you what they think a friend is. Tell them a simple definition of friendship. (Friendship is when you like a friend and you have fun together and even help each other.) Have children talk about their friends. Ask them to tell you what love means. (Write down some of the responses for a class newsletter.)

Materials a photocopied worksheet of a heart, one per child
red crayons
scissors

Procedure As children color and cut out their hearts, talk about Valentine's Day and hearts. Valentine's Day is a day for love and friendship.

Valentine's Day Cards and Envelopes

Language targets
- Verb forms: I'm verb + -ing: Teachers make a card AT THE SAME TIME as the children, telling what they are doing and then asking the children.
  past tense regular: folded, glued, colored, decorated
  past tense irregular: drew, wrote, made
- Vocabulary and concepts: biggest, message
- Possessive nouns: Jessica's, Henry's, etc.
- Prepositions: *onto, for* (This is *for* my mother/father/sister, etc.)

Materials small (6") paper plates (one per child)
red and white paper
glue
markers
12" x 18" white construction paper (one sheet per child)

Preparation	1. Cut three different-sized heart shapes (one set per child), the largest big enough for the plate to fit on (see diagram).
2. Make envelopes: draw a line 1" from the edge on the large white construction paper sheets (see diagram).
Procedure	Tell children:
1. Find the big*gest* heart. Glue the plate *onto* the biggest heart.
2. Then glue the two other hearts *on* the plate.
3. You may decorate your card with markers.
4. I will write a *message* on your card. Do you want "I love you" or "Happy Valentine's Day" or another message?
5. While your card is drying, fold the large white paper to the line and glue both sides to make your envelope.

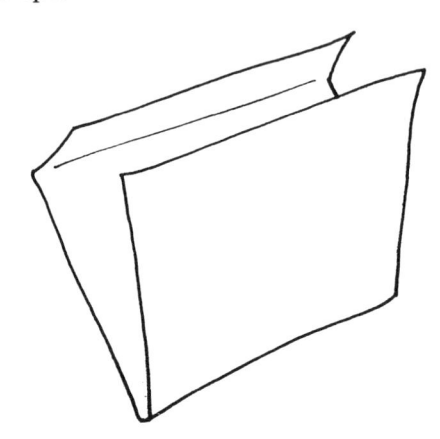

Favorite Things Collage

Language targets	• Make an effort to model at least two forms for each child you work with.
• WH question: What are your favorite toys?
• Irregular plural nouns: people, food
Materials	magazines for each child
large white construction paper
glue
scissors
Preparation	Gather sufficient magazines for each child to have one.
Procedure	1. Have children cut out pictures of their favorite things (food, toys, people, etc.).
2. The children can then glue the pictures on their white paper.

March Bulletin Board

Language targets
- Plural and possessive nouns: St. Patrick's Day, coins in the pot of gold
- Vocabulary and concepts:

    Leprechauns are make-believe elves. Ireland is a country like the United States. People who live in Ireland or whose families used to live in Ireland are called Irish people.

    Green is the color of Ireland. St. Patrick was a special person who lived in Ireland.

    A story in Ireland is that if you see a rainbow and go to the end of it, you will find a pot of gold. *What is a rainbow?*

    A rainbow is an arch of colors made when the sun is shining through clouds or water in the air.

- After discussion, ask older children to define *rainbow, leprechaun, St. Patrick's Day, Irish*

Source   Wasserman, F., and S. Medow. 1984. *Early Childhood Seasonal and Holiday Activities.* Compton, CA: Educational Insights.

Materials   large sheet of white bulletin board paper
crayons and markers
gold foil for coins

Preparation   Draw a rainbow, a leprechaun, a pot of gold, and shamrocks to make a mural for the children to color.

Procedure
1. Discuss St. Patrick's Day, rainbows, pots of gold, and leprechauns with the children.
2. Have children color in the mural and hang it on the wall.

Painting a Fire Engine

Language targets
- Basic and more advanced concepts and vocabulary
- Colors: red and black
- Names and functions of parts: hose (pours water on fire), ax (chops down doors and windows to save people from the fire), ladder (helps firefighters to climb up high to rescue people upstairs in a burning building), etc.
- Parts/directional terms: front, back, right side, left side, etc.

Materials   1 or 2 very large boxes
red and black paint
brushes
scissors or knife for adult to cut cardboard
picture of a fire engine

Preparation	1. Obtain large boxes.
	2. Find adequate space to paint.
	3. Have children wear old clothes.
Procedure	1. Today we will paint these boxes red and make a fire engine. We also have black paint to paint some things that go on a fire engine.
	2. Look at the picture. Tell me about what a fire engine looks like (big, red). Tell me the different things on a fire engine (wheels, steering wheel, bell, axes, hoses, ladder, headlights, seats). Why does a fire engine have a bell or a siren? What is the hatchet for? What are the hoses for? What is the ladder for?
	3. Assign areas for painting: front, right side, left side, back, hood, etc.

Tracing Shapes with Stencils

Language targets	• Plural nouns: shapes, stencils
	• Verbs: trace, will trace, traced, I'm tracing
	• Locatives: inside, outside
	• Adjectives: same/different
	• Shape names: circle, square, triangle, rectangle, half circle
Materials	shape stencils pencils drawing paper crayons and/or markers
Preparation	Draw some of the shapes on a piece of paper.
Procedure	1. Display the stencils and have the children talk about the different shapes. Ask children to match stencil shapes with the shapes you traced on paper.
	2. Have the children trace shapes on the inside of the stencils and/or around the shape.
	3. Children may fill a paper with all the same shape or put different shapes on one sheet of paper.

Paper Plate Bunnies
(For Spring Bulletin Board)

Language targets	• Vocabulary and concepts: colors each side eyeballs, whiskers, soft, puffy tail inside and outside (ear) larger and smaller (plate and ear)
	• Prepositions: *on, under, over, next to*

Source   Hazell, B. G. 1982. *Paper Plate Animals (Cut and Paste Patterns)*. Malvern, PA: Instructo/McGraw, Inc.

Materials
6" and 9" paper plates
pastel ("spring") colors of construction paper
white cotton balls (for tail)
white, pink, and black construction paper
tape
pencils
glue
stapler

Preparation   For each child, cut out two ears (from pastel colors), two white inner ears, two pastel eyes, two smaller black eyeballs, white feet, black eyebrows, one pink nose, one white tail, and four white whiskers.

Procedure
1. Glue white inner ears on large colored outer ears.
2. Glue ears under top side of 6" plate.
3. Overlap 6" plate on 9" plate and glue or staple (see diagram).
4. Glue colored eyes on 6" plate. Glue black eyeballs on eyes.
5. Glue nose on face.
6. Glue two whiskers on each side.
7. Glue feet under bottom of 9" plate.
8. Glue tail under 9" plate. Glue cotton balls on tail.
9. Draw a mouth of the face and fold one ear forward.

Making Kites

Language targets
- Vocabulary and concepts:
  kite is a *diamond shape*
  corners
  lines
  names of all materials (streamers, crepe paper, colors)
- Narrative sequence: Have the children who come early start working on their projects immediately. Then ask them to tell (and show) latecomers how to make the kites.
- Verb tenses:
  future: *will*
  past (regular): colored, stapled, glued
  past (irregular): cut
- Auxiliary: I'm coloring, stapling, etc.
- WH question: What color paper do you want?
- Yes/No question: Do you want red? (etc.)

Materials	kite shapes to trace (to fit 12" x 18" paper)
	construction paper (12" x 18" sheets, white or colored, one per child)
	stapler
	glue
	scissors
	crayons
	crepe paper streamers (for tail)
	construction paper scraps

Preparation
1. Precut enough bows from scrap construction paper to attach five to each kite tail.
2. Cut crepe paper streamers into 3' lengths.

Procedure
1. Children will trace kites on colored or white paper and cut out.
2. Children will color designs on their kites.
3. Staple a crepe paper streamer to the kite.
4. Children may color bows, then glue them to the streamers.

Easter Chicks

Language targets
- Verbs:
  I'm shaking/gluing, making ___. She's ___, He's ___.
  past (regular): glued
  past (irregular): shook, made

- Vocabulary and concepts:
  Chicks are *little* and *soft*.
  Chicks are baby hens/roosters.
  Yellow, orange beak, black eyes.
  Are in their nests.

- Narrative sequence: Have early arrivals explain the project and the steps to late arrivals.

Source Warren, J. 1983. *Crafts: Early Learning Activities.* Palo Alto, CA: Monday Morning Books.

Materials cotton balls (yellow if possible)

yellow tempera paint powder and baby powder (if yellow cotton balls are not available)

egg cartons
orange and black construction paper scraps
hole punch
glue
lunch bags (if yellow cotton balls are not available)

Preparation
1. Cut out individual cups from egg cartons.
2. Use hole punch to make black construction paper dots for eyes.
3. Cut out orange triangles for beaks.
4. If yellow cotton balls are not available, put two teaspoons of yellow tempera paint powder and one teaspoon of baby powder into a lunch bag. (The children can each shake the cotton balls themselves, taking turns to use the bag of paint and powder.)

Procedure
1. Have children glue three or four cotton balls to the inside of the egg carton cup.
2. Have children glue on eyes and a beak.

Easter Basket

Language targets
- Vocabulary and concepts: Naming materials and guessing what they are for. Cotton is *for* the bunny's tail, white is *for* eyeballs, grass is *for* inside of basket, *for* Easter eggs.
- Plural and possessive nouns
- Following one- and two-step directions
- Verbs:

  future tense in describing to latecomers what they *will* do

  auxiliary (I'm/he's/she's) in sharing what they're doing, what their friends are doing with someone just arriving or teacher coming over to table

  regular and irregular past tense in telling what they *did* (You can bring in another child or adult so a few children can tell what they *did*. The children can tell their parents later.)

Materials
lunch bags (brown or white; one per child)
crayons or markers
scissors
artificial grass
cotton balls
stapler
glue
white paper
black paper (optional)

Preparation
1. Cut out two white ovals for each bunny's eyes. Black whiskers may also be cut if desired.
2. Cut both sides of each bag halfway down (see diagram).
3. Draw outline of ears on the bag for the children to cut (see diagram).

Procedure
1. Tell and show the children what to do (you can give instructions two steps at a time for older children; for youngest children, give instructions one step at a time). Early arrivals can tell latecomers. Younger children may need assistance in cutting ears.
2. Have the children:
   - cut out around the ears.
   - flatten the bag on the table and glue on the white eyeballs.
   - draw in eyes, nose, mouth, and whiskers (older children may cut out and glue on whiskers).
   - color middle of ear pink or red.
   - glue cotton ball to back for a tail.
   - put "grass" inside.
   - staple ears together at the top.

Pussy Willows

Language targets
- Concepts:

  Changes that tell us spring is coming. Pussy willows grow. Other changes: warmer weather, birds come back, buds on tree branches

  Can they talk about the real pussy willow? Branches are hard. Gray buds are SOFT like a pussy cat.

- Naming items needed: blue paper, brown crayon, cotton, glue

Materials
blue construction paper (9" x 12" sheets, one per child)
white cotton balls
brown crayons
real pussy willows (optional)

Preparation
Draw branches on the blue paper.

Procedure
Have children glue small pieces of cotton on each side of the branches to resemble pussy willow stems.

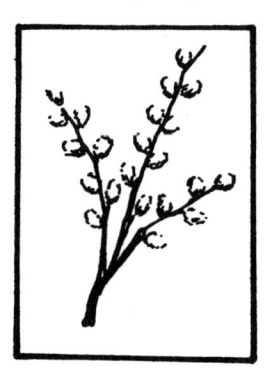

Butterfly, Butterfly, Fly Away

Language targets
- Vocabulary and concepts: half/halves vs. whole (whole thing); each side, middle, antenna, antennae
- Comprehension of WH questions
- Verbs:
  present: decorating, coloring, drawing, making
  past (regular): colored, finished, marked, glued
  past (irregular): drew, made
- Sequential narrative: Have early arrivals explain to late arrivals what to do in correct order.

Materials
yellow and black construction paper scraps
blue construction paper (12" x 18" sheets, one per child)
pencils
markers
glue

Preparation
1. Cut out butterfly halves from yellow paper (two per child) and butterfly bodies (one per child) from black paper.
2. In the left corner of each sheet of blue paper, write "Butterfly, butterfly, fly away."

Procedure
1. Using future tense, tell the children what they *will* make and let them "guess" or look at and name the materials they *will* need. (What will you need to make your butterfly?)
2. Have children glue the two halves together on the blue paper.
3. They may decorate the wings with markers, then glue a black body in the middle and draw an antenna on each side of the body.
4. Older children may also want to draw grass, a sun, flowers, etc., on the blue paper.

Ladybugs

Language targets
- Vocabulary and concepts: ladybug, red wings, black dots, circle (half/whole), head, antenna
- Possessive noun: ladybug's back
- Plural noun: dots

Materials
white construction paper (9" x 12", one sheet per child)
red construction paper
glue
markers

Preparation
Trace 7" circles on the red construction paper; draw a line down the middle to divide the circle in half. Precut the half-circles, or have the children do the cutting.

Procedure
1. Have children glue the two halves side by side on the white construction paper.
2. Guide them to draw a head on the ladybug and color it in with black.
3. Have them draw two antennae coming out of the head.
4. Let the children put black dots on the ladybug's wings with a black marker.
5. Older children may wish to draw in a sun and other features.

Daffodils

Language targets
- Narratives: have early arrivals guess *what* and *how* the flowers will be made. Have early arrivals *tell* late arrivals *what* to do (use buddy system).
- Vocabulary and concepts: parts of flower (stem, leaves, petals), colors being used, middle/center. Daffodils grow in the spring.
- Verbs:
  future: we *will* glue, we *will* paint
  present: I'm painting, I'm gluing
  past (regular): painted, glued

Materials
blue construction paper (9" x 12", one sheet per child)
green construction paper for stems and leaves
yellow paper for daffodils
glue
orange tempera paint and brushes (optional)
egg cartons (note: if children are going to paint egg-carton cups, use cardboard egg cartons)

Preparation
1. Cut daffodil petals from yellow paper, stems and leaves from green paper. The flower should be at least 5" across.
2. Cut apart egg cartons.

Procedure
1. Display the components of the project (or a model), and ask children to guess what they will make today. See if they can guess *how* they will make it.
2. Have children glue stems and leaves on blue paper.
3. Have children glue on the yellow flower.
4. They will then center an egg-carton cup in the middle of the yellow flower, and glue it on.
5. The children may paint the center cup, if desired.

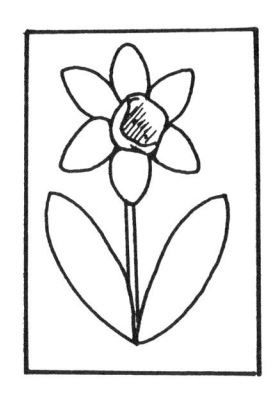

Cupcake Flower Vase (Mother's Day Gift)

Language targets
- Vocabulary and concepts: blossoms/flowers, stems, leaves, vase
- Present for Mother's Day
  Why do we have a day called Mother's Day?
  Why do we make presents for our moms?
- Noun plurals:
  regular: flowers, stems
  irregular: leaves
- Verb tenses:
  We *will* cut out, glue, draw (in telling late arrivals)

  regular and irregular past: I cut, glued, drew, made (in telling someone who wasn't there)
- I'm + verb + -ing: I'm cutting, gluing, drawing

Materials
construction paper (12" x 18", one sheet per child)
construction paper scraps
cupcake papers (colored, three per child)
scissors
glue
markers

Preparation
Trace vases (one per child) and leaves (two or three per child) on pieces of colored paper.

Procedure
1. Have the children cut out the vases and leaves.
2. Guide the children to arrange the leaves on the large sheets of construction paper, then lay the vase over the lower ends of the leaves.

3. Have the children glue down the leaves and then the vase.

4. Children may draw stems and glue the cupcake papers at the ends of the stems, using markers to add any desired detail on the flowers.

Caterpillars

Language targets
- Vocabulary and concepts:

  What is a caterpillar? (An *animal*. It spins a cocoon and *inside* the cocoon it *grows* into a butterfly with wings.)

  Does a caterpillar have wings? How does it move? (It crawls.)

  What is an *antenna* for? To see? Feel? (So it can get around.)

  When do we see caterpillars? (In the *spring*.)

- Names of all the arts and crafts materials. (We made the caterpillar from an egg carton. The antenna is a pipe cleaner.)

- Verbs: We *will* paint, I'm painting, I painted (also for *glue*)

Source
Warren, J. 1983. *Crafts: Early Learning Activities*. Palo Alto, CA: Monday Morning Books.

Materials
cardboard egg cartons (one carton for every two children)
paints
pipe cleaners
markers
picture of a caterpillar turning into a butterfly (optional)

Preparation
1. Cut egg cartons in half lengthwise.
2. Punch two small holes in the "head" end of the caterpillar for the pipe-cleaner antennae.

Procedure
1. Let the children paint their caterpillars, and allow the paint to dry.
2. Show the children how to insert a pipe cleaner in and out of the front cup to make antennae.
3. Have children use paint or markers to draw on two eyes and a mouth.

Paper Plate Fish

Language targets
- Vocabulary, word retrieval: mouth, triangle, shape, tail, names of all materials
- Third person singular verb agreement: a fish swims, eats seaweed, steers with its tail, lives in the ocean or in a river or lake
- Third person singular irregular verbs: *has* (This fish has a mouth, has a tail, has eyes.)

Source Warren, J. 1983. *Crafts: Early Learning Activities.* Palo Alto, CA: Monday Morning Books.

Materials paper plates (one per child)
markers
stapler
scissors

Preparation Mark with a dotted line a triangular section on the paper plate (see diagram).

Procedure
1. Have each child cut out the triangle on the dotted lines. This area is the fish's mouth.
2. Show the child how to staple the cut-out triangle section onto the back of the plate to make the fish's tail.
3. Have the child draw in an eye and color the fish.

Circle Time

The circle-time activities are grouped according to seasonal and/or holiday themes, and include suggestions of language targets to work on while the children are engaged in these tasks.

Introduction

Seasonal

Fall
    Poems and Fingerplays about Fall
    Columbus Day
    Halloween Fingerplays and Poems

Winter
    Gobble Gobble (auditory discrimination game)
    What Is Thanksgiving (discussion)
    What I Am Thankful For (discussion)
    Thanksgiving Dinner (discussion)
    The Chanukah Menorah
    Martin Luther King, Jr.

General
    Me and My Family
    Special Name Song
    Our Places to Play
    Addresses: Where Do You Live? (recognition)
    Discussion of Class Field Trip
    Tell Me What You Heard (familiar-sounds auditory training tape)
    Following Directions (following directions activity cards)
    What Part Is Covered? (body parts)
    My Feelings

Poems and Finger Plays about Fall

Language targets
- Listening skills
- Acting out verbal images
- Vocabulary related to fall
- Concepts of seasons (winter following fall)

Source Wasserman, F., and S. Medow. 1984. *Early Childhood Seasonal and Holiday Activities* (cards 12 and 13). Compton, CA: Educational Insights.

Procedure
1. Do the fingerplays (it is probably best to work on only one new fingerplay per day).
2. Have several teachers read the different poems.
3. Discuss: "Before, it was summer. Now it is fall. It will get colder and colder and then it will be winter."

Poem *Crackling Leaves*
Crisp fall leaves make a crackling sound
When I stomp them on the ground.
Squirrels and birds soon hurry away,
I'm making so much noise today!

Fall is Here!
There's a brand new crispness in the air.
I feel it more each day!
It tells me that fall is finally here.
And winter's on the way!

Fall Chore
Red, yellow, orange, and brown,
Those pretty colors make me frown.
I rake them up and pile them high,
Why couldn't it be some other guy?

Finger play *Fall Leaves*
The leaves are falling from the trees.
   (arms raised, fingers wiggling, lower arms to ground)
They make a pillow for my knees.
   (fluff up imaginary pile of leaves on ground)
I jump and land on the pillow there
   (jump and land gently on "pillow" of leaves)
And send leaves flying in the air.
   (move arms quickly out and up away from the body)

In the Fall
Leaves with fingers waving by
   (wiggle fingers and move arms from left to right)
Paint their colors in the sky.
   (move arms and fingers like a brush, get larger with each stroke)

Pumpkins in their patches lie,
> (make an oval shape with arms and lower to floor)

And Halloween witches come out to fly.
> (bring hands together as if holding a broomstick and stand up, ready to fly)

Columbus Day

Language targets
- Following one-step directions
- Sequential narratives (comprehension of Columbus story)
- Preposition: *for*
- Verbs:
  past (regular): looked, rowed
  past (irregular): found, saw
- Question forms: yes/no (Do you see land?)

Source Wilmes, L., and D. Wilmes. 1982. *The Circle Time Book.* Dundee, IL: Building Blocks Publishers.

Materials
for flannel board presentation: three sailing ships, water, land
bathroom tissue tubes (two per student for binoculars)
glue
plastic sled for a ship (optional)
sailor hats (optional)

Preparation
1. Lay out ships, water, and land on flannel board.
2. Make binoculars: Glue two bathroom tissue tubes together side by side.

Procedure
1. Use the flannel board and ships to assist in telling the story of Christopher Columbus.
2. Sing (to the tune of *Row, Row, Row Your Boat*):
   Sail, sail, sail your ship;
   Sail it night and day.
   Look, look, look for land
   All along the way.
3. Give each child a set of "binoculars" and have the children act out the following directives (you or one of the children can give the "orders"):
   Row the boat!
   Pull those ropes!
   Wash the deck!
   Look for land!
   Raise the sail!
   Quiet, please!
4. If desired, set the sled in the center of the circle and have two or three children at a time pretend they are in a real ship.

Halloween Finger Plays and Poems

Language targets
- Auditory memory training
- Motor imitation with verbal/visual cues
- Verb Tenses:
  irregular past: said, went
  is/are copula and noun/verb agreement
- Plural nouns:
  regular: witches, ghosts, goblins, black cats, costumes
  irregular: children

Source Wasserman, F., and S. Medow. 1984. *Early Childhood Seasonal and Holiday Activities.* Compton, CA: Educational Insights.

Materials pictures of witches, goblins, ghosts, black cats, jack-o'-lanterns (to display during poem)

Procedure
1. Read the poem, using dramatic voice inflection and appropriate facial expressions. Display or point to the pictures and objects as they are mentioned in the poem.
2. Have children repeat and imitate the poem and associated finger play. It is a good idea to start poems and finger plays weeks in advance. Have children practice every day if possible. They love and need the repetition.

Finger play *Five Little Pumpkins*
Five little pumpkins sitting on a gate.
   (hold up five fingers)
This one said, "My, it's getting late!"
   (take hold of thumb)
This one said, "There are witches in the air!"
   (take hold of index finger)
This one said, "There is mischief everywhere!"
   (take hold of middle finger)
This one said, "Oo-oo, let's run!"
   (take hold of ring finger)
This one said, "It's only Halloween fun!"
   (take hold of little finger)
Ooo-ooo went the wind, out went the lights;
   (clap hands)
Away went the jack-o'-lanterns on Halloween night.
   (hands behind back)

My Pumpkin
See my pumpkin round and fat.
   (make circle with hands, fingers spread wide, touching)
See my pumpkin yellow.
   (make smaller circle)
Watch him grin on Halloween.
   (point to mouth which is grinning wide)
He's a very funny fellow.

Poem   *Halloween Time*
Witches, ghosts, and goblins and black cats in a row,
When they come around each year, it's Halloween time I know.
But I'm not really scared of them, they never frighten me.
They're children dressed in costumes, for Halloween time, you see.

Gobble (Auditory Discrimination Game)

Language targets
- Auditory discrimination skills
- WH question: where
- *Are* as main verb
- Past tense irregular: heard

Source   Wilmes, L., and D. Wilmes. 1982. *The Circle Time Book,* p. 41. Dundee, IL: Building Blocks Publishers.

Materials   large picture of turkey and two or three little turkeys (optional)

Procedure
1. *We are going to play a new game. Our game is called "Gobble." I will pick a mommy turkey or a daddy turkey to go* [somewhere outside the circle where group activities cannot be overheard]. *Then I will pick two baby turkeys. Everyone will hide your mouth. ONLY the two baby turkeys will say "gobble." The mommy or daddy turkey will come out and try to find the baby turkeys.*
2. The "baby turkeys" continue to gobble as the parent turkey walks around the circle to find them. *Where are the baby turkeys? You heard them!*

What Is Thanksgiving?

Language targets
- Maintaining conversational topic and turn-taking skills
- Auditory focus and discrimination
- WH questions: what, why

Materials   pencil and paper to note children's responses

Procedure
1. Ask each child (or several children): *What do you do on Thanksgiving? Why do we have Thanksgiving?*
2. Write down the children's responses, to be included in a class newsletter for Thanksgiving.
3. Explain: *The Pilgrims were people who came to the United States a long, long time ago before it had roads and cars and towns. It was just woods. They came on a boat across the ocean. There were no supermarkets. They were so hungry. They needed some food. The Indians already lived here. They helped the Pilgrims find food for the first Thanksgiving.*

What I Am Thankful For

Language targets
- Pronoun: *I*
- Main verb: *am* (I am thankful for ___.)
- Preposition: *for*
- Concept: thankful

Source Wilmes, L., and D. Wilmes. 1982. *The Circle Time Book,* p. 41. Dundee, IL: Building Blocks Publishers.

Materials a reproducible turkey worksheet
colored markers
flannel boards
tacks

Preparation Make photocopies of a turkey worksheet (one per child).

Procedure
1. Discuss Thanksgiving and ask the children to tell you what they are thankful for: *Thanksgiving is a time for saying thank you. We say thank you because we are thankful or full of thanks for good things that make us happy. For our nice families who take good care of us, for our toys, our friends. Let's take turns telling something we are thankful for and I will write it on your turkey.*

2. Write each child's name on a turkey picture and record the children's responses on their pictures. (You may want to select another adult in the classroom to go first and demonstrate.) Pin each worksheet to the flannel board so the children can watch as you write down their responses.

3. The children may use the markers or crayons to color outside the turkeys, if desired.

Thanksgiving Dinner

Language targets
- Complex sentence with prepositional phrase "for ___"
- Modal *would*
- Infinitive *to eat*
- Vocabulary: naming picture food items

Materials magazines (with pictures of food)
scissors
glue
paper plates

Procedure
1. Prior to circle time, give children magazines with pictures of food. Children cut out pictures of food their families might eat on Thanksgiving, and glue the pictures to the paper plates.

Procedure
1. Today I will tell you a poem called "How Many."
   How many people live at your house?
   How many people live at your home?
   One, my mother.
   Two, my father.
   Three, my sister.
   Four, my brother.
   There's one more, now let me see.
   Oh yes, of course. It must be *me*.

2. Read the poem, then have each child repeat the poem with you, adjusting the poem according to the number of people in the family.

3. After reciting and discussing the poem, give each child a picture of a family doing an activity. Have the children stand, one at a time, and hold up their pictures so that everyone can see them. Let the children talk about what the family is doing. Continue until all the children have had a chance to share their pictures.

4. Talk about chores that you do around the house. Ask the children what they do to help around their homes.

5. Once you have discussed household chores in general, ask the children to select the chores they enjoy the most. Have each child say the name of the job into a tape recorder. After everyone has had an opportunity to talk into the recorder, play it back and see if the children can recognize the voices. When someone identifies the voice, have the child whose voice has been recognized stand up.

Special Name Song

Language targets
- WH question with inversion: *Where is ___?*
- Pronoun: *I*
- Uncontractible copula: Here I am.
- Contractible copula: I'm fine.
- Social discourse and conversational turn taking

Materials none

Preparation Have the children sit on their mats in the circle area. To the tune of "Frere Jacques," everyone will sing the words of the song (given below), inserting the name of the next person in the circle (include teachers and other adults in the classroom). The named person will stand and sing the appropriate responses, then sit as the turn moves on to the next person. Have one or two of the adults go first, to demonstrate the procedure.

Procedure Group: Where is [name]? Where is [name]?
Person: Here I am. Here I am.
Group: How are you today?
Person: I'm fine, thank you.
Group: Welcome back. Please sit down.

Our Places to Play

Language targets
- Following one- and two-step directions
- Requesting help
- Concepts: new, moved
- Prepositions: *behind, for*
- Comprehension of WH questions: What is it? Where does it go?
- Irregular past tense: found

Materials
large plastic or paper bag
one item from each play area in the classroom
laminated photographs of each play area, flannel-backed for flannel board use

Preparation
Use this activity to introduce children to classroom changes as new activity centers and furniture are added, or furniture is rearranged. The dialogue below is a sample.

Procedure
1. Say: *Here are pictures of places to play in our room. Some of our places to play were moved. What place is this?* [Show a picture of the block-building area.] *The blocks are in a new place.* [Point it out.]
2. Repeat for the book area and the circle area.
3. Show the picture of the arts and crafts area. *What do we do in arts and crafts? Our arts and crafts table is behind our new shelf.* [Point it out.]
4. Show pictures of new interest center(s). *We have two new places to play:* [name of fast-food restaurant visited on field trip] *and science.*

Addresses: Where Do You Live?

Language targets
- Goals:
  Recognition of street and town; recognition of address
  Child can repeat address, one line at a time
  Child can repeat entire address
  Child can give address without prompts
- WH questions: Who lives at this address? Where do you live?
- Comprehension and expression

Materials
construction paper (9" x 12" sheets, one per child)
ball or beanbag (optional)

Preparation
Print each child's address on a separate sheet of construction paper. You will be asking the children to recognize their addresses as you read them aloud. (You may also want to print the child's name lightly on the back of the sheet, so that you can prompt in case some children fail to recognize their addresses.)

Procedure
1. Read out an address and ask, *Who lives at this address?*

2. After a child "claims" the address, read the address again and have the child repeat it with you. Then ask, *What is your address?* and have the child repeat the address.

3. Hand a child a ball or a beanbag and ask, *What is your address?* After the child responds, have the child ask the same question of the next child in the circle while passing the child the beanbag. The next child responds, and so on. The goal is for the children to repeat their own addresses with minimal prompting.

Discussion of Class Field Trip

Language targets
- Questions/prompts:
  Tell me what you saw. (I saw ___.)
  Write: Mary saw ___ and ___ and ___. Marco saw ___ and ___.

  Tell me what you ate. (I ate ___.)
  Write: Landon ate ___.

  Tell me what you drank. (I drank ___.)
  Write: Kelley drank ___.

  Tell me what you played on. (I played on ___.)
  Write: Andrew played on ___.

- Past tense forms: saw, ate, drank, *-ed* (played)

- Vocabulary: food names, people names (cashier, cook, etc.), playground items

Materials
for each group of two or three children:
a flannel board covered with a white sheet of paper
a marker
a copy of appropriate questions about the field trip

Preparation
1. Divide children into groups of two or three with an adult leader for each group.

2. Each adult will be leading the children in discussing a recent field trip. (The sample below assumes a field trip to a local fast-food restaurant; however, any subject can be substituted.) Prepare copies of four or five questions about the field trip for each adult group leader to refer to during the discussion (see Language Targets, above, for examples).

Procedure
1. Each teacher leads a group of children in discussing and answering the following questions.

2. Tell me where we went yesterday. *We went to [name of fast-food restaurant].*

3. Let's take turns talking about [restaurant] and I will write down what you say.

4. Ask each child the same question (see Language Targets, above), writing down the responses and correcting the grammar. Then move on to the next question.

5. After you have recorded the children's responses to all the questions, headline your story with: *Yesterday we went to [restaurant]. We rode on a yellow bus. Our teachers went with us.*

6. All groups return to the main circle. Each teacher can "read" the group's stories to the whole class, or you can invite others in and read the stories to them.

Tell Me What You Heard

Language targets
- Irregular past tense: heard
- Pronoun: *I*
- Identification and naming of common sound-producing objects without a picture cue

Materials auditory training tapes (such as *Auditory Training Familiar Sounds* from DLM/Teaching Resources)

picture cards of sounds on the tape

Procedure
1. Play one taped sound at a time.
2. Ask one child at a time, *Tell me what you heard.*
3. Then show the card to see if the child was right.

Following Directions

Language targets
- Vocabulary: bend down, shake hands, move over, close your eyes, run, lie down, walk backward, walk forward, stand up, raise your hand, sit still, jump forward, jump backward, turn around, march, open your eyes, etc.
- Yes/No questions: Can you ___?
- Teacher models: Were they right?

Materials following directions activity cards (such as *Look 'n' Do: Following Directions Activity Cards,* Trend Enterprises)

masking tape or sheet of paper

Preparation
1. For each group, make an X on the floor with masking tape (or lay down a sheet of paper).
2. Divide the children into groups of no more than four, and have an adult lead the activity in each group.

Procedure
1. The first child comes and stands on the X and selects an activity card, shielding it from view.
The child asks the group, "Can you ___?"
The group follows the child's directions.
The child then shows the group the picture.
Ask the child, *Were they right?*

2. Repeat with other children in the group.

What Part Is Covered?

Language targets
- Comprehension of WH question with inversion: What part did I cover?
- Contractible copula: I'm (advanced level)
- Verb + -*ing:* I pointing (basic level)
- Naming large and small body parts
- Complex sentences
- Body parts
- Following directions

Source
Wilmes, L., and D. Wilmes. 1983. *Everyday Circle Time*, p. 14. Dundee, IL: Building Blocks Publishers.

Materials
different-sized pieces of paper (12" x 18" construction paper down to 3" x 5" index card)

Procedure
1. Select a child to come to the front of the circle and have the others close their eyes. Use a large sheet of paper to cover up one of the child's legs. Have the children open their eyes and quietly call out what part is covered up. Do this several more times with large body parts (arm, hand, head, foot, fanny, etc.) on different children. Ask, *What part did I cover up?*

2. Use the smaller pieces of paper to cover up smaller body parts (eye, nose, ear, finger, etc.) on other children. Let the children guess what part is covered up.

My Feelings

Language targets
- Vocabulary and concepts: happy, sad, angry, sleepy, surprised
- Pronoun: *I*
- Auxiliary *am* or verb: *feel/felt*
- Complex sentences: I feel ___ because ___; When I feel ___, I ___.

Materials
paper plates
tongue depressors or craft sticks
glue
markers

Preparation
1. Draw faces on the paper plates displaying the emotions *happy, sad, angry, sleepy, surprised* (make enough duplicates of the faces, if necessary, for each child to have one).

2. Glue the plates to the tongue depressors or craft sticks to make puppets; let dry.

Procedure
1. Show children the puppets.

2. Have them guess how each puppet is feeling.

3. Make up a short anecdote, if necessary, either to give clues or to confirm their answers. For example: *This puppet just made a big block house. He was so proud. Then his baby brother crawled in and knocked it over. The puppet was very ___.*

4. Lay puppets out on the floor and allow each child to select one. Have them hold the puppet faces up in front of their own faces and say, *I feel ___*, matching their statements to the emotions displayed on the puppet faces.

5. Sing, "If you're happy and you know it, ___."

Cooking

The cooking activities include suggestions of language targets to work on while the children are engaged in these tasks.

Introduction
   Recipes
      Fruit Salad
      Applesauce
      Dip for Raw Veggies
      Pumpkin Bread
      Pumpkin Cookies
      Banana Wheat Germ Snacks
      Apple Muffins
      Chocolate/Vanilla Pudding
      Egg Salad
      Cinnamon Toast
      Macaroni and Cheese
      Baked Potatoes
      Peanut Butter and Jelly Sandwiches
      Muffins from a Mix
      Open-Faced Heart Sandwiches
      Heart-Shaped Finger Gelatin
      Ziti with Butter and Seasoning

Source (unless otherwise noted): Warren, J. 1982. *Super Snacks: Seasonal Sugarless Snacks for Young Children.* Alderwood Manor, VA: Warren Publishing House.

Introduction

Cooking activities provide a concrete way of teaching sequencing, vocabulary, colors, quantity concepts, and cause/effect relationships. The structure provided by planned cooking activities, combined with the high interest level of working with food and eating the results, makes such activities very stimulating and educational for the children.

A good time for cooking is the first half hour of class (unless a dish needs to be eaten immediately after being prepared). Unless you are using a recipe where all the children prepare the food right at snack time, take three or four "cooks" to the kitchen or other suitable area, keeping track of your "cooking crew" so as to rotate everyone through the cooking activities as the weeks progress.

It is important to teach the children from the beginning of the school year to prepare food in a healthy and sanitary manner. Hands should be washed before preparing any food. Discourage licking of fingers and utensils until projects are finished. Then, hands should be washed again. All fruits should be thoroughly washed and scrubbed, if appropriate, to remove residual insecticides and other chemical substances.

Wherever knives are indicated in the list of materials, table knives should be used if at all possible. If a sharp knife is required, each child must have one-to-one direct supervision during the cutting portion of the activity.

It is a good idea to have children and adults wear plastic aprons, to keep their clothing as clean as possible. If plastic aprons are not available, plastic painting smocks may be substituted. Large plastic garbage bags with head and arm cut-outs can be used, with children's sleeves pushed up.

Most activities are enhanced and more easily understood by preschool children if a picture activity chart is made for the project. This provides visual directions as the teacher gives verbal instructions. The picture activity chart should show the steps necessary to complete the activity in simple line drawings, with one or two words under each step. The pictures should be presented in a sequential order, left to right and top to bottom, as on a printed page. Picture charts may also be used when the activity is finished or at the end of the day to retell the sequence of the activity to the group, or to some person not present for the activity. As the children become more competent at following verbal directions, these activity charts may be faded, if the purpose is to increase the children's ability to follow oral directions.

Fruit Salad

Language targets
- Vocabulary: stems, core of apple, skin, names of all utensils and fruits
- Sequencing skills: children will tell the rest of the class how they made the salad.
- Verbs:
  past tense (regular): peeled, cored, sliced, mixed
  past tense (irregular): cut, took off, chose fruit

Materials
variety of fresh fruit (seedless grapes, naval oranges, apples, pears, bananas)
table knives (plastic or dull metal; one per child)
cutting boards or paper plates
bowl
large wooden or plastic spoon
apple corer/slicer
sharp knives (for teachers)
1 Tbsp. honey (optional)
small cups (one per child)
spoons (one per child; optional)

Preparation
1. Prepare picture activity chart illustrating steps.
2. Have children name all the fruit.
3. Have all the fruit on a plate in the center of the work place.
4. Have all the children wash their hands first, making sure that all soap is rinsed thoroughly.
5. Give each child a cutting board or paper plate and a dull knife.

Procedure
1. Introduce: *Today we will make a fruit salad. What kind of fruit will we have? What do we have to do to fix the fruit salad?* [cut, slice, take core out of apples, peel the oranges and bananas, take grapes off stems, etc.]
2. Have children choose an orange or banana to peel. Help them get started.
3. Adults should core and slice the apples and pears and have children cut up the slices into smaller pieces.
4. Have the children pull grapes off the stems and add them last to the salad.
5. Mix fruit with wooden spoon. (If desired, you may stir in a tablespoon of honey.)
6. Serve the fruit in small cups. The children may eat the fruit with their fingers or use spoons, depending on their ability.

Applesauce

Language targets Vocabulary: names of utensils; parts of apple (skin, peel, stem, seeds, core)

- Verbs:

  future tense: Tell early arrivals what we will do. Ask them to repeat this for late arrivals.

  am/is verb + *-ing:* Ask children to tell each other what they are doing—cutting, chopping, mixing.

  At snack time, have children tell what we did.

- Concepts: smell, taste, texture, consistency (especially for one or two who assist in putting cooked apples through strainer in kitchen; later the whole group can compare a raw apple to the cooked applesauce during snack: How are apples different? hard/soft, mushy; cold/warm; can smell applesauce (cinnamon); white/brown).

Materials
apples (at least one per child; Mackintoshes are the best)
large cooking pot with cover
smaller bowls
table knives (one per child)
paper plates (one per child)
paring knives for teachers
strainer
cinnamon
cups/bowls and spoons (one of each per child)

Preparation
1. Set out knives and plates.
2. Cut apples in half first.

Procedure
1. Introduce: *We will make applesauce. We need these things* [point to utensils]. *What is this?* Ask children to name items or point to them when you name them. *We will cut the apples into little pieces. Then we will cook them. Later we will mash them up into applesauce.* (Reserve at least part of one apple to keep raw, for comparison with the cooked applesauce during snack time.)

2. Give each child a plate, a knife, and half an apple. Let them cut and throw everything into the large cooking pot. Cook over low to medium heat (or microwave) until the apples are soft (time varies). Have two or three children mash the cooked apples through a strainer to remove the seeds and skin. Add cinnamon to taste.

3. Serve applesauce warm.

Dip for Raw Veggies

Language targets
- Vocabulary: tofu, cottage cheese, yogurt, soup mix, names of vegetables
- Verbs:

  past tense: We mashed the tofu, then added the cottage cheese and yogurt. Lastly, we stirred in the soup mix.

  Future: Later we *will* dip our veggies.
- Prepositions: Pass the bowl *to* Sarah. The fork is *for* mashing. The spoon is *for* stirring. We eat vegetables *with* dip.
- Possessive and contracted copula: Now it's Henry's turn.
- Describing ingredients (copula *is*): Tofu is soft and white. Cottage cheese is lumpy. Yogurt is smooth. The soup mix smells good.
- Following one- and two-step directions.

Materials

large bowls
forks
spoons
extra bowls for ingredients
soft tofu (16 oz.)
cottage cheese (8 oz.)
yogurt (one pint, unflavored)
dry onion soup mix (one package; not instant-lunch types)
raw vegetables (celery, carrots, cucumbers, zucchini, green peppers, cauliflower, broccoli)

Preparation
1. Set up two work stations; divide the ingredients in half and place half at each work station.
2. Set out one bowl, a fork, and a large spoon at each work station.
3. Wash and cut up vegetables; refrigerate until snack time.

Procedure
1. Introduce: *We will make a special dip to eat with our vegetables at snack. We will dip our vegetables in the dip.*
2. Help children name the ingredients (tofu, cottage cheese, yogurt, soup mix).
3. Have the children first mash the tofu with the fork, then add the cottage cheese, then the yogurt. Stir in the soup mix.
4. Refrigerate until snack time. Serve with raw vegetables.
5. Have children give the names and colors of the vegetables at snack time.

Pumpkin Bread

Language targets
- Vocabulary: pumpkin, spices (nutmeg, cinnamon, cloves), oil, eggs, molasses, brown sugar, flour
- Following instructions: *First* we will ___, *then* we will ___, *next* we will ___.
- Possessives: It's Jason's turn.
- Copula: Eggs *are* yellow. The flour *is* dry.
- Present tense: The spices *smell* good. It *looks* gooey.
- Future tense: We *will* add ___; we *will* bake ___.

Recipe
Preheat oven to 350 degrees.
4 eggs
½ C water
1 C vegetable oil
1 C cooked/canned pumpkin
1¼ C molasses
1 C brown sugar
3 C whole wheat flour
1½ tsp salt
2 tsp baking soda
2 tsp cinnamon
1 tsp nutmeg
½ tsp cloves
shortening or margarine (for greasing pans)

Break eggs into mixing bowl and beat with egg beater until fluffy. Then add remaining ingredients. Stir everything together until batter is smooth. Grease two loaf pans and fill two-thirds full with batter. Bake for 45-60 minutes. Let cool in pans for at least 15 minutes before removing. Slice to serve.

Utensils
large mixing bowls
smaller bowls (for premeasured ingredients)
large spoons
2 bread pans (approx. 5" x 9")
measuring spoons
rubber spatula
large knife (for slicing the bread)

Preparation
Measure out all the ingredients (except the eggs and spices) and divide into halves (to set up two work stations). For this activity, the children will add premeasured ingredients, and measure out only the spices, baking soda, and salt.

Procedure
1. Introduce: *We will make pumpkin bread for snack. We need lots of ingredients to put in our bread.* [Name and discuss.] *We need special utensils, too.* [Name them: beater/mixer, measuring spoon/teaspoon, scraper/spatula, bread pans, etc.] *First we break the eggs. Then we add oil, pumpkin, molasses, and sugar. Last we stir in flour, salt, soda, and spices. Then we will pour the batter into a pan and bake it.*

2. Let the children take turns adding the premeasured ingredients and stirring (all wet ingredients are mixed first, then add dry ingredients). Since the ingredients are premeasured, each child simply selects the bowl containing the indicated ingredient and adds it. The children will be measuring the spices, baking soda, and salt, however. Give children the correct measuring spoons and let them spoon the ingredients out of the can. (Minor measuring errors are unimportant.) Encourage the children to sniff the different spices as they are measuring. Does salt (or baking soda) smell? Do cinnamon, nutmeg, and cloves smell the same?

3. Have one of the children in each group grease the group's bread pan while others are mixing and measuring.

4. Pour in the batter, and bake.

Pumpkin Cookies

Language targets
- Vocabulary: Names of all utensils and ingredients; "cooking verbs" (preheat, grease, cream, beat in, sift together, drop, bake)
- Verbs:

  future tense: *will*

  past tense: reviewing the activity, telling the other children: we preheated, beat (irregular), sifted, added, dropped, baked

Recipe
½ C butter or margarine
¾ C honey
1 egg
1 tsp vanilla
1 C cooked/canned pumpkin
2½ C flour
1 tsp baking powder
1 tsp baking soda
1 tsp nutmeg
1 tsp cinnamon
shortening or margarine (for greasing cookie sheets)
raisins

Cream together butter and honey; add the egg, vanilla, and pumpkin. Sift dry ingredients together and add to creamed mixture. Drop by teaspoons onto greased cookie sheets. Bake 15 minutes. When cookies come out of the oven, make faces on them with raisins.

Utensils
mixing bowl
measuring cups and spoons
flour sifter
electric mixer
rubber spatula
cookie sheets
spoons

Preparation	Gather all utensils and ingredients in the kitchen area. Work with a selected small group of children.
Procedure	1. Introduce: *Today we will make pumpkin cookies.*
	2. See if children can name all utensils and ingredients.
	3. Describe steps, using *we will:* preheat the oven (*why?*), grease the cookie sheet, beat in, sift together, add to, drop by teaspoons full

Banana Wheat Germ Snacks

Language targets	• Future tense: We *will* make banana snacks.
	• Concepts: half milk and half honey. Milk is thin liquid, honey is thick.
	• Vocabulary: naming all ingredients. Smelling milk and honey (before mixing) with eyes closed and guessing which is which.
	• Plurals: pieces of bananas, toothpicks
	• Past tense verbs: talk about what you *did* in the circle to tell the others. (We cut, shook, put the pieces on a tray, etc.)
Source	Croft, D. J., and R. D. Hess. 1975. *An Activities Handbook for Teachers of Young Children,* 2nd edition. Boston: Houghton Mifflin.
Materials	bananas milk honey toasted wheat germ table knives (one per child) shallow bowl or small tray (for dipping mixture) plastic bag serving trays or plates toothpicks or forks
Preparation	1. Wash the bananas.
	2. Lay out ingredients and utensils on table for children to see.
Procedure	1. Let children peel and cut bananas into bite-sized pieces
	2. Mix equal parts of milk and honey; pour into shallow dish or tray.
	3. Have children dip each piece of banana into the milk-honey mixture.
	4. The pieces of banana are dropped into a plastic bag filled with wheat germ and shaken until well coated. Serve on trays or plates with colored toothpicks (or have children use small plastic forks to serve themselves).
	5. Refrigerate until ready to serve.

Apple Muffins

Language targets
- Following directions
- Vocabulary: names of ingredients and utensils
- Cooking verbs: sift, grate, mix
- Verbs (future and past tense): will sift, sifted; will grate, grated; will mix, mixed; will pour, poured, etc.
- Narrative sequence: Children explain the steps to the others.

Recipe

Preheat oven to 350 degrees.
1½ C flour
1¾ tsp baking powder
½ tsp cinnamon
⅓ C sugar
⅓ C shortening
1 egg, beaten
⅓ C milk
2 raw apples, grated
1 tsp cinnamon (for topping)
2 Tbsp sugar (for topping)
shortening or margarine (for greasing muffin pans)

Sift first four ingredients together; cut in shortening. In a separate bowl, mix egg, milk, and grated apples. Add to dry ingredients and stir only until mixed. Fill greased muffin tins; sprinkle with cinnamon-sugar topping. Bake for 20 minutes. Makes 1 dozen muffins.

Utensils

large mixing bowl
measuring cups and spoons
additional bowls and cups for premeasured ingredients
flour sifter
pastry cutter (or two knives)
large spoon
rubber spatula
grater
muffin pan

Preparation
1. Premeasure ingredients into small bowls and cups.
2. Quarter and core the apples; store in slightly salty water or orange juice until ready for use.

Procedure
1. Tell children what they will do.
2. Have them look at and smell the different ingredients and attempt to identify the ingredients and utensils.
3. Have one or two of the children grease the muffin pan.
4. Sift the first four ingredients together.

5. Cut in shortening.
6. Grate the apples.
7. Mix together egg, milk, and grated apple.
8. Add the apple mixture to the flour/shortening mixture and stir only until all ingredients are moistened.
9. Fill greased muffin tins 2/3 full.
10. Sprinkle top of muffin batter with mixture of cinnamon and sugar.
11. Bake for 20 minutes.

Chocolate/Vanilla Pudding

Language targets
- Vocabulary: ingredients (*What are ingredients?*), names of ingredients, utensils (electric mixer, bowls, spoons)
- Verbs (future and past tense): will open package, opened; will pour, poured; will mix, mixed
- Yes/No questions: Please may I ___?

Materials
chocolate and vanilla instant pudding mixes (one package serves 5-6 children)
milk (2 C per package)
small colored marshmallows
large mixing bowls (one bowl for each flavor)
electric mixer
small bowls or cups (one per child)
spoons (one per child)

Procedure
1. Talk about the ingredients and utensils.
2. Children will open the packages, pour the mixes into the mixing bowls, and add milk.
3. Children will take turns beating mix for required time.
4. Let the children pour or spoon the pudding into serving bowls or cups and top each with marshmallows. If appropriate, you might want to suggest that the children count out a given number of marshmallows for the top of each serving, in order to work on number concepts, and to ensure that all puddings have the same number of marshmallows.

Egg Salad

Language targets
- Future tense: we *will* make, we *will* stir
- Copula: the eggs *are* cooked
- Past tense: we peeled, chopped, stirred, added
- Vocabulary: shells, yolks, whites, colors (yellow, white)

Materials	hard-boiled eggs (cook two per child) large bowls plate or cutting board (for chopping eggs) spoon (for mixing and serving) mayonnaise dull knife
Preparation	1. Boil the eggs a day ahead of time. To keep eggs from cracking during cooking, fill pot with cold water, add eggs, bring water to a boil, then turn down heat to maintain a gentle boil. To make eggs easier to peel, stir in at least 1 C of salt to the cooking water. Cook for 20 minutes; rinse eggs and refrigerate. 2. Set out eggs, plate, bowls, spoon, mayonnaise.
Procedure	1. Introduce: *We will make egg salad for snack today. First we will peel the shells off the eggs. Put shells together in one bowl, eggs in another. Then we will chop the eggs and stir in mayonnaise. We will eat the egg salad for snack.* 2. Have the children use half the eggs to make egg salad. Save the other half to eat as plain hard boiled eggs. Ask the children to compare the eggs in the salad with the whole hard-boiled eggs.

Cinnamon Toast

Language targets	• Vocabulary and concepts: bread, toast; soft and cold, warm and crunchy; halves, shapes (triangle, rectangle; first slice of bread was square) • Yes/No questions: Is it toast yet? Do you want me ___? • Following two- and three-step directions. • Past tense (regular and irregular): talking about it afterwards (We pushed down the toaster handle. The bread toasted. It popped up. We took it back to our place. We spread margarine on it. We shook cinnamon and sugar on it.)
Materials	1 slice of whole wheat bread for every two children margarine cupcake papers (one per child) cinnamon and sugar in shakers (one or two per table) toasters trays or small paper plates plastic knives
Preparation	1. This activity will occur at the beginning of snack time. An extra few minutes should be allotted for snack. 2. Set up toasters at available room outlets. 3. Put pats of margarine in individual cupcake papers and set out with individual plastic knives at each place. 4. Set cinnamon/sugar shakers at each table.

Procedure
1. Introduce: *Today we will make toast.* Group children in pairs; each pair will toast one slice of bread.
2. *What do we have to do first?* Children: "Put the slice of bread in the toaster."
3. *This is bread. Is it toast yet?* Children: "No."
4. *What do we have to do to make it toast?* Children: "Push down the lever."
5. *Now it's toast* [after it pops up]. *Now it's warmer and crunchier.*
6. *I will cut it in half. Do you want me to cut it into rectangles or triangles?*
7. *Now you can take it back to your place and spread margarine on it. Then you can shake cinnamon and sugar on it.*

Macaroni and Cheese

Language targets
- Vocabulary and concepts: names of ingredients and utensils; function of strainer (to drain); idea of measuring (telling how much); counting to six; concepts of taste or flavor (salty/cheesy); compare uncooked and cooked macaroni (uncooked is hard, brittle, breaks, and is cool, children can touch it; cooked is warm/hot, wet, slippery, soft)
- Verbs:
  future tense: Tell what you *will* do, what you *are* doing, what you *did*.
  past tense: opened, poured, measured, cooked, drained, added, mixed

Materials
packaged macaroni and cheese (one 7-oz. box serves approximately eight preschoolers)

water
salt
¼ C butter or margarine
¼ C milk
2-3 quart saucepan
measuring cup
strainer

Preparation
Prepare an activity chart which has little sketches of the ingredients and the activity steps numbered, for the children to refer to as they proceed. The children can also show this to the group and tell what they did during play time or snack time.

Procedure
1. Children measure/count six cups of water, pouring it into the saucepan.
2. Bring water to a boil, telling children what you are doing, but keeping them well back from the stove.
3. Have children open the package of macaroni and remove the sauce envelope. Have an adult add the macaroni to the boiling water and cook for 7 to minutes. (Reserve a few pieces of uncooked macaroni for children to handle while the other is cooking.)
4. An adult should drain the cooked macaroni in the strainer.

5. The children can assist in returning the macaroni to the pan and adding ¼ C margarine or butter, ¼ C milk, and the cheese sauce mix from the envelope. Mix well. Makes three cups.

Baked Potatoes

Language targets
- Verb tenses:
  future: *will* bake, *will* scrub, *will* poke, etc.
  past (regular): baked, washed, scrubbed, wrapped, poked
- Vocabulary and concepts: light vs. heavy, hot oven to bake, names of utensils
- Prepositions: *with, to*
- Question forms:
  WH questions: Where are, What do we need?
  Yes/No questions: Is it light or heavy?

Materials
small baking potatoes (one per child)
vegetable brushes or sponges (for washing potatoes)
3 large bowls or dishpans
aluminum foil (cut into 8" squares)
3 forks
large baking dish for serving potatoes
pot holders
activity chart
potato toppings (optional): butter, bacon bits, cheese, sour cream, etc.
This activity is for three children working with an adult.

Preparation
1. Prepare an activity chart, illustrating the steps in preparing baked potatoes: washing the potatoes, wrapping in foil, poking holes with fork, putting in oven
2. Put the potatoes in a bag.
3. Preheat oven to 350 degrees.

Procedure
1. Introduce: *Today we will make baked potatoes for our snack.*
2. *Where are the potatoes?* [in the bag] *Let's pick up the bag. Is it light or heavy?* [heavy]
3. *What do we need to bake these?* [name all utensils]
4. Refer to chart. *First we have to wash the potatoes in these bowls. Each one can take a bowl. What do we need?* [water] Fill bowls with water.
5. *We will scrub the potatoes with these brushes.* Comment on clean versus dirty water.
6. *Now we will wrap each potato in foil. We will poke holes with a fork.*
7. *Now we will put them in the oven for one hour.* Comment on the hot oven.

Peanut Butter and Jelly Sandwiches

Language targets
- Verbs:
  future tense: *will*
  past tense (regular): shared, finished, covered
  past tense (irregular): spread, cut, made
- Vocabulary and concepts: quarter, slice of bread, loaf of bread
- Noun plurals: knives, loaves, slices
- Narrative sequence: Telling others about their cooking project at the circle after snack (may use the activity board as a guide)

Materials
loaf of whole wheat bread
peanut butter
jelly or fruit conserve
plates or cutting boards
plastic knives
serving plates or trays
foil (to cover tray of sandwiches)

Preparation
1. This activity calls for a team of three children to be making one or two sandwiches each, with each sandwich serving four children.
2. The children will all work from one container of peanut butter and one of jelly, thus having to ask each other for the appropriate ingredients.
3. Optional: Prepare an activity chart showing the steps needed to make sandwiches and cut them in quarters.

Procedure
1. Introduce: *Today we will make peanut butter and jelly sandwiches for our snack. We will make big sandwiches and then we will cut them into four quarters.*
2. Have children spread the peanut butter and jelly on the bread, then add the top slice of bread. Show them how to cut the sandwich into quarters.
3. Have the children arrange the sandwiches on trays or plates, and cover with foil.

Muffins from a Mix

Language targets
- Telling a sequential narrative using the picture activity chart
- Verbs:
  past tense (regular): mixed, stirred, blended, baked, poured
  future tense: telling latecomers what we *will* do
- Names of all ingredients and utensils. Children should be able to name them all without a model, after one initial introduction.

Materials
cupcake papers
packaged muffin mix
egg, milk (as required by mix)
mixing bowl
muffin pan

Preparation
1. Prepare an activity chart, following the instructions on the muffin mix package.
2. Preheat oven to temperature specified on muffin mix package.

Procedure
1. Tell children about preheating the oven.
2. Have the children follow the directions on the package: mix, blend in bowl.
3. Have them place the cupcake papers in the muffin pan, then spoon in the mix.

Open-Faced Heart Sandwiches

Language targets
- Vocabulary: names of utensils and ingredients; heart-shaped, open-faced, press, shake, spread, valentine
- Telling a narrative sequence using the activity chart
- Verbs:
  past tense (regular): pressed, stirred
  past tense (irregular): spread, put, shook

Materials
loaf of whole wheat bread
heart cookie cutters
cutting board
cream cheese (soft, whipped variety, or softened ahead of time)
red food coloring
bowl
wooden spoon
plastic knives
serving plates or trays
foil

Preparation
1. This activity is for a three-member team of children.
2. Set out ingredients and utensils.
3. Make an activity chart to illustrate the steps.

Procedure
1. Introduce: *Soon it will be Valentine's Day. Today we will make heart-shaped sandwiches.*
2. *Everyone can cut out hearts on a slice of bread.* Lay out bread slices on the cutting board; work out the most economical arrangement of heart shapes on the slice. Press down and then shake out the bread.
3. Shake one or two drops of food coloring into the cream cheese after spooning it into a larger bowl. Mix it up with the wooden spoon.
4. Carefully spread the pinkish-red cream cheese onto the heart-shaped bread slices. Leave the slices open-faced. Arrange on serving trays or plates.
5. Cover with foil and refrigerate until snack time.

Heart-Shaped Finger Gelatin

Language targets
- Vocabulary and concepts: gelatin, liquid, boiling water, powdery grains, dissolve, chill, firm, mold
- At each stage of preparation, discuss: What is the difference between the gelatin now and when we will eat it? (powdery, dry; hot, liquid, can pour; harder, firmer, can pick it up, can't pour it)
- Verbs:

  future tense: *will* in describing activity

  past tense: in reviewing activity with entire class after the snack is eaten (have children refer to the activity chart): opened, poured, boiled water, stirred, dissolved, chilled, pressed, made a mold, heart-shaped
- WH questions children can ask each other: Why is this a valentine snack?—because it is shaped like a heart and because it is red.

Materials
4 envelopes unflavored gelatin
3 packages cherry, raspberry, or strawberry-flavored gelatin
4 C boiling water
large bowl
13" x 19" baking pan
heart-shaped cookie cutters

Preparation
1. For a morning preschool, the gelatin will need to be prepared the day before it will be eaten, to allow the gelatin to thicken sufficiently. The next day, the children will use cookie cutters to cut out heart shapes for snack.
2. Prepare an activity picture chart (if gelatin will be eaten the following day, emphasize this on the chart).
3. Assemble ingredients.

Procedure
1. This activity involves all the children in the gelatin-making process and in pressing out the heart-shaped pieces.
2. Tell the children what you will do using an activity picture chart. Describe what you and they are doing using "I'm [verb + *-ing*]" and ask them to do the same.
3. Have children open all the packages and envelopes of gelatin and mix them in the large bowl.
4. Add four cups of boiling water and let the children stir gently until the gelatin is dissolved.
5. Pour carefully into the baking pan and chill until firm.
6. Have the children cut out heart-shaped pieces of the firm gelatin. The hearts can be arranged on a plate and chilled until snack time.

Ziti with Butter and Seasoning

Language targets
- Vocabulary: names of ingredients and utensils
- Concepts: hard ziti is uncooked. Cooked is softer. Boiling water is very hot.
- Verbs: stirring/ed, measuring/ed, pouring/ed, cooking/ed, boiling/ed

Materials
1 package of ziti (16 oz.)
1-cup measuring cups (or pitcher with "one quart" marked)
large pot
spoons to stir
butter
salt
pepper
colander

Preparation Assemble all ingredients.

Procedure
1. The children will prepare the pasta right before snack time and serve it warm to the rest of the class.
2. Explain and demonstrate that 4 cups is the same as 1 quart.
3. Have children measure 4 quarts (16 cups) of water into a large pot; have an adult bring the water to a boil on the stove.
4. Let the children open the package; an adult can pour the ziti into the boiling water. (Reserve a few pieces of uncooked ziti for the children to examine while the other is cooking.) Stir until the water boils again (approximately 30 seconds).
5. Cook for 12 to 16 minutes. DO NOT OVERCOOK.
6. Drain in colander; return to pan. Allow children to add butter, toss, add salt and pepper.

Music

Some of the music activities are grouped according to seasonal and/or holiday themes; all include suggestions of language targets to work on while the children are engaged in these tasks.

Introduction

Three Favorite Songs:
    Put Your Finger in the Air
    Where Oh Where Is [name of child]?
    Eensy Weensy Spider

Open Shut Them (Hap Palmer record)

Singing with a Guitar or Autoharp
    Names and Clothes

Moving to Music (Hap Palmer record)

Halloween Movement Songs and Dances
    This Is the Way the Witches Dance (song)
    Black Cat, Black Cat (chant and dance)

Hokey Pokey (song and dance)

Thanksgiving Songs:
    Smells Like Dinner (Tune: Frere Jacques)
    Ten Little Indians

Christmas Songs:
    Rudolph the Red-Nosed Reindeer
    Jingle Bells (looking at bells and playing them)

Chanukah (Bowmar Records: December Holidays)
    Chanukah is Here
    Dreidles of Chanukah
    Chanukah March

Songs about Winter
    The Snow Came Down
    On a Winter Day
    Ice Skating
    Five Little Snowmen

Riding in My Car (Woody Guthrie)

Easter Eggs

Introduction

The music activities presented in this section accomplish many objectives: learning music, language remediation, gross and fine motor movements, sequencing, and repetition. In addition to being enjoyable for the staff and children, music has been found to be therapeutic for language-impaired children.

> Both language and music are forms of communication that generally are transmitted auditorily. There may be a more significant connection between music and language, however. Recent literature indicates that language is processed in the left hemisphere of the brain, whereas music is processed in the right hemisphere. Some researchers speculate that undeveloped language areas may exist in the right hemisphere which may be stimulated by joining music with language. (Shanin 1984, p. 1)

During music activities, the children should be allowed to make noise and be physically active. Music is a good activity to plan either before or after a series of more structured and sedentary activities. The children have fun and you can target language objectives at the same time.

Many of the activities outlined in this section are based on specific songs from published records. Consider the suggestions as samples of what can be done with these types of music, and generate activities from the records and tapes you have on hand.

Shanin, S. J. 1984. *Songs for Language Learning*. Tucson, AZ: Communication Skill Builders.

Three Favorite Songs
(Hap Palmer record)

Language targets
- Body parts: in, on
- Where is ___? Names, next to
- Verbs:
  past tense (regular): crawled, washed, dried
  past tense (irregular): came

Record
Hap Palmer. 1972. *Getting to Know Myself.* Freeport, NY: Educational Activities, Inc.

Materials
large cards with children's names

Preparation
Have the children sit in a circle.

Procedure
Introduce the songs.

"Put Your Finger in the Air" (Tune: "If you're happy and you know it")
Other body parts: finger on knee, finger on head, finger on chin, etc.

"Where Oh Where Is [child's name]?"
Use large name cards to help children recognize their own and others' names. Last line of song: "Sitting next to [child's name]."

"Eensy Weensy Spider"

Open, Shut Them
(Hap Palmer record)

Language targets
- Vocabulary: opposites (open, shut); actions (clap, put, creep, crawl)
- Prepositions: *in, up, to*
- Following directions
- Pronouns: *them, your*
- Body parts: chin, mouth, lap
- Negatives: do not

Record
Hap Palmer. 1972. *Getting to Know Myself.* Freeport, NY: Educational Activities, Inc.

Procedure
Demonstrate movements for "Open, shut them," have children imitate you.

Open, shut them; open, shut them;
Give a little clap.
Open, shut them; open, shut them;
Put them in your lap.

Creep them, crawl them; creep them, crawl them
  (crawl hands up chest to under the chin)
Right up to your chin.
Open wide your little mouth (dramatic pause)
But do not put them in. (hands go in back)

Singing with a Guitar or Autoharp

Language targets
- Vocabulary: clothing items, guitar/autoharp strings, wood, case, musical instrument
- Plural nouns: shoes, socks, etc.
- WH question: What did you wear today?
- Verb tenses:
  past tense (irregular): made, wore
  future tense: will pluck, will sing
  copula *is*:: A guitar/autoharp is a musical instrument.

Materials guitar or autoharp

Procedure
1. Talk about the guitar or the autoharp: *A guitar/autoharp is a musical instrument. It makes a pretty sound. I will pluck the strings. We will sing a song.*
2. If possible, play some of the old songs the children know and have them sing along with you.
3. Introduce the following song (tune: "Mary Had a Little Lamb"): *We will sing a song about the clothes you have on.*
   Sarah wore a pink shirt, a pink shirt, a pink shirt.
   Sarah wore a pink shirt all day long.
4. Change the name and clothing item for each child around the circle.

Moving to Music
(Hap Palmer record)

Language targets
- Vocabulary: body parts (hands, nose, hips, lap, head, toes)
- Prepositions: *in, on, around, up and down, to*
- Directionality: right/left
- Plurals: hands, hips, toes, both hands
- Verbs: put, turn, jump, walk, bow

Record Hap Palmer. 1969. *Learning Basic Skills through Music* (vol. 1). Freeport, NY: Educational Activities, Inc. The song for this activity is "Put your hands up in the air," Side 1, Band 2.

Preparation
1. Preview music to be familiar with the actions called for in the song.
2. Push tables aside so there is room for children to move and sit down.

Procedure
1. Introduce: *We will listen to the record and do what it tells us.*
2. Demonstrate the actions the song will have the children do: Put your hands up in the air, on your nose, on your hips, in your lap. Turn around, jump up and down, walk quietly. Right, left hand, both hands, bow head.
3. Play the music and lead the group in the movements.

Halloween Movement Songs and Dances

Language targets
- *Witches Dance:*
  Body parts
  Pronoun: *they*
  is as main verb

- *Black Cat:*
  Following directions
  Prepositions and locatives
  Concepts: turn around; high/low

Source
Warren, J. 1984. *Movement Time,* pp. 12, 17. Palo Alto, CA: Monday Morning Books.

Materials
props (witch's hat, cat's whiskers, pumpkins, etc.)

Preparation
This is a good activity to channel energy on Halloween Day after a costume parade and before snack or party time. Arrange children in a circle to do the motions. Use the chant below to feature the different children in their costumes.

Procedure
1. Introduce the children to the song (tune: "Here We Go Round the Mulberry Bush"), encouraging them to do the activities the song mentions.

    This Is the Way the Witches Dance
    This is the way the witches dance,
    Witches dance, witches dance.
    This is the way the witches dance
    On Halloween night.

    Other verses:
    This is the way they kick their heels . . .
    This is the way they hook their arms . . .
    This is the way they turn around . . .

2. Repeat first verse.

3. Introduce the "Black Cat" chant, below. Change "black cat" to any of the Halloween characters the children represent, or use props (witch's hat, pumpkins, etc.).

    Black Cat, Black Cat
    Black cat, black cat, turn around.
    Black cat, black cat, touch the ground.
    Black cat, black cat, jump up high.
    Black cat, black cat, touch the sky.
    Black cat, black cat, reach down low.
    Black cat, black cat, touch your toe.

Hokey Pokey

Language targets
- Body parts: hand, foot, head
- Vocabulary and concepts: whole self; right hand/foot; left hand/foot

Materials small pieces of paper, masking tape

Preparation Tape a small piece of paper to each child's right hand and right foot.

Procedure
1. Have the children stand in a circle. Explain that it is their *right* hand and *right* foot that are labeled.
2. Start the song:
   Put your right foot in,
   Put your right foot out.
   Put your right foot in
   And shake it all about.
   Do the Hokey Pokey and
   Turn yourself around.
   That's what it's all about.
3. Repeat with all parts (left foot, right and left hand, head, body)

Smells Like Dinner

Language targets
- Modal: *can*
- Third person singular: smells
- Vocabulary: food names

Source for pictures National Dairy Council. 1977. *Food . . . Your Choice: A Nutrition Learning System,* Level 2. Rosemont, IL.

Materials pictures of foods (foods for any regular meal, or foods for specific holiday feasts, such as Thanksgiving, Christmas, or Passover)

box for picture cards (optional)

Preparation Select pictures for appropriate meal. Place the pictures in the box (optional).

Procedure
1. *Smells like dinner* (tune: "Frere Jacques")
   Smells like dinner,
   Smells like dinner.
   Mmmm, mmmm, good!
   Mmmm, mmmm, good!
   I can smell the ___.
   I can smell the ___.
   Mmmm, mmmm, good!
   Mmmm, mmmm, good!
2. Have the children name their favorite dinner foods (or any other meal).

3. Optional: Children take turns reaching in box and pulling out a food picture (you may need to cue the food names). This item then is the basis of the next verse.

Ten Little Indians

Language targets
- Concepts: counting to ten, then counting backwards from ten; one-to-one correspondence (standing up when pointed to)
- Future tense: we *will* sing, we *will* move, we *will* march

Record *Sing the Happy Romper Room Songs.* Newark, NJ: Peter Pan Records; taped or recorded Indian dance music

Materials Indian feathers (made earlier by the children; see "November: Indian headdress" in the Arts and Crafts section of this manual)

Procedure
1. Help the children put their headdresses on as they gather for this activity.
2. Introduce: *We will sing a song about Indians. We will count them.* Practice singing the song, then sing the song again and have one child stand up with each number as you point to the appropriate children.
3. Sing the song with the record, having the children stand.
4. Play Indian dance music and have the children march and move around the room.

Christmas Songs

Language targets
- Memorization
- For "Rudolph the Red-Nosed Reindeer": adjectives (red-nosed, shiny, foggy), past tense (loved, shouted, used)

Record Use any recording of children's Christmas songs such as "Rudolph the Red-Nosed Reindeer."

Materials pictures of items mentioned in the song

Procedure Introduce only one new song in any session. Play the song and sing the words, encouraging the children to sing along with you as they become familiar with the words.

Jingle Bells

Language targets
- Plurals: bells, triangles, sticks
- Copula: This bell *is* ___; these bells *are* ___.
- Concept: same, different
- Vocabulary: bell, triangle; ring, shake, tap (hit), jingle

	• Adjectives: large, small; large, larger, largest; small, smaller, smallest
Record	A recording of "Jingle Bells"
Materials	bells of different sizes and varieties triangles from rhythm instruments
Preparation	Set up record or tape player; lay out bells.
Procedure	1. Introduce "Jingle Bells" and say, *We will sing "Jingle Bells," then we will play the bells and sing.* 2. Play the record and help children learn the words. 3. Show children the bells and triangles. Talk about them and allow the children to choose bells to play. 4. Play and sing "Jingle Bells."
Chanuka	See the Circle Time section for songs and dances using the Chanukah theme.

Songs about Winter

Language targets

The Snow Came Down

- Verbs:
  past tense (regular): covered
  past tense (irregular): came, left

- Past tense time concepts: last night

- Color/Adjectives: sparkling white

On a Winter Day

- Third person singular verb: comes, covers

- Pronouns: *we*

- *is* as a main verb: This is the way

- Verb vocabulary: comes, covers, shovel, throw, roll

Ice Skating

- Complex sentences: ___ and ___

- Prepositional phrases: in the sky

Five Little Snowmen

- Verbs:
  past tense (regular): melted
  past tense (irregular): came

- Number concepts: 1 through 5

- Irregular plural nouns: snowmen

Record	Wood, L. 1971. *Rhythms to Reading Picture Songbook.* Glendale, CA: Bowmar Publishing Co.
Materials	either a record player or a piano
Procedure	1. Children should each have a chair or mat to sit on while learning the songs, before they dance and move to the music.
	2. After the children are familiar with the words, teach the motions to the songs.

The Snow Came Down
   The snow came down and covered the town,
   The snow came down last night.
   The snow came down and covered the town,
   And left it sparkling white.

On a Winter Day
   This is the way the snow comes down,
   Snow comes down, snow comes down.
   This is the way the snow comes down,
   On a winter day.

Other verses:
   This is the way it covers the town
   This is the way we shovel the snow
   This is the way we roll the snow
   This is the way we throw the snow

Ice Skating
   On ice and snow, skating we go.
   Skates sing a dance song as we glide along,
   Turning and turning around like a top.
   Turning and turning, then quickly we stop.
   Running, we fly like a bird in the sky.
   We go sailing by.

Five Little Snowmen
   Five little snowmen fat.
   Each with a funny hat.
   Out came the sun and melted one.
   What a sad thing was that,
   Down, down, down.
   Four little snowmen fat . . .
   Three . . .
   Two . . .
   One . . .

Riding in My Car (Woody Guthrie)

Language targets	• Vocabulary (limited only by imagination): snowplow, snowmobile, motorboat, horse, racing car, motorcycle, airplane, helicopter, etc.
	• Prepositions: *for, in, on*

- Verbs: show how a snowplow pushes, how a horse bounces, how an airplane flies, etc.
- Past tense: We rode in a ___

Materials
guitar (optional)
pictures of different vehicles (optional)

Procedure
1. Teach children the first verse of the song:

    Riding in My Car
    Take me for a ride in your car, car;
    Take me for a ride in your car, car;
    Take me for a ride in your car, car;
    Take me for a ride in your car, car.

2. Ask children to suggest different types of vehicles to use in the song. Have them add motions, if desired. Vary the speed and loudness of the song to correspond to the different vehicles they suggest. If children have difficulty thinking of vehicles spontaneously, have a few pictures to choose from, or cue by function. (See vocabulary list above.)

Easter Eggs

Language targets
- Irregular past tense: found
- Number concepts: 1 through 8
- Prepositional phrase: in the grass
- Plural noun: eggs
- Color names

Songbook
Wood, L. 1971. *Rhythms to Reading Picture Songbook.* Glendale, CA: Bowmar Publishing Co. "Five Easter Eggs," p. 105.

Materials
large Easter eggs (cut from different colors of 9" x 12" construction paper)
sitting mats
piano and pianist (optional)

Procedure
1. Select children to be Easter eggs; give each a paper egg, and have them "hide" around the room (stand in the various areas, in full view of the circle). The remainder of the children will take turns later.

2. Play and sing the song: *Five pretty Easter eggs, hiding in the grass (repeat). Five pretty Easter eggs hiding in the grass. I found a blue one.* Look around for the children holding the eggs. Point out the child who is holding the blue egg; that child then returns to a chair or mat.

3. Start with five and go down to one, each time selecting the color of one of the remaining eggs. You might want to ask the children in the circle to suggest which color to name next, or to identify which color eggs are still out "in the grass."

Science

The science activities include suggestions of language targets to work on while the children are engaged in these tasks.

Introduction
Projects:
    Introducing a Pet Turtle
    Autumn Walk to Find Leaves
    Autumn Leaves Bulletin Board
    Seed Collection
    Carving Pumpkins
    Touch Center: Textures
    Touch Center: Size and Shape Discrimination
    Touch Center: Thickness Discrimination
    Touch Center: Common Objects (arts and crafts tools)
    Filmstrip: Fall
    Filmstrip: Winter
    Bird Feeder Construction
    Shadow Walk and Shadow Tag (for Groundhog Day)
    Fire Experiment
    Bird and Worm (picture to color)
    Filmstrip: Spring
    Coloring Easter Eggs
    Mr. Grass
    Carrot-Top Garden
    Egg-Carton Nursery
    Farm and Zoo (bulletin board)
    Farm and Zoo Animals
    Farm and Zoo Animal Books

Introduction

With preschool children, the introduction of science activities is directed toward exposure, not mastery of skills. With language-impaired children, such activities provide a concrete means of teaching cause/effect relationships. By using manipulative objects in most activities, the children can feel and/or see changes created by the activities.

The preschool science curriculum should emphasize activities and objects found in the children's natural environment. The immediate relevancy of these activities is critical.

In addition to teaching cause/effect relationships, the science theme activities address concept learning, classification, and preacademic skill development. Temporal concepts are stressed in the activities involving seasons. Classification skills are found in the animal activities. Colors, along with visual and tactile discrimination skills, are emphasized in several of the suggested activities, as are direction-following skills.

Carefully planned science activities can be coordinated with other theme topics and/or theme areas. The controlled presentation of the activities can stimulate the children's curiosity to examine the world around them.

Introducing a Pet Turtle

Language targets
- Concepts: reptiles, protects, live on land, live under water. Different kinds of turtles (hard vs. soft, fast vs. slow)
- Vocabulary: jaw, beak, shell, carapace
- Basic sentences describing turtle's appearance and actions
- Comprehension of WH questions and yes/no questions: Where do turtles live? What do turtles eat? What is the turtle doing?
- Possessive nouns: turtle's head, eyes, etc.
- Third person singular verbs: the turtle crawls, eats, drinks, lives, etc.

Materials
box turtle
book about turtles (*Book of Turtles* by John F. Waters, esp. pp. 23, 28)
plastic or glass aquarium
large rock
rug for underneath aquarium
dish for water
desk or table for aquarium
food (fruit, vegetables, worms, etc.)

Preparation
1. Place the turtle in a fairly sunny area of the room so children can see and enjoy.
2. Have instructions for care (feeding and cleaning) posted nearby. Use simple words and pictures to communicate what the children should do to care for the turtle.

Procedure
1. Discuss all aspects of a turtle (feeding habits, habitat, body parts, shape, size, texture, etc.).
2. Let children feel and observe their new pet.
3. Discuss the turtle book, showing pictures, etc.
4. See Cue Cards on wall of Science Section for specific language targets and suggestions for conversation.

Autumn Walk to Find Leaves

Language targets
- Negative construction: Leaves haven't fallen down yet. Some haven't turned color yet. Evergreens won't turn colors.
- Verbs:
past tense (regular): turned yellow/brown/orange, stayed green
past tense (irregular): found, fell down
- Concepts:
same/different (leaves, seeds)
damp, dry (leaves)
hard, bumpy (pine cones)
sharp (pine needles)
round, pointy (leaves)

Materials lunch bags

Procedure
1. Take the children on a walk through an area with mixed deciduous and evergreen trees, if possible, and let them collect leaves, pine needles, pine cones, seeds, and twigs they find on the ground. Return to the room and have the children display their collections.
2. Talk about the fall. It comes after summer. It gets cooler.
3. Cooler weather makes leaves turn colors and they fall to the ground. What color were the leaves last summer? They were green and now some are starting to turn brown, yellow, and orange. Ask children to identify colors of leaves they find. Trees have different shaped leaves.
4. Some trees do not lose their leaves. They stay green. They are called evergreens. Evergreens don't have leaves, they have needles.
5. Trees have seeds. Evergreen trees make pine cones. The seeds are in the cones.

Autumn Leaves Bulletin Board

Language targets
- Concepts: fall, cooler weather, colors, high/low, same/different colors
- Prepositions: *in, on, through, with* (tape)
- Question forms: May I ___ please?
- Vocabulary: fall, branch
- Plural nouns: leaf/leaves; branch/branches

Materials leaves from autumn walk (activity above) or colored leaves of different shapes cut from construction paper

masking tape
bulletin board decorated with bare tree

Procedure
1. Lay out leaves on a table near the bulletin board you are going to complete.
2. Select children by name to tape colored leaves to the branches. Cue them to ask for a leaf by color: *May I have an orange/a brown/a yellow leaf?* You can model the question: *Ask me, may I have ___?*, putting the words in the right order. They can also ask for tape or for help. They can tell which branch they will tape the leaf to (for example, a high branch or a low branch), or whether they will put the leaf on the ground or falling through the air.

Seed Collection

Language targets
- Vocabulary and concepts:
  Fruits and vegetables grow from seeds
  A pumpkin grows from a pumpkin seed
  How seeds grow; takes time
  Plant them in the ground
  Need warm sunshine and water
  Some plants take a long time to grow from a seed
  Some take shorter time

Materials
: fruits and vegetables (both snack items and others—such as pumpkins, dry bean pods, tomatoes, green peppers, ears of corn—that have seeds)

paper towels or paper plates
pictures of fruits and vegetables used (seed catalogs have wonderful pictures)
plastic sandwich bags
stapler

Procedure
: 1. Over the course of a few weeks, have children who are preparing snack items save the seeds of the various fruits and vegetables used for snacks (apples, pears, oranges, peaches, plums, cucumbers).
  2. Bring in other fruits and vegetables and have the children remove the seeds, wash them, and lay them out to dry on paper towels or paper plates. (Label the paper towels or plates as to the identity of the drying seeds.)
  3. After the seeds have dried, have the children place the seeds in plastic sandwich bags, and label what the seed is from (or what it would become if planted) by finding pictures of the fruit or vegetable in a seed catalog, cutting out the picture, and either putting the picture in the bag or stapling both the bag and the picture on a bulletin board.

Carving Pumpkins

Language targets
: - Future tense: *will*
  - Modal: *can*
  - Parts of pumpkin: outside, inside, seeds
  - Concepts: pumpkin as food; how it grows
  - Vocabulary: bake, cook, mash, crisp, mushy, sharp, carve

Materials
: pumpkins (one pumpkin for every three children)
large pot for pumpkin pulp and seeds
carving knives
markers
large spoons
glue
tempera paint
scraps of cloth
buttons
yarn

Preparation
: Cut out the tops of the pumpkins around the stems, so the "caps" are removable. Cover tables with newspapers and set pumpkins out.

Procedure
: 1. The children will take turns scooping out the pumpkin seeds. They can then take turns marking the face of the pumpkin and watch as you cut out the facial features they have drawn. At no time should the children handle the knife. It should be kept out of reach at all times. After the face has been carved, the children can decide on further decoration of the face with media of their choice (paint, marker, scraps of cloth, buttons, yarn for hair, etc.).

2. *What is this?* (A pumpkin.) *We will carve this. We will cut off the top. We will scoop out the insides and make a face. A pumpkin with a face is called ___* (a jack-o'-lantern).

3. *What is inside the pumpkin?* (Seeds.) *We can bake the seeds in a hot oven. They will get crisp. We can eat them. We can cook the pumpkin and mash it up and make bread and pumpkin pie with it.*

4. *Where does a pumpkin come from?*

Touch Center: Textures

Language targets
- Vocabulary and concepts: texture labels (bumpy, smooth, silky); texture names (corduroy, silk, terry cloth, etc.); concepts of: feeling, touching, same/not same
- WH questions: Which ones feel the same?
- Yes/No questions: Is that the same? Are these the same?

Source Doan, R. L. 1979. *Science Discovery Achievement Activities.* West Nyack, NY: The Center for Applied Research in Education, Inc.

Materials "Touch box" (large covered box with handholes in the sides)

5 pairs of objects or materials with matching textures: cotton cloth, corduroy, velvet, silk, sandpaper, paper towels, etc.

Preparation
1. Cut 4" or 5" holes in each side of the box, and decorate it. You might want to tape or glue the tops of 6" to 8" squares of fabric across the handholes (inside the box). Hands can still be inserted into the box, but children will not be able to see into the box and possibly identify the materials.

2. Gather the samples of different textures, and cut two of each texture.

    Note: Introduce only two pairs of textures at the beginning, and gradually work up to five. Always show the children the fabrics and let them feel the textures and discuss them before you place the texture samples in the box.

Procedure
1. *Here is a Touch Box. We will put our hands inside and feel these cloths.* Show the different fabrics to the children. *Before I put the cloths in the box, let's feel them.* Feel and name the textures. Name a texture and ask the children to find the fabric that matches.

2. Use the handholes on the opposite side of the box to put two sets of texture samples in the box while the children close their eyes. *Reach into the box and try to find two that feel the same. Feel them. Then you can pull them out and see if they are the same.*

3. Children may want to see one sample and try to locate the other by touch in the box.

Touch Center: Size and Shape Discrimination

Language targets
- Vocabulary and concepts: round—circle/ball; square—block/box
- Comparative adjectives: big, bigger, biggest; small, smaller, smallest
- Order of adjectives when viewing an object: a big red square; a big red block; the small yellow circle/ball
- Order of adjectives when object is hidden from view: I feel/felt a big block.

Name shape (two-dimensional) =	*Name object* (three-dimensional)
round/circle	ball
square	block/box/cube

Source Doan, R. L. 1979. *Science Discovery Achievement Activities*. West Nyack, NY: The Center for Applied Research in Education, Inc.

Materials Touch Box (see instructions in the preceding activity)
1 pair of large spheres
1 pair of large cubes
1 pair of small spheres
1 pair of medium cubes
1 pair of small (1") cubes

Procedure
1. *We have some new things in our Touch Box.* Remove shapes and show them. *Before we put them inside, let's touch and look at them.* Name shapes and characteristics (round, square).
2. Proceed as in the activity above, initially introducing two pairs, working up to all five.

Touch Center: Thickness Discrimination

Language targets
- Concepts: same/different; thick vs. thin; thick, thicker, thickest

Source Doan, R. L. 1979. *Science Discovery Achievement Activities*. West Nyack, NY: The Center for Applied Research in Education, Inc.

Materials Touch Box (see above)
6 pairs of circles cut from materials of different thicknesses

Procedure
1. Show children the circles and have them feel the differences in thickness.
2. Proceed as described in the two preceding activities.

Touch Center: Common Objects

Language targets
- Vocabulary and word-retrieval skills: naming all items and identifying what they are used for; describing differences among pencils (thicker, bigger, with holder, etc.)

- Past tense verbs: I felt it, I touched it
- Yes/No questions: Is it the same? Is it different? Is it a ___?
- WH questions: What is it?

Source — Doan, R. L. 1979. *Science Discovery Achievement Activities.* West Nyack, NY: The Center for Applied Research in Education, Inc.

Materials — Touch Box (see above)

2 each: primary pencils, preprimary pencils, regular pencils with erasers, scissors, erasers, markers

Procedure — *We have something new in our Touch Box.* Show the objects to the children; have them feel the differences in size and shape of the pencils. Then put the objects inside the box, and proceed as described above.

Filmstrip: Fall

Language targets
- Vocabulary: explain the meaning of underlined words in captions; fall, autumn, frost, harvest, gathers, thick coat (of fox), valley, drift
- Concepts: of how weather and plant life change in the fall and of how animals get ready for winter

Materials — filmstrip projector
screen
filmstrip: "Fall" (captioned version), 1981, National Geographic Society.

Preparation — Load filmstrip projector and focus the image.

Procedure
1. Tell children about what they will see.
2. Discuss briefly what things happen in the fall that they are familiar with.
3. Read captions that appear below each picture (do not read italicized captions, only the captions in regular print).

Filmstrip: Winter

Language targets
- Basic vocabulary and concepts:
Winter brings cold weather and snow to many parts of the country.
Winter activities include sledding, skiing, and ice fishing.
Many birds fly south in the winter.
Some birds stay.
They and other animals have to search hard for food in winter.
Some animals sleep all winter.
Evergreen trees stay green all winter.
Other trees are bare.

Materials — filmstrip projector and screen
filmstrip: "Winter" (captioned version), 1981, National Geographic Society.

Preparation	Load filmstrip projector and focus the image.
Procedure	1. Tell children about what they will see. 2. Discuss briefly what things happen in the winter that they are already familiar with. 3. Read captions below each picture and discuss.

Bird Feeder Construction

Language targets	• Concepts: winter, cold weather, food hard to find for birds. We help the birds by making a bird feeder. Snow will cover seeds that are on the ground so we put them up in a bird feeder so birds can get to them. • Vocabulary and metaphors: neck of the bottle, pie pan, cord, birdseed • Verbs: past tense (regular): glued, filled past tense (irregular): cut, hung • WH questions: Why do birds need bird feeders in the winter? • Yes/No questions: Do birds need feeders in the summer? Why not?
Source	Doan, R. L. 1979. *Science Discovery Achievement Activities*. West Nyack, NY: The Center for Applied Research in Education, Inc.
Materials	plastic bleach bottle or milk jug aluminum pie pan strong cord knife glue birdseed funnel (optional)
Preparation	You will make the bird feeder as the children watch and help, discussing each step.
Procedure	1. Discuss the need for a bird feeder in the winter, and examine the materials together. 2. Cut six small holes (no larger than 2" inches in diameter) in the plastic bottle near the base. 3. Children help glue the pie pan to the bottom of the jug. 4. Children help tie the cord on the neck of the bottle. 5. Children can fill the bottle with bird seed. (A funnel may be necessary here.) 6. While making the feeder, talk about the importance of assisting birds in the winter. 7. Put the feeder on an outside windowsill or hang in a nearby tree for children to watch birds eat. Refill feeder as necessary.

Shadow Walk and Shadow Tag (for Ground-Hog Day)

Language targets
- Vocabulary and concepts: shadow, shapes, same shape. Shadows are caused by sunlight and something getting in between.
- Prepositions: *in between, behind, in front of*
- WH questions: Where is your shadow? Whose shadow is that? What is that a shadow of?
- Yes/No questions: Can you step on his/her shadow?
- Pronouns: *they* have shadows; *he/she/it* has a shadow; *their/his/her* shadows

Materials Plan to take a walk on a sunny day; use a powerful flashlight for optional indoor demonstration.

Preparation Ask parents to make sure children are dressed warmly and wear boots (if necessary) for a walk the next day, weather permitting.

Procedure
1. Dress the children for outdoor play.
2. Shadow Walk:

   What is a shadow? It is a dark shape on the ground, the floor, or the wall. You make the shadow when you get in between the sunshine and the ground or the floor or the wall. Everything makes shadows. Things make shadows.

   Let's find shadows. Find shadows of trees, cars, the children.

   Move your leg or your arm and watch the shadow move.

2. Shadow Tag:

   Try to step on someone else's shadow. Pick one person to be "IT."

   Remember, your shadow follows you, so if you move away, it will move with you.

Fire Experiment

Language targets
- Vocabulary: *Starter Fire Words Picture Dictionary* with page references, on p. 23, can be used to review vocabulary with individual children.
- Verb forms:

  third person singular: Daddy makes (p. 1); lights (p. 2); fire/wind needs (p. 3); fire burns (p. 3); makes, keeps, cooks (p. 6), cools, puts (p. 11); melts, cuts (p. 21)

  past tense irregular: made, sent (p. 7)

  past tense regular: rubbed (p. 9), burned (p. 14)

  future tense: *will* (pp. 12, 32)
- Copula *is* (pp. 4, 13, 15); *are* (p. 12); *is* (pp. 18, 19)

Materials	candle holder matches glass jar that covers candle and holder story: *Fire: Wonder Starters* (Wonder Books, Grosset and Dunlap 1971)
Preparation	Read *Fire: Wonder Starters* to the children for circle time or story time. This coordinates with the Fire Engine and Putting out a Fire theme areas.
Procedure	1. Read the story, discuss the ideas, and show the pictures. 2. Do the experiment on p. 22: Light a candle. Put a jar over the candle. Soon the air in the jar will be gone and the flame will go out.

Bird and Worm

Language targets	• Concepts: winter/spring; weather in the south; first; lays eggs in nest • Pronouns: *it, they* • Verbs: third person singular agreement: He/It flies/comes, looks for worms/eats. past tense (regular): He/They looked for worms to eat. past tense (irregular): He/They flew/came back. • Advanced levels only: See if the children can say what these words mean (that is, can they define them in their own words): *first, hungry*
Materials	line drawing of a bird with a worm crayons scissors glue colored construction paper (9" x 12") picture of robins (optional) nest
Preparation	1. Make copies of the picture for each child. 2. After the discussion (see below), the children will color their birds and cut them out to glue on a colored sheet of construction paper. Title the pictures "First Robins."
Procedure	1. Talk briefly about spring. *It is the season after winter when the days start to get a little warmer. The first birds to fly back might be robins.* 2. *Where were the robins when it was very cold out?* They flew south just before winter. *Where is the south?* Talk about children's (or grandparents') trips to warmer areas (Florida, Arizona, California, Hawaii). *In the south, the weather is warmer when places in the north are having ice and snow.* 3. *The robins are hungry. They look for worms to eat.* You (and other classroom adults) may copy a short "story" about each picture on the bottom or back as dictated by the child.

Filmstrip: Spring

Language targets
(The following is from the guide that accompanies the filmstrip):

Spring is a time of growth and change for many living things. In spring, flowers bloom, trees sprout new leaves, and the weather becomes warmer. Many insects lay their eggs in spring. Cows, sheep, and other animals have their babies.

- Vocabulary: buds, bloom, gather, insects, tadpoles, trout, hatch
- Verb forms:
  future: *will*

  third person singular agreement: robin sits, farmer plants seeds, boy fishes, water strider walks, cow feeds, baby lamb drinks, boy works in his garden
- Plural nouns: flowers, things, cows, plants, leaves, buds, nests, eggs, insects
- Prepositions: *on, in, for, beside, under, to, through*

Materials
filmstrip projector
screen
filmstrip: "Spring" (captioned version), 1981, National Geographic Society.

Preparation
Load filmstrip projector and focus the image.

Procedure
1. Tell children about what they will see.
2. Discuss briefly what things happen in the spring (see Language targets above).
3. Read captions that appear below each picture.
4. Optional: After reading the caption, have the children take turns telling what they see in the picture or talking about the picture.

Coloring Easter Eggs

Language targets
- Future tense: Have the children guess what they will do. *We will choose a color. I will write your name on your eggs with a crayon. You will dip the egg into the colored water and the egg will turn color.*
- Past tense: Describe to the children (or have early arrivals describe) what you already did to get ready: You boiled the water. You added 20 drops of color. You measured one teaspoon of vinegar. You poured the vinegar in the water.
- Pronouns: *I, he, she* (in describing own and others' actions)
- Vocabulary: name all the ingredients and utensils
- Auxiliaries: Model *I'm* during your preparation in telling what you are doing, then ask children to tell others what they are doing.
- Special vocabulary: dyeing, dipping, coloring, choosing

Materials	2 hard-boiled eggs per child
vinegar
styrofoam or ceramic coffee cups
boiling water
food coloring
crayons (light colors)
measuring spoons
spoons for dipping eggs in dye
newspapers or paper towels
cookie racks

Preparation
1. Add 20 drops of desired coloring to ½ cup boiling water and 1 teaspoon vinegar in a cup. (Note: styrofoam cups tend to tip; sturdy coffee mugs work better.)
2. Early arrivals can watch the preparation and help you count the drops.

Procedure
1. Have children guess what they will do and name all the utensils and ingredients.
2. Describe the preparation of the dye in past tense.
3. Describe the activities the children will be doing: *We will color two eggs each.*
4. Write each child's name on two eggs with light-colored crayon before the children dip them in the dye. Have children rest an egg on a spoon and lower the egg into the dye. Remove the egg and let it drain on paper towels or cookie racks laid out on newspapers.

Mr. Grass

Language targets
- Sequential memory: tell the sequence to the children. See if the older ones can retell it to the others.
- Vocabulary: names of all the materials
- Concepts:

    Seeds grow in soil, need sunlight and water.

    "Looks like"—grass looks like hair in these cups.

    What else looks like something else? (apple looks like a ball, paper plate looks like a steering wheel, etc.)
- Past tense verbs: decorated the cup, planted the seed, watered the dirt, poured the water

Materials
styrofoam cups (one per child)
markers
potting soil mixture
grass seed

Procedure
1. Have children use markers to decorate cups to resemble a face.
2. Have the children fill their cups with the potting soil mixture.
3. Let them sprinkle grass seed on top of the soil.
4. Water the cups of grass seed.
5. Place the cups on a shelf where the sun shines, and have the class watch the "hair" grow.
6. Water as needed to keep soil moist.

Carrot-Top Garden

Language targets
- Vocabulary: shallow dish vs. deep dish; parts of carrot (tops, part we eat); watering can
- Questions: Where is the watering can? How do the carrots look?
- Yes/No questions: May I water the sprouts? Are they growing? Do they need water? Is that enough water?
- Quantity terms: enough water, too much, not enough, more, less

Materials
3 or 4 carrots
shallow dish
water
container for watering

Preparation
1. Mark a line ¼" from the bottom of the dish.
2. Cut off carrot tops and place them on a shallow dish or baking pan. Add water to ¼".

Procedure
1. Have children water the carrots daily, keeping water at ¼" at all times. (Show them the water-level mark.)
2. Children can then watch green sprouts in days to come.

Egg-Carton Nursery

Language targets
- Vocabulary: names of all materials and parts (soil, sections of the egg carton, seeds, teaspoon, measuring, tray)
- Concepts: how plants grow. (You can use flannel board materials during circle time to explain this also.) Seed has to stay moist, not too wet, not too dry; needs to be warm. After a seedling appears, it needs light.
- Verb forms (basic level): I'm putting in potting soil/seeds. I'm measuring water. I'm covering the seed. More advanced level (past tense): put, measured, covered

Materials	cardboard egg cartons with tops potting soil marigold seeds teaspoon container of water tray to set cartons on
Procedure	1. Have each child put soil in two sections and carefully plant two marigold seeds in each section. (Have adults label each child's carton sections.) Water each section with a teaspoon of water. 2. Seeds will sprout more quickly if egg carton top is down. (Seeds stay warmer and moister that way.) 3. Check planters daily to see that soil stays very most. 4. When seeds sprout, children may take them home and plant in larger containers. (Cut containers apart with scissors or knife.) When weather is warm enough, marigolds may be planted outdoors.

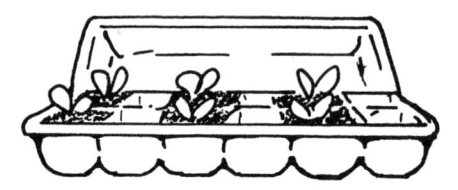

Farm and Zoo
(Bulletin Board)

Language targets	• Concepts and vocabulary: Barns and cages are places to live. Which animals live in barns? Why? Which animals live in cages? Why? If the wild, dangerous animals were not in cages, where would they live? (in jungles) Where are jungles? Are jungles near cities? Where are zoos? (zoos are near cities where people live) Why are wild animals put in zoos? • Plural nouns: barns, cages, towns, jungles, animals
Materials	barn and zoo cage (cut out of construction paper)
Preparation	Put the barn and the zoo cage on a bulletin board.
Procedure	This activity is to be coordinated with step 3 in the activity below, when the children will be coloring worksheets of zoo and farm animals. The language targets below may be implemented when the children are deciding where their individually prepared animals should go.

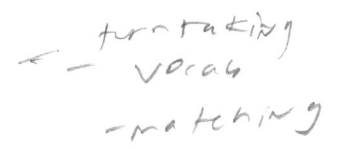

Farm and Zoo Animals

Language targets
- Concepts and vocabulary: Talk about the differences between farm and zoo animals. Zoo animals might be wild and dangerous. What does that mean? You should not pet wild animals. They might bite, etc.
- Third person verb agreement: Describe each animal as you are attaching it to the bulletin board (He eats hay. He lives in a zoo. He bites. He *has* stripes. He *doesn't* bite.)

Source   For patterns, see Forte, I., 1982, *The Kid's Stuff Book of Patterns, Projects, and Plans,* Nashville, TN: Incentive Publishing, Inc.

Materials   photocopies of farm and zoo animals
crayons
scissors
markers

Preparation
1. Have the Farm and Zoo bulletin board ready (see above).
2. Make one photocopy of each farm and zoo animal to be used.

Procedure
1. Have children select one zoo animal and one farm animal apiece.
2. Have them color and cut out their animals.
3. Let the children determine where on the bulletin board their animals belong and select places for their animals to be placed.

Farm and Zoo Animal Books

Language targets
- Concepts and vocabulary: names of animals; describe their color, size, sounds they make, any other special features: horses gallop, pigs squeal and are fat, cows give milk and say "moo," etc.
- Third person singular verb agreement: A horse lives on a farm, a zebra lives in a zoo, etc.

Materials   photocopies of farm and zoo animals
construction paper (12" x 18", one sheet per child)
paper fasteners or stapler
crayons
markers

Preparation   Photocopy one set of zoo animals and farm animals for each child (see the activity above for animal worksheets). Fold construction paper in half, insert set of photocopies, and fasten with paper brads or staples.

Procedure
1. Talk about farm and zoo animals.
2. Have children color the animals in their books. The first week the children can color the farm animals, and the next week they can color the zoo animals.

Story Time

The story-time activities are grouped according to seasonal themes, and include suggestions of language targets to work on while the children are engaged in these tasks.

General Instructions

September and October
Me and My School
All about Me
Me and My Family
Me and My Feelings, Me and My Friends
Halloween Stories

December
Christmas Stories

January
Winter Stories

February
Ground-Hog Day Stories and Games

March
Spring Stories
A Story about the Wind

March or April
Easter Stories

May or June (or any time)
Stories about Animals: Pets, Farm, Zoo, and Jungle Animals
Mothers and Baby Animals
Teddy Bear Stories for Teddy Bear Week

General Instructions

During Story Time, children should be divided into small, cozy groups according to language level, preferably no larger than four children per adult if staffing permits. Children like to sit in nooks and corners on the floor and cuddle up close to each other and the adult reading to them. Read the exact words of the story or tell it in your own words, simplifying when necessary, depending on the language comprehension abilities of the children and the complexity of the story. Stop for comments and conversation. Talk about the pictures. Encourage conversational digression and remind children entering an ongoing conversation of what the topic was. To help children direct their remarks to each other and not always to you, look away from the child who is talking and look towards the person the child should be responding to.

If a story is being read to the entire class during Circle Time, have the storyteller sit on a small chair slightly higher than the children, and make sure all the children can see each page of pictures as it is slowly displayed.

Children love repetition. As they become familiar with certain books, ask them to tell the story, using the pictures as a cue. Alternately, you can display the pictures and ask them questions about the story.

Display Story Time books (and others) prominently in the Book Nook. Have children make use of the following times to sit down with a book:

> During the transition between interactive play or bathroom and the Circle, children can select a book from the Book Nook and sit on a mat in the circle to look at it.

> During Free Play, a limited number of children (one to three) may be allowed to select the Book Nook.

> If parents are delayed in picking up a child, encourage the child to select a book to "read."

Experience with books during the preschool years is related to successful literacy development during the elementary school years. Story reading demonstrates to children how books work, that print makes sense, that print and speech are related in a specific way, that book language differs from speech, and that books are enjoyable. Additionally, it demonstrates patterns of interacting characteristic of behaviors expected in a school setting (Schickedanz 1986).

An additional contribution of story reading is the pleasure that it can bring to children. In discussing the emotional pleasure and nurturing of attention and physical closeness during story reading, Taylor (1986), states that "the seemingly benign activity of reading bedtime stories to the preschool child can permeate years of family life" (p. 83).

> It probably permeates years of school life, too. If experience with books is enjoyable, and if it occurs under especially nurturant conditions, the feelings associated with reading and books are likely to be highly positive. The development of such positive attitudes toward books and reading may be one of the most important contributions that early book-reading experiences can make. (Schickedanz 1986, pp. 50-51)

The book titles included in the following activities should serve only as suggestions. Encourage children to bring in their own favorite books on a given theme or subject, and use the public library to expand your collection. (Check for seasonal books at the public library as far in advance of the holiday as possible, since selection dwindles as the holiday approaches.) Constantly upgrade the class's stock of books, as funds permit. Be aware of which books are favorites among your children, and consider adding other titles by those authors, or books of similar type. (Many libraries have used-book sales, where older versions of some of the classics are available at minimal cost.)

Schickedanz, J. A. 1986. *More than the ABCs: The Early Stages of Reading and Writing.* Washington, DC: National Association for the Education of Young Children.

Taylor, D. 1986 *Family Literacy: Young Children Learning to Read.* Portsmouth, NH: Heinemann.

Me and My School (September and October)

Language targets *Monster Goes to School*

- Talk about "make believe." Are there really monsters? Do they go to school? Why did the monster in the story want to go to school with the boy? Talk about being lonely and missing people. Past tense verbs (regular and irregular); negatives (pp. 18, 19)
- Complex sentences with *because, if*
- Copula past tense: *was, were*

Grover Goes to School

- Excellent pictures and straightforward but not simple text. Talk about the pictures with younger children.
- Past tense (regular)
- Past tense (irregular): thought, shook, forgot
- was + verb + *-ing;*
- Complex sentences with *so, if*
- Reflexive pronoun: *himself*
- Copula: *was, were*

The Teacher Who Could Not Count

- Number recognition and counting (have the children be the numbers)
- Negatives weren't, didn't
- Past tense (regular and irregular)
- Modal: *can*

Show and Tell

- Familiar Sesame Street characters, but fairly complex text. Good pictures the younger children can discuss.
- Conditional verbs: wouldn't
- Complex sentences with *after, when*
- Compound sentences
- Past tense (regular and irregular)

First Day in School

- Real photos of racial mixture of preschool children; simple text
- Copula: *is*
- Third person singular noun-verb agreement

Sources Binzen, B. 1972. *First Day in School*. Garden City, NY: Doubleday and Co.

Blance, E., and A. Cook. 1973. *Monster Goes to School*. Glendale, CA: Bowmar Publishing Co.

Elliot, D. 1982. *Grover Goes to School.* New York: Random House/Children's Television Workshop.

McKee, C., and M. Helland. 1981. *The Teacher Who Could Not Count.* New York: School Book Fairs, Inc.

Relf, P. 1980. *Show and Tell.* Racine, WI: Western Publishing Co., A Sesame Street/Golden Press Book.

Preparation: The first week of school, these books might be prominently displayed in the Book Nook section.

Procedure:
1. Encourage children to relate the stories to their own experiences.
2. Talk about what we do in school. Older children can talk about what is the same and what is different about their own school and the schools in the stories.

All about Me
(September and October)

Language targets

Who am I?
- Pronoun: *I*
- Copula: *am*
- Talking about the pictures

The Shape of Me and Other Stuff
- Ask children to identify the silhouettes.
- *and*
- Plural nouns

The Magic of Growing Up
- Complex sentences
- Reasoning skills
- Good discussion

My Head-to-Toe Book
Excellent pictures and simple text for the youngest children.
- Body parts
- Verb vocabulary
- Verb + *-ing*
- Preposition: *for*

Me
Large, simple, manipulative pictures, simple text. The youngest children will love this.
- Body parts
- Preposition: *for*

- Pronoun: *I*
- Verb + *-ing*

Sources

Behrens, J. 1968. *Who Am I?* Elk Grove Press, Inc.

Clure, B., and H. Runsey. 1968. *Me.* Glendale, CA: Bowmar Publishing Co.

Geisel, T. 1973. *The Shape of Me and Other Stuff.* New York: Random House, Inc.

Tymms, J. 1974. *My Head-to-Toe Book.* New York: Golden.

Walley, D. 1970. *The Magic of Growing Up.* Kansas City, MO: Hallmark Cards, Inc.

Preparation

Display the books for this theme prominently in the Book Nook, along with other preselected books for September and October.

Procedure

1. Using the books listed above as models, have children identify various body parts. Have children identify children of different ages in the books, and then have them try to place the students in the class in chronological order. This might be incorporated into a class bulletin board by using photographs of the children and birth dates.

2. Once children can identify their own body parts, have them identify body parts on other children.

3. Use a slide projector (or other light source) to generate shadows and trace children's silhouettes. Have the children identify and mark the various silhouettes.

Me and My Family (September and October)

Language targets

Waiting for Baby
No text; wonderful pictures of a young child curious about mother's tummy, grandmother coming to care for child, parents leaving for hospital, talking to mother on telephone, visiting hospital to see mother and new baby. Excellent for discussions when a new baby is expected in a child's family.

A Baby Sister for Herry
Emphasis on the new "herry" baby at home and all the extra attention it gets and special responsibilities of older siblings.

- Past tense (regular and irregular)
- Pronouns

People in My Family
"Monster" Muppet family; good lead-in for children to discuss own family.

- Vocabulary
- Counting to five
- Adjectives: furry, scary, fuzzy, hairy

Mommies Are for Loving
- Talk about feelings among family members.
- Preposition: *for*
- Verb vocabulary

What Kind of Family Is This: A Book About Stepfamilies
Rather complex text. Good even to simplify if you have children whose parents have divorced and remarried. Conflicts among children could trigger discussion about getting along with brothers or sisters.
- Complex and compound sentences
- Question and negative forms

Families Live Together
Excellent photographs of different families that will trigger much discussion. Very simple text. (Book is written in present tense.)
- Animal families, human families, new baby, anger in families, family outings, children in families
- Third person singular noun-verb agreement

Sources

Endersby, F. 1985. *Waiting for Baby*. Holland: Child's Play International.

Kingsley, E. 1984. *A Baby Sister for Herry*. Racine, WI: Western Publishing Co., A Sesame Street/Golden Press Book.

Meeks, E. K., and E. Gabwell. 1969. *Families Live Together*. Chicago, New York: Follett Publishing Co.

Moss, J. 1983. *People in My Family*. Racine, WI: Western Publishing Co., A Sesame Street/Golden Press Book.

Penn, R. 1962. *Mommies Are for Loving*. New York: G. P. Putnam's Sons.

Seuling, B. 1985. *What Kind of Family Is This? A Book About Stepfamilies*. Racine, WI: Western Publishing Co., A Golden Learn About Living Book.

Preparation
1. Have preselected books prominently displayed in the Book Nook.
2. Children could bring in pictures of themselves and their families for Show and Tell. These pictures could also be displayed on paper cutouts shaped like houses, one per child, with the child's name, symbol, and address on the bottom for a bulletin board or front door display.

Procedure

Encourage children to digress freely and relate story elements to their own families and experiences.

Me and My Feelings, Me and My Friends (September and October)

Language targets

Monster Looks for a Friend
A book for older preschool children.
- Complex sentences with *but, because, and* and infinitives

- third person singular noun-verb agreement (goes, comes, thinks, plays, etc.)

Best friends
- Talk about the pictures.
- *was* + verb + *-ing*
- Past tense regular *-ed* and irregular verbs

Will I Have a Friend?
- Question forms
- Regular and irregular past tense verbs
- Concept of "making a new friend." How do we make a new friend? How do we feel if we are a new child in a school?

Two Good Friends
- Verb + *-ing*
- Regular and irregular past tense verbs
- Talk about what we do with our good friends. How did the good friends in the story help each other? How can we be helpful and kind?

Friends
Wonderful photographs to discuss.
- Concepts: names of family members, brothers and sisters, boys and girls together

I Had a Bad Dream: A Book about Nightmares
Parents' guide explains how waking fears can be translated into bad dreams. The pictures and simple text explain this to the children.
- Question forms
- Regular and irregular past tense verbs
- Vocabulary to describe feelings and qualities
- Telling reality from dreams

Why Are People Different? A Book about Prejudice
Being different from the perspective of a black boy and his grandmother. One child in the story stutters. Complex sentence structures and reasoning suitable for older preschool children. Excellent for discussion of differences and feelings.

Nobody Cares about Me
This story has some complex language but can be told to children on lower language levels, using the pictures.
- Regular and irregular past tense verbs

Tony and His Friends
- Plural nouns
- Agent-action-object sentences
- Regular and irregular past tense verbs
- Modal verb *can*

Sometimes I Get Angry
- Past tense verbs
- Pronouns
- Talk about times when children might get angry at home and in school.

Sources

Clure, B., and H. Runsey. 1968. *Monster Looks for a Friend.* Glendale, CA: Bowmar Publishing Co.

Cohen, M. 1979. *Best Friends.* New York: Macmillan.

_____. 1967. *Will I Have a Friend?* New York: Macmillan.

Delton, J. 1974. *Two Good Friends.* New York: Crown Publishers, Inc.

Dunn, P. 1971. *Friends.* Mankato, MN: Creative Educational Society, Inc.

Hayward, L. 1985. *I Had a Bad Dream: A Book about Nightmares.* Racine, WI: Western Publishing Co., A Golden Learn About Living Book.

Hazen, B. *Why Are People Different? A Book about Prejudice.* Racine, WI: Western Publishing Co., A Golden Learn About Living Book.

Roberts, S. 1982. *Nobody Cares about Me.* New York: Random House, Inc.

Wagner, K. 1969. *Tony and His Friends.* Racine, WI: Western Publishing Co.

Watson, J., R. E. Switzer, and J. C. Hirshbery. 1971. *Sometimes I Get Angry.* Racine, WI: Western Publishing Co.

Preparation

Display these books prominently in the Book Nook to encourage the children to look at them at other times than Story Time.

Procedure

1. Encourage children to talk about their feelings. See if children can "interpret" feelings of people pictured in the stories. Older children can talk about why characters felt a certain way.

2. For stories about friends, ask younger children concrete questions based on the pictures in the stories. Encourage all to talk about "what is a friend" and "what we can do with our friends." Role play "polite" forms.

Halloween Stories (October)

Language targets

Mousekin's Golden House
- Nature themes
- Complex sentences

It's Halloween
Introduces main vocabulary for the Halloween season with several short story sequences.

Gus Stories
Long and interesting narratives with lots of past-tense regular and irregular verbs, contracted auxiliary verb forms, pronouns

Sources Miller, E. 1964. *Mousekin's Golden House*. Englewood Cliffs, NJ: Prentice Hall, Inc.

Prelutsky, J. 1977. *It's Halloween*. New York: Scholastic Book Services.

Thayer, J. 1972. *Gus and the Baby Ghost*. New York: William Morrow and Co.

Thayer, J. 1961, 1962. *Gus Was a Friendly Ghost*. New York: William Morrow and Co.

Preparation
1. Display books prominently in the Book Nook.
2. Invite children to bring in their own books about Halloween themes. Add them to the story curriculum.

Procedure Little children may become fearful around Halloween time. Talk about "pretend" and make-believe. Have them try on costumes, and urge parents to send in makeup and hats rather than masks.

Christmas Stories (December)

Language targets

Madeline's Christmas
A straightforward narrative with many pictures. Good for general vocabulary and verb tenses. All children.

The Bears' Christmas
Simple language.

- Plurals
- Irregular past tense verbs
- Rhymes

Encourage children to imitate and "read" along with you.

Jingle bells
Simple narrative. Good for all children.

- Third person singular noun-verb agreement
- Regular past tense verbs

Tiny Bear and His New Sled
Simpler yet. Encourage children to repeat ("read") after you. You can ask one to be the "teacher" and "read" this to the others (repeating after you).

- Yes/No questions
- Irregular past tense verbs

Mousekin's Christmas
Complex sentences in this narrative. Good for the oldest or most language-advanced in the high-risk group. Condense and simplify for the others.

- Regular past tense verbs

Sources
: Bemelmans, L. 1985. *Madeline's Christmas*. New York: Viking Press.

Berenstain, S., and J. Berenstain. 1970. *The Bears' Christmas*. New York: Random House Beginner Books.

Daly, K. N. 1964. *Jingle Bells*. Racine, WI: Western Publishing Co., A Little Golden Book.

Long, R. 1969. *Tiny Bear and His New Sled*. Racine, WI: Golden Press.

Miller, E. 1965. *Mousekin's Christmas*. Englewood Cliffs, NJ: Prentice Hall, Inc.

Preparation
: Display the books prominently in the Book Nook so the children may look at these books at playtime or before Circle Time and request an adult to read to them individually.

Procedure
: See remarks above for specific books.

Winter Stories (January)

Language targets
: All of the books listed below incorporate the following:

- Simple and complex sentence structures
- Regular and irregular past-tense verbs
- Vocabulary and concepts related to winter
- Question forms: WH questions and yes/no questions

Sources
: Bedford, A. N. (retold by). 1979. *Frosty the Snowman*. Racine, WI: Golden Press.

Fox, P. 1962. *When Winter Comes*. Chicago, IL: Reilly and Lee.

Hader, B., and E. Hader. 1948. *The Big Snow*. New York: Macmillan.

Keats, E. J. 1962. *The Snowy Day*. New York: Viking Press.

Long, R. 1969. *Tiny Bear and His New Sled*. Racine, WI: Golden Press.

Wood, L. 1971. *Winter Days*. Glendale, CA: Bowmar Publishing Co. (coordinated with a record)

Preparation
: 1. Display books prominently in the Book Nook prior to being used for Story Time.

2. Wait for a winter snow before presenting these stories. This Story Time could be coordinated with a walk in the snow, Arts and Crafts activities such as making a cotton puff snowman, a science experiment involving bringing snow inside in a plastic bucket to "see what happens," or playing with snow brought inside in a big tub (children wearing mittens).

Procedure
: All of the stories listed above have a simple text. *Winter Days* has an alternate and more complex text on the left-hand page and is coordinated with a Bowmar Record in the same set. The most complex story is *The Big Snow*.

Ground-Hog Day Stories and Games (February)

Language targets   *Shadows* (and general discussion)

- Vocabulary and concepts: burrow, colors, furry, fall, winter, sunshine, shadows
- Pronouns: *they, we* (talking about their walk and about the ground hogs in the story)
- Verbs:
  past tense (regular): rolled, jumped, ducked, dodged, tumbled, snored
  past tense (irregular): ran, crept
  third person singular: it copies, it makes, it stays
- Negative forms: don't, can't, doesn't

The Ground Hog

- Verbs:
  past tense (regular): wiggled, looked
  past tense (irregular): left, shook, ran, crept, slept, saw
  past tense of copula *was*
- Compound sentence with conjunction *and*
- Vocabulary and concepts: shy, fright, left, right, shadow, burrow

Sources   Devendorf, A. 1986. Shadows. *Turtle Magazine.* February. Indianapolis, IN: Children's Better Health Institute.

Wilmes, D., and L. Wilmes. 1982. *The Circle Time Book,* p. 65. Dundee, IL: Building Blocks Publishers, Inc.

Shadows

It was Ground-Hog Day. Three little ground hogs—Chuck, Chuckie, and Chuckles—popped out of their holes.

"Oops," said Chuck. "I see my shadow. That means six more weeks of winter."

"And I see mine," said Chuckles.

"I don't want six more weeks of winter," said Chuck.

"I don't want one more week of winter," Chuckie said.

"I don't want one more day of winter," said Chuckles.

"Quick," said Chuck. "Let's cover our shadows. Then maybe spring will come faster."

"Yes," said Chuckie. "Let's bury our shadows under snow."

The three little ground hogs began heaping snow on their shadows.

"My shadow stays on top of the snow," Chuck said.

"Yes," said Chuckie, "My shadow refuses to be buried."

"No matter how much snow I use," said Chuckles, "my shadow doesn't disappear at all."

"I'm going to try to roll my shadow like a window shade," Chuck said.

"I'm going to fold my shadow like a sheet," said Chuckie.

"And I," said Chuckles, "am going to wad my shadow into a ball and throw it away!"

"I can't roll my shadow," said Chuck, as he bent over his shadow. "It doesn't roll at all. It only copies me."

"I can't fold my shadow," said Chuckie with a sigh. "It makes fun of me. It does what I do."

"I can't wad my shadow into a ball," said Chuckles. "It stays as flat as a pancake."

"There must be something good about a shadow," said Chuck.

"What?" asked Chuckie.

"I know what's good about a shadow," answered Chuckles. "Shadow tag is!" He jumped on Chuckie's shadow. "You're IT!" he said.

"What do I do!" asked Chuckie.

"You try to catch my shadow and step on it or you try to catch Chuck's shadow and step on it," said Chuckles. "Whoever's shadow you step on is IT!"

The three little ground hogs ran and jumped. They ducked and dodged. They rolled and tumbled. They got so tired that they crept back to their holes and snored through the six more weeks of winter!

The Ground Hog

A shy little ground hog left his bed.

He wiggled his nose and shook his head.

He looked to the left, he looked to the right.

The day was clear and the sun was bright.

He saw his shadow and ran in fright.

Then back to his burrow he crept, he crept.

And six more weeks he slept, he slept.

(variation of poem by Marguerite Gode)

All About Ground Hogs (a suggested narrative)

Ground hogs are little furry animals.

They are black or brownish red.

(show a picture, if available)

In the fall, they eat a lot of plants and vegetables.

They eat so much so they won't get hungry all winter.

They don't eat in the winter.

They sleep in a hole in the ground.

Their hole is called a burrow.

Sometime around Ground-Hog Day on February 2, they wake up and they come out of their holes to look around.

If they see their shadows on the ground from the winter sun, they run back to their holes and sleep for six more weeks. Then everyone thinks that there will be six more weeks of snowy, cold winter weather.

Preparation
1. Find pictures of ground hogs, both sleeping and awake.
2. Plan several coordinated activities:

   Ground-hog snack: raw veggies (carrots, celery, green peppers), *because ground hogs like to eat these and they are good for you.*

   Shadow Tag or Shadow Walk (see Science Activities section).

Procedure
1. Before the Story Time or at Circle Time, tell the children all about ground hogs, using pictures if possible.
2. Bring a box to be used as a burrow. As you read "The Ground Hog," have the children take turns being the ground hog and doing the actions mentioned in the story.
3. Before Story Time, during gross motor play, plan to have a Shadow Walk or play Shadow Tag. When you read "Shadows," encourage discussion about the children's shadows. Were they scared of their shadows?

Spring Stories (March)

Language targets *Splish, Splash*

- Verbs:
  copula *is* and contracted copula *it's*
  future tense: *will*

- Vocabulary: excellent science vocabulary (skunk cabbages, catkins, crocus, shadbush trees)

- Rhyming verses: children might like to repeat some

A Springtime Walk
See notes for the records to which this book is keyed.

Sources Kessler, E., and L. Kessler. 1973. *Splish, Splash.* New York: Parents Magazine Press.

Wood, L. 1971. *A Springtime Walk.* Glendale, CA: Bowmar Publishing Co. (coordinated with record)

Preparation
1. These stories can be coordinated with a springtime walk where the children identify signs of spring, and with a filmstrip about spring (see Science Activities section).
2. Save *Splish, Splash* for a rainy day.
3. Encourage children to bring in pussy willows or other spring harbingers such as crocuses.

Procedure	As an alternative to small-group stories, either story can be presented to the entire group at Circle Time. *A Springtime Walk* can be coordinated with the music during Music Time.

A Story about the Wind (March)

Language targets	*The Wind Blew*

- Verbs:
  past tense (regular): turned, snatched, satisfied, whipped, grabbed, tossed, plucked, lifted, whirled, pulled, mixed
  past tense (irregular): blew, took, swept, kept, stole, sent, found, threw

- Prepositions: *from, inside out, up, with, upward*

- Vocabulary: Ask, "What does this mean?" (show pictures for a clue: content, satisfied, plucked, fluttering)

Source	Hutchins, P. 1974. *The Wind Blew.* New York: Macmillan Publishing Co.
Preparation	1. Save this story for a blustery day.
	2. The children might go out for a walk in the wind or they could take turns standing on a stool and looking out the window to see the trees blowing in the wind.
Procedure	1. This is a good story to tell to a larger group of children sitting in one or two semicircles. It has big pictures and a short, rhyming text on each page.
	2. Talk about spring and the windy weather. For older children, explain the meaning of *March comes in like a lion and goes out like a lamb.* Have the children blow puffs of cotton or pinwheels to make "wind."

Easter Stories (March and April)

Language targets	*The Easter Lady* (right-page text):

- Three-element sentences with irregular past tense verbs (made, grew, became)

- Three-element sentences with uninflected present tense verbs (go, find, listen)

- Prepositions and prepositional phrases: comprehension and use (*from, for, in, with*)

- Question comprehension: Do you know ___? Where?

- Concepts:
  Easter comes in the spring. In spring, a bulb grows into an Easter lily. Sun and rain make flowers grow. We hide Easter eggs and find them. New baby animals (ducklings) are born in the spring.

The Enchanted Egg
Talk about the pictures. Simplify the text.

- Concept of "make believe": do robins wear aprons and dust?

Peter Rabbit
Following a retelling of the narrative sequence, ask the children questions about what you've just read. Have them look at the pictures and predict what is going to happen next.

The Golden Egg Book

- Verbs:
past tense regular: pushed, jumped, climbed, rolled, yawned
irregular: shook, threw, thought
- WH questions: Where is my egg? Where did you come from? What was it?

The Easter Lady (left-page text)

- Narrative sequences with same concepts as basic level, but more advanced language structures (complex and compound sentences, conditional verbs)

The Runaway Bunny

- Conditional sentences (*if . . . then*). Ask the children to retell these as an answer. Ask, "*What will the mommy do if she ___?*" Children answer, "If she ___, then ___."

Sources   Brown, M. W. 1947, 1962. *The Golden Egg Book*. New York: Golden Books.

Brown, M. W. 1942. *The Runaway Bunny*. New York: Harper and Row.

Burrows, P. 1956. *The Enchanted Egg*. New York: Rand-McNally.

Potter, B. 1958, 1970. *Peter Rabbit*. New York: Golden Books.

Wood, L. 1971. *The Easter Lady*. Glendale, CA: Bowmar Publishing Co.

Preparation   Display these stories prominently in the Book Nook and encourage the children to look at the pictures during Circle Time or Playtime.

Procedure   These books vary greatly in difficulty and comprehension demands. Present the stories to the following age groupings for high-risk language-impaired children, six to twelve months delayed or deviant in development:

2½- to 3½-year level:
The Easter Lady (right-page text), *The Enchanted Egg, The Golden Egg Book*

3½- to 4½-year level:
Peter Rabbit, The Golden Egg Book, The Easter Lady (left-page text)

Over 4½-year level:
The Runaway Bunny

Stories about Animals: Pets, Farm, Zoo, and Jungle Animals (May or June)

Language targets

For all texts:

- Vocabulary: concepts of pets, indoor vs. outdoor animals, animals that live on farms vs. those that live in jungle; compare and contrast these groups.
- Verb forms: action verbs describing movements of animals
- Prepositions: regarding locations of animals
- Adjectives: describing animals (ferocious, wild, tame, scary, soft, furry, etc.)
- Pronouns and possessive noun forms: in talking about animals, activities, appearance

Sources

Very simple texts; large pictures or photographs:

Bonforte, L. 1981. *Farm Animals.* New York: Random House.

Golden Press. 1980. *Pet Friends.* Racine, WI: Golden Press, A Golden Book (photo).

O'Callahan, K. 1983. *Look with Us at Animals: A First Guide to Animals.* England: Newmarket-Brimax Books.

Rojankovsky, F. (illus.). 1951. *The Great Big Wild Animal Book.* Racine, WI: Golden Press.

Moderately difficult language and text:

Bonaforte, L. 1981. *Who Lives in the Zoo?* Racine, WI: Western Publishing Co.

Your Big Backyard. February 1986. Vienna, VA: National Wildlife Federation (Magazine with stories about turtles, koala bear, ground hog, newborn zebra, red fox, etc.)

More challenging language and concepts; more complex texts:

Davis, A. V. 1940. *Timothy Turtle.* New York: Harcourt, Brace and World, Inc.

Dunn, P. *Animal Friends.* Mankato, MN: Creative Educational Society, Inc.

Waters, J. F. 1971. *Turtles.* Chicago: Follett Publishing Co. (A Follett Beginning Science Book)

Whitley, B. *Safari Adventure: A Hallmark Pop-Up Book.* Hallmark Cards, Inc.

Preparation

1. Coordinate animal stories with field trips to farms and zoos. Encourage children who go to the circus to bring in pictures of wild animals and talk about them.

2. Coordinate with Arts and Crafts and Science animal projects. Display models of animals, especially when presenting the stories to younger children.

3. Encourage pet hamsters, turtles, frogs, etc., to visit the classroom.

Procedure — Introduce stories about just one category of animals at a time (jungle animals, farm animals, mother and baby animals [see "Are You My Mother?" below], etc.).

Mothers and Baby Animals

Language targets
- Verbs:
  future: he *will* look
  past tense (regular): jumped, looked, shouted, walked
  past tense (irregular): came, ran, found
  copula: *Are* you my mother? No, I *am* not. I *am* a dog.
- Pronoun: *I*
- Yes/No questions: Are you ___? Will he find ___?
- Negative forms: I am *not* your mother. You are *not* a cow.

Source — Eastman, P. D. *Are You My Mother?* New York: Random House Beginner Books.

Preparation
1. This is a good story to present to the entire group at Circle Time as well as in Story Time.
2. Prepare flannel board sets or models of mother and baby animals to show to younger children.

Procedure — Talk about mothers and babies. They look the same sometimes, sometimes not. For older children, ask, How the same? How different?

Teddy Bear Stories

Language targets
- Vocabulary: based on the plots of the stories
- Verb forms: *-ing*, copula *is*, past tense regular and irregular
- Pronouns: especially subjective pronouns *he, she, I, they*
- Negative forms: especially *can't, won't, don't*

The following list of books is included for use during Teddy Bear Week (see Theme Days and Weeks for additional "teddy bear" activities for Teddy Bear Week).

Sources

Asch, F. 1978. *Sand Cake: A Frank Asch Bear Story.* New York: Parents Magazine Press.

Berenstain, S., and J. Berenstain. *Berenstain Bears Books.* New York: Random House.

1973. *Almanac.*	1981. *Moving Day.*
1984. *Christmas Tree.*	1975. *Nature Guide.*
1982. *Go to Camp.*	1974. *New Baby.*
1981. *Go to the Doctor.*	1977. *Science Fair.*
1982. *How to Get Along at School.*	1984. *Shoot the Rapids.*
1984. *And Mama's New Job.*	1983. *To the Rescue.*
1984. *Meet Santa Bear.*	1981. *Visit the Dentist.*
1983. *And the Messy Room.*	1983. *And the Wild Wild Honey.*

Also Bright and Early Books:
1971. *Bears in the Night.*
1969. *Bears on Wheels.*
1964. *The Bike Lesson.*

Duplaix, G. 1947. *The Big Brown Bear.* New York: Golden Press, Western Publishing Co.

Elias, J. 1972. *Yogi Bear and the Colorado River.* 1972. *Yogi Bear and the Pie Bomb.* 1974. *Yogi Bear Teaches Boo Boo some Ecology.* New York: Modern Promotions.

Freeman, D. 1968. *Corduroy.* New York: Viking Press.

Gross, R. 1980. *A Book About Pandas.* New York: Scholastic, Inc.

Hoffman, G. 1978. *Who Wants an Old Teddy Bear?* New York: Random House.

Hubert, A. 1983. *Sweet Dreams for Sally: A Tale from the Care Bears.* U.S.: Parker Brothers.

Kahn, P. 1983. *The Care Bears: "Try try again."* New York: Random House.

Kay, S. 1986. *Care Bears comic book.* New York: Marvel Comics Group.

Kuskin, K. 1961. *The Bear Who Saw the Spring.* New York: Harper and Row.

Ludlow, M. 1983. *The Trouble with Timothy: A Tale from the Care Bears.* U.S.: Parker Brothers.

Milne, A. A. Walt Disney Presents. *Winnie-the-Pooh and . . . .* Racine, WI: Golden Press.
1974. *Eeyore's Birthday.*
1979. *A Honey Pot Book, Jokes and Riddles.*
1965. *The Honey Tree.*
1973. *Tigger.*

Minarik, E. 1968. *A Kiss for Little Bear.* 1957. *Little Bear.* 1960. *Little Bear's Friend.* New York: Harper and Row.

Reich, A. 1983. *The Care Bears and the Terrible Twos.* New York: Random House.

Scott, E. 1973. *The Fourteen Bears Summer and Winter.* Racine, WI: Golden Press.

Watts, M. 1971. *Never Pat a Bear: A Book About Signs.* Racine, WI: Golden Press.

Werner, J. 1973. *Smokey the Bear.* Racine, WI: Golden Press.

Preparation Remove the books in the Book Nook and replace with teddy bear stories if you have enough. If not, put teddy bear stories on the top shelf.

Procedure
1. Have stories available for Book Nook, for transition time at the Circle before Good Morning routines, for ten-minute Structured Language Therapy sessions as per instructions, or for regularly scheduled time for small groups to read stories.

2. Encourage children to tell what happened by using the "cloze" technique (do not finish the sentence; rather, use vocal inflection to indicate an incomplete sentence, and allow the children to finish the sentence).

Theme Areas

The theme areas activities include suggestions of language targets to work on while the children are engaged in these tasks.

General Instructions

Themes:
- Fast-Food Restaurant
- Little Folks Hair and Beauty Gallery
- Department Store
- Get-Well Hospital
- United States Post Office
- Fire Station
- Supermarket

General Instructions

The primary purpose of theme areas within the classroom is to promote naturalistic interpersonal speaking time. The secondary goal is to introduce the preschoolers to basic social studies through learning about the community around them. The areas, when properly used, teach about community workers, vocabulary in a variety of contexts, and basic grammatic/syntactic structures through modelling and expansion. As with the Theme Days and Weeks, the theme areas provide a continuity of framework in which to teach a variety of language and preacademic skills.

Only one theme area should exist in the classroom at any given time. A specific area of the classroom should be set aside for the theme area space. Although the theme may change throughout the year, the physical location should remain the same. The length of time a theme area is set up depends on the severity of the students' deficits. The more severely language impaired the children are, the longer the theme area should be retained. The least amount of time suggested would be one week, with most themes in language-disordered classes remaining for up to one month. The specific space for the theme area is to be used only for language therapy targets and should not be used for unstructured play purposes. The idea of these areas is not exposure, but directed discourse among the students, with modeling and expansion of language by the adults. As with other sections of this curriculum, the ideal ratio is three students for one adult, although this can vary with the activity and the specific behaviors of the children.

Most props and materials for the theme areas are readily available at no charge from local businesses or from parent solicitation. Grocery stores provide meat trays, bakers' hats, baskets, and shopping bags; the Post Office lends hats, bags, and shirts. Many manufacturers are willing to provide packaging and other items bearing their logo. Buildings and counters can be constructed from large appliance boxes supplied by local stores; adults can do the major cutting and construction, with painting and decorating done as a class project.

Large cue cards with lettering at least one inch in height should be hung on a wall behind the theme area at adult eye level. These cards contain generic scripts appropriate to the particular theme with language targets specified for each child.

To initiate the theme area, the adults role play the situations. After two or three "rehearsals," one adult remains as a participant and the others verbally guide the children through the role routine. Once the children appear to understand the general procedure, the adult then retires to a supervisory/modeling role.

Theme areas should be used as child-generated verbal language facilitators. Once the children have mastered the scenarios presented or outlined by the teacher, they should be allowed to generate their own roles and scripts as they play in this area. The adult assigned to the theme area will be present to gently direct the children's discourse and model language appropriate to the individual children.

Class field trips to local stores or community services depicted in the theme areas provide realistic, concrete introductions to the theme areas. Most businesses are pleased to show children how their facility operates and usually give the children some sort of item that can then be used as a prop back in the schoolroom. It is suggested that these field trips be scheduled the week before preparation for a specific theme area.

Additional suggestions for guiding children through the theme area are given in the chapter on Planning and Scheduling.

Fast-Food Restaurant

Language targets
- Yes/No and WH questions
- Plural nouns
- Future tense marker: *will*
- Negatives
- Copula: *is/are* as main verb

Materials Consult the manager of a local fast-food restaurant; ask to borrow uniform jackets and hats, place mats, trays, straws, individual packets of salt, ketchup, and honey, empty hot- and cold-drink cups, and empty sandwich, French fry, salad, children's meal, and/or dessert containers.

ordering counter (puppet stage or small table)
cash register and play money
construction paper
poster board
laminating material
old magazines

Preparation
1. Cut out of construction paper and laminate hot dogs, hamburgers, carrot sticks, tomatoes, lettuce, cheese, and French fries.
2. Cut out pictures of menu items (from magazines or nutrition publications) and paste onto poster board to make a "menu." Post this on the front of the ordering counter.
3. Set up small desks and chairs to serve as the "dining room" of the restaurant.
4. Arrange the empty food containers and drinking cups on shelves behind the counter. Put laminated food items in small trays or boxes. Lay out a tray with straws, napkins, and condiments; place this on top of the shelves out of the customers' reach. Put a toy cash register on the counter.
5. Help the children choose roles (see below) and obtain the necessary props. Explain the poster menu to the "patrons" and show the "food servers" the food and serving containers.

Procedure Roles:
   One or two servers (wearing uniforms; one can take the food orders and the other can select the food items and put them on the tray)

   Up to three customers (children could dress up and come into the restaurant as mother and father, bringing their baby [doll] or child)

Script ideas:

Ordering food:
   If a family is ordering together, have one family member ask the others what they want and order for them all.

   Server: May I help you?/What do you want today?

   Customer: What's good today? I'll have _____ [sodas, hot dogs, etc.].

Server: Do you want ketchup/sugar with your _____ or _____?

Customer: May I have ketchup with my hot dog/cheese (or tomatoes) on my hamburger/sugar with my coffee?

Server #1 may tell Server #2 what to get; Server #2 places the items on a tray.

Customer: How much is it?

Server: That will be _____ dollars, please. [Note: The server should not be concerned with making correct change, as this concept is above preschool abilities for children in general.]

Complaining about unsatisfactory items served:
Customer: This coffee is cold./This hamburger doesn't taste right.

Server: I'm sorry. Do you want another one?

Little Folks Hair and Beauty Gallery

Language targets
- Vocabulary and concepts: grooming, manicure, names of items in beauty kit, barber/beautician, receptionist, tip
- WH and Yes/No questions
- Topic maintenance and conversational turn-taking skills
- Polite forms/indirectives
- Would, future tense marker: *will*

Materials

Children will bring their own personal grooming kits from home. Label each kit and as many items as possible in each with the child's name and symbol. Girls' beauty kits may contain real or play makeup, comb, brush, emery board, nail polish, polish remover, face cloth, cold cream, hand lotion. Boys' kits may contain a razorless shaver (safety razor without the blade), shaving cream, after-shave lotion, comb, brush.

Provide:

small chairs

large tilted mirrors set on low tables

counters or boxes

smocks or plastic covers borrowed from a hair salon

white or pastel beautician/barber smocks

plastic basins for water

towels

table with cash register for appointment desk

large doll(s) with yarn wigs for supervised hair cuts (optional)

poster with pictures illustrating the various services (shaves, comb-outs, makeup, manicures, special doll haircuts)

Note: scissors should be kept in possession of adult staff at all times to avoid real haircuts.

Procedure It is very important that an adult constantly supervise this activity, and that children understand clearly the list of "services" offered, so that this theme area doesn't result in disastrous amateur hair-chopping of the children's hair. Emphasize that hair comb-outs are offered, not haircuts (except for the practice dolls), and that for the shaves, manicures, and makeup, the children will use their own grooming kits.

Roles:
barber

beautician

receptionist (this is a good role for the teacher, who may double as a beautician or barber to model responses and provide constant supervision of all activities)

male and female customers

Script ideas:

Greeting receptionist:
Receptionist: Do you have an appointment? (If no) Let me see if we have time. What would you like today? (showing pictures) Do you want a hair comb-out? Do you want a facial and makeup? Do you want a manicure?

Customer: Today I want a _____/Today I would like a _____.

Receptionist: (calls over barber/beautician and introduces the customer) This is Mary, our beautician. Mary, this is Mrs. _____. (to beautician) Mrs. _____ would like a _____.

Receiving beauty or grooming services:
Customer converses with barber/beautician who gets the customer's grooming kit from the shelf and performs the service. They can talk about the ongoing service or make conversation about the weather, etc., as cued by the adult receptionist, who might walk over to check on them and ask the customer if everything is all right.

Bringing in one's "child" (doll with yarn hair) for a haircut:
A customer brings in a little child who needs a haircut. Use the two scripts above, with the receptionist providing the barber/beautician with scissors. The "parent" helps to prop up the child and tells the child to sit still. The barber/beautician can actually cut off a little of the yarn hair.

Paying for the service and tipping the barber/beautician:
Receptionist: That will be _____.

Customer: Here. May I have some change for a tip? (customer goes to barber/beautician) Here is a tip. Thank you very much.

Department Store

Language targets
- Vocabulary
- Yes/No and WH questions: correct word order
- *for* in a phrase
- Pronoun: *they*

- Negative: *don't*
- Social language and conversational interaction
- Possessive nouns: *'s*
- Concepts: *striped, spotted, plain, patterned*

Materials

low desks
shelves
table
toy cash register
rack for ties
small chair for shoe department

merchandise—shoes and slippers in shoe boxes, shoe sizer or ruler, ties, belts, men's shirts, ladies' blouses, men's or boy's hats, ladies' hats, pocketbooks, small stand-up mirror, jewelry (necklaces, bracelets, earrings, rings)

hangers, rack, or other arrangements to hang shirts and blouses

department store "signs" with pictures illustrating *shoes, ties and belts, men's shirts, ladies' blouses, jewelry, pocketbooks, hats*

Preparation

Arrange departments. Display the appropriate sign in each department. The shoe department should be near a shelf for shoes, with two small chairs and a foot-measuring device. Hang ties and belts on small easels or other hangers and display on a shelf along with the pocketbooks. Jewelry can be on a small desk in little boxes. Hang men's and ladies' clothing separately and near the hat display with a mirror nearby.

Procedure

Participate in various roles. At first, children may want to be customers and the cashier, so you may have to take the role of salesperson.

Roles:
  salesperson(s)
  customer(s)
  cashier

Script ideas:

Trying on and selecting shoes:
  Salesperson: Can I help you?

  Customer: I'm looking for shoes/slippers. Do you have _____?

  Salesperson: What size shoe do you wear? May I measure your foot? You are size _____. Do you like this pair of _____?

  Customer: May I try them on? They fit!/They don't fit!

  Salesperson: Please pay the cashier.

Selecting ties and belts:
  Customer: I want to buy a tie for myself/my brother/father/husband, etc.

  Salesperson: This week we have striped ties and polka-dotted ties, plain/solid color ties, and patterned ties.

  Customer: I'll buy this/these tie(s).

Selecting jewelry:
    Customer: I'm looking for some new jewelry.

    Salesperson: Do you want to try on this/these ring(s), bracelet(s), necklace(s), earrings? There's a mirror. You can look at yourself. Please pay the cashier.

Shopping for clothes or hats:
    Salesperson: Can I help you?

    Customer: I am looking for a lady's/man's blouse/hat/shirt.

    Salesperson: Here they are. Here's a mirror. What size/color do you want?

    Customer: Can you help me try this on?

    Salesperson: Yes. That looks nice, etc.

Get-Well Hospital

Language targets
- WH and Yes/No questions
- Negative forms: *don't, won't, can't*
- Vocabulary and concepts: thermometer, stethoscope, blood pressure cuff/gauge, heart, lungs, reflexes, doctor's hammer, eye chart, vision, all body parts, fever, hot/cold, fast/slow

Materials

doctor or hospital kits (should include toy thermometers, blood pressure cuffs, pill bottles, eye charts, reflex hammer)

child-size doctors' and nurses' uniforms (or use white blouses or shirts)

real stethoscope

baby scale

fold-out mattress covered with a sheet

low table covered with a sheet or white paper

hospital gown and/or pajamas (at least one should fit the adult as children enjoy having the teachers be the patients)

Homemade props can be integrated (for example, a doll, dress-up clothes, pocketbooks for the children playing adults).

Preparation
1. Arrange an "examination table" for the infant. The adult will be examined on the mattress (which should be large enough for either an adult or a preschool child).
2. Use another low desk covered with white paper or a sheet to display the instruments. Post the list of roles and the scripts on large poster paper at adult eye level.

Procedure
1. *Let's play hospital.* Allow children to choose the roles. Most will be reluctant to be the patient. A teacher or a doll can be the patient.
2. One adult can put on a "sterile gown" and be the doctor's helper (medical assistant) in order to coach the children through the various scripts and give the names of the instruments.

Script ideas:

History:
What is your name? How old are you? Where do you live?

Illness history:
What is the matter? Are you sick? Do you/does your baby need a checkup? What hurts you? Do you have a cold/fever/tummyache? Are you dizzy? (Patient or patient's "parent" answers.)

Examination:
I have to take your temperature. I'm going to put this under your arm (place thermometer in patient's armpit). Don't be scared. It won't hurt. Your temperature is high/low, _____ degrees.

Take blood pressure (blood pressure cuff, gauge).

Weigh baby on the scale; _____ pounds.

Listen to your heart (use stethoscope); it sounds fast/slow/okay.

I will check your/baby's reflexes (hit knee *gently* with doctor's hammer).

Use the eye chart to give an eye test.

Treatment:
shot, pills, hospital bed rest, operation

United States Post Office

Language targets
- Basic concepts through role playing, related story books and discussion:
  Our country is the United States of America.
  This is a United States Post Office.
  We mail letters. Letters and packages are called mail.
  Postal workers are the people who work in the post office.
  They sort mail. They deliver mail.
  We can mail letters in the post office. We can buy stamps.
  We can ask the postal clerk to weigh our packages.
  Heavy packages and letters cost more money (need more stamps) to mail.
- Sorting by size/weight: big, bigger, biggest; small, smaller, smallest; heavy vs. light
- Yes/No questions, WH questions:
  Can I buy a stamp?
  How many stamps do you want?
  What kind of stamp do you want?
  How much money is that?
  Will you please weigh my package?
  How much does my package weigh? Does it weigh a lot?
  Is it heavy? Is it light?

- Third person singular verb agreement and irregular forms:
  It weighs, it does/doesn't, Does it
  He/She delivers the mail, sorts mail, sells stamps
- Address: street number, street, town

Materials service counter (puppet stage, store counter, large box, or desk)
various colored stamps
cash register
box with mail slot
small scale
larger scale for packages
mail carrier uniform and sack (borrowed from an actual post office)
signs
American flag
props for customers (pocketbooks, hats, play money, coins)
large supply of used envelopes of various sizes

Set up several large, upturned boxes in the back of the theme area for storing larger packages and envelopes.

Preparation Duplicate as closely as possible the main features of an actual post office (for example, service counter in the front, rear area for sorting mail, and appropriate props such as a cash register, a mail slot, and scales).

Procedure Roles:
  postal clerk who works at the counter

  postal worker who sorts the mail

  mail carrier who delivers the mail

  customers who come into the post office to buy stamps, get mail, etc. (Adults can take any of the roles.)

Script ideas:

Writing/addressing letters:
  Have children "write" letters (scribbles) or draw pictures for someone else in class. Show them how to fold paper, stuff envelopes, and seal envelopes. Have children address envelopes from a model or use color-coded shapes to designate a specific child (for example, blue circle = Jim, black square = Sue). If some children are too young or lack ability for the above, distribute envelopes that are already addressed and coded.

Buying stamps and mailing letters:
  Customers come in and request stamps. The clerk tells them how much money they cost; the customers put stamps on their envelopes and mail them or give them to the clerk to mail.

  Clerk: Can I help you?

  How many stamps do you want?

  What kind of stamps do you want? (show selection)

  Customer: I need to buy _____ stamps.

  I want the red/blue/big ones.

How much money is that?

Clerk: That's _____ dollars/cents.

Customer: Where do I mail this/these letter(s)?

Clerk: You can put them in the mail slot next to you/I can mail them for you.

Sorting mail:

Postal worker(s) sort large boxes and different sized envelopes and put them in the mail sack. The mail carrier goes around the classroom "delivering" them.

Weighing mail:

A customer comes in with a large package or heavy envelope. The postal worker weighs it.

Postal Worker: I have to weigh your package/envelope.

Customer: How much does it weigh? Does it weigh a lot?

Postal Worker: No it doesn't/Yes it does. It weighs _____ pounds.

Delivering mail:

Valentines and packages, etc. The mail carrier "checks" the addresses (this will require teacher prompting).

Fire Station

Language targets
- WH questions: Where's the fire?
- Verb forms:
  contracted copula: There's a fire. I'm the driver.
  contracted auxiliary: I'm verb + -ing.
- Plural nouns: hatchets, firefighters, wheels
- Prepositions: *with, in, on, for*
- Firefighting vocabulary and concepts
- Topic maintenance, conversational turn taking to plan rescue activities

Materials

fire engine (large refrigerator-sized box or boxes painted red, decorated with paper plates for wheels and steering wheel)

light (flashlight covered with red cellophane)
bell to ring
ladder
chair (for the fire engine seat)
cardboard "hatchets" attached to outside of fire truck
corner of large cardboard "house" with paper flames
hose
telephone
slickers and boots (have children bring their own)
dolls
paper fire hydrant
pad of paper

Preparation   Set up a corner for the telephone and dispatch pad to write down address of fire when person calls in. The fire engine should be in the center of the theme area, with the accessories appropriately arranged on and around the fire truck. Place slickers and boots to the side by the dispatch area, and in one corner set up the burning house with dolls hanging from the windows.

Procedure   Roles:
  firefighters

  dispatcher

  driver

  fire chief

Script ideas:

Dispatcher gets report of fire:
  Where's the fire? Announces: There's a fire on Main Street. Hurry, we need _____ firefighters. Take the hose, ladder, and hatchets.

Ride to the fire:
  Negotiate roles: I'm the driver. I'm standing up in the engine. I'm ringing the bell.

Putting out the fire:
  Hook the hose to the fire hydrant. Put the water on the fire. The people are trapped. The fire is too hot to go in. Set up the ladder. Let's rescue the people. Break the window with the hatchet. I'm giving first aid to these people.

  Encourage the dispatcher and the fire chief to give orders. Let firefighters engage in dialogue among themselves to sequence events and organize their activities.

Supermarket

Language targets
- Yes/No questions: Can I _____?
- WH questions: Where is the _____? What did you buy today?
- *is* as main verb: This is _____.
- Negatives: It *isn't* fresh. I *can't* find the _____.
- Vocabulary and concepts: names of items and item categories, produce, fruit, vegetables, refrigerator section, frozen, fresh, defrosted

Materials   a variety of plastic play fruit and vegetables, canned goods, empty boxes of crackers, cereal, etc.

empty egg cartons
milk and orange juice cartons
empty bottles/boxes of cleaning supplies
toothpaste boxes, etc.
uniforms borrowed from local store
meat clerk hats
scale for weighing produce
paper bags

cash register

variety of shelves and boxes on which to display food

partitions to create aisles

refrigerator from home play area to hold foods which must be kept cold or frozen (play boxes of frozen chicken, waffles, etc.)

plastic play shopping carts

Preparation Display food on shelves and aisles by "departments" with the scale near the produce section. Create aisles. Line up carts at the "entrance" and have the cashier stationed at a small table near the "exit."

Procedure Roles:
    shoppers

    supermarket manager

    supermarket clerk

    cashier

Teachers may be clerks and managers initially if the children all want the other roles.

Script ideas:

Shopping for food:
Children have the option of going in family groups (for example, mother and baby, husband and wife) so they can discuss what to purchase.

Asking the manager or clerk where items are located:
I can't find the _____.

Where is the _____?

Complaining to the manager:
Shopper: This _____ is spoiled. It isn't fresh. May I have a fresh one?

This _____ is defrosted. It isn't frozen. May I have a frozen one?

Manager: I'm sorry. Of course. I'll get you a fresh/frozen one.

Checking out with cashier:
Cashier: Please, can you put your purchases on the counter? What did you buy today? Tell me what you bought today.

Shopper: I bought _____/This is a _____.

Theme Days and Weeks

The theme days and weeks activities include suggestions of language targets to work on while the children are engaged in these tasks.

Introduction

February
    Red, White, and Blue Day (Lincoln's Birthday)
    Red, White, and Blue Snack (cooking lesson)
    Red, White, and Blue: The Colors of Our Flag (Circle Time lesson)
    Coloring Pictures (Arts and Crafts lesson)
        The flag
        George Washington
        Abraham Lincoln
    Making an American Flag (Arts and Crafts lesson)
    Marching to American Marches (Music lesson)
        Three Cheers
        Yankee Doodle
        Stars and Stripes
        Jimmy Cracked Corn

March
    Green Day (St. Patrick's Day)
    Making Green Playdough (Arts and Crafts lesson)
    Experiment with Green Water (Science lesson)

Teddy Bear Week
    Fuzzy Teddy Bears (Arts and Crafts lesson)
    The Bear Went Over the Mountain (Music lesson)
    Teddy Bear Contest

Introduction

The use of theme days and weeks provides the opportunity to concretely teach holidays to preschool children. The idea of theme can also be extended to include the children's interests, as in Teddy Bear Week. In emphasizing a special theme, the teacher is able to incorporate that topic in all activities from arts and crafts to preacademic instruction. With language-impaired children, much repetition of material is needed for successful integration of the information. Using a theme as the basic structure allows the teacher to concentrate on the specific information to be presented in a consistent framework. The interest level of the children is especially heightened in all subject areas when they can democratically vote on interest themes to be used.

The learning of abstract concepts is particularly difficult for language-impaired children. Using the holiday theme approach to teaching helps make temporal concepts more concrete. During all activities, constant reference can be made to a classroom calendar prominently displayed in the room. Not only does such a calendar help teach temporal concepts, it also helps children learn rote numbers and sequencing skills.

Use a classroom weekly newsletter to increase communication with parents, as well as to solicit materials needed for projects. Through the newsletter, you can make specific requests of the parent, such as dressing the child in a certain color or costume. The newsletter also creates an atmosphere of sharing between home and school. Current and upcoming themes can be included, so that the child is reinforced at home. The additional discussion at home generates continued interest.

February
Red, White, and Blue Snack
(Cooking lesson)

Language targets
- Vocabulary and concepts:

  fresh vs. frozen food (Frozen food is good to eat. Freezing it keeps it fresh. You have to eat fresh food right away. You can keep fresh food in the refrigerator for a few days but then it spoils. Frozen food does not spoil.)

  colors, mixing, thawing

  names of utensils

- Verbs:
  future tense: to describe what we *will* do
  past tense: we opened, poured, stirred, mixed, sprinkled

Materials
fresh or frozen blueberries
frozen cherries or strawberries
whipped cream or dessert topping
small paper snack cups
3 bowls for main ingredients
3 spoons

Preparation
1. Set out all ingredients but do not open the packages.
2. Arrange materials so that three children can share them around a table in the kitchen. Set out snack cups and a tray.

Procedure
1. *Today we will fix a red, white, and blue snack.*
2. *Where is the red food? What is it? Is it fresh or frozen?* Repeat for the blue and the white foods.
3. *What do we have to do first?* (Must open packages and dump fruits into bowls.)
4. *The fruit is icy and frozen.* (Must separate/break it apart it in the bowl.)
5. Give the children the snack cups (one per child in the class) and have them spoon in equal parts of cherries and blueberries, then top the mixture with a spoonful of whipped cream.

Red, White, and Blue: The Colors of Our Flag
(Circle Time)

This activity is intended to be done on Lincoln's Birthday, February 12.

Language targets
- Verb form: I'm wearing ____.
- Colors and vocabulary: names of clothing items; colors (red, white, blue); stripes, checks, ruffles, etc.
- Past tense irregular verb: wore
- Concepts: our country, our flag, our Presidents
- Preposition: *to* ("Happy birthday to you")

Materials
: a large United States flag or banner with the colors of the flag
calendar page of February
pictures of George Washington and Abraham Lincoln (optional)

Request that parents dress the children in red, white, and blue clothing for class this day.

Procedure
1. *Today we all wore red, white, and blue clothes.* Have children tell about the clothes they wore that are these colors.
2. *What country do we live in?* (the United States of America or the U.S.A.)
3. *The U.S.A. has a flag. This is our flag. It is red, white, and blue.*
4. *The U.S.A. has a special leader called a President. Our first President was George Washington. His Birthday is on February 22.* Show on calendar. *Another special President was Abraham Lincoln. His birthday is today. Let's sing happy birthday to these Presidents.*

Coloring Pictures of the American Flag, George Washington, and Abraham Lincoln (Arts and Crafts lesson)

Language targets
- Vocabulary and concepts: red, blue, white, stars, stripes; soldier, white hair; slaves, freed
- Verbs:
  irregular past tense: was, were, had, rode
  regular past tense: lived
- WH questions: Who is this? What color is this? What is this?

Materials
: outline pictures of flag and Presidents
crayons
felt markers
white chalk
real American flag (optional)

Procedure
1. Talk about the pictures as the children color them. *The flag is red, white, and blue. It has white stars on a blue background, and has red and white stripes.*
2. *George Washington lived to be an old man with white hair. He was a good soldier. He led the army. He rode on a horse. He was the first President.*
3. *Abraham Lincoln was another President; he was very tall. He helped to free the black people so they didn't have to work with no money. They were slaves, then they could be regular workers. Abraham Lincoln had a beard.*

Making an American Flag (Arts and Crafts lesson)

Language targets
- Vocabulary and concepts:
  United States of America; our country
  Which is more—six or seven?
  stripes, stars, red, white, blue

- See also Arts and Crafts general language targets.

Materials
photocopies of the American flag on 8½" x 11" paper (one copy per student)
5" squares of blue construction paper (one per child)
gummed stars
paste or glue sticks
red crayons or markers

Preparation
1. Make photocopies of the American flag, and mark the seven stripes to be colored red with lightly printed X's.
2. Either make a sample flag, or have on hand a real flag for the children to examine.

Procedure
1. Tell the children: *Today we will make an American flag. This is the flag for our country, the United States of America.* Show an American flag or your completed sample. *What colors are in the American flag?*
2. *First we will color all these marked stripes red and leave the others white.* Have the children count the red and white stripes. *Which one is more?*
3. *Then we will glue the blue square in this* (upper left-hand) *corner. A real American flag has 50 stars, but you can put as many as you want to on the blue paper.*

Marching to American Marches (Music lesson)

Language targets

Three Cheers:
- Prepositions: *for, of*

Yankee Doodle:
- Irregular past tense: came, stuck
- Past tense: called
- Preposition: *to*

Stars and Stripes:
- We will march, we marched

Jimmy Cracked Corn:
- Negative: *don't*
- Conjunction: *and*

- Irregular past tense: *gone*
- Concepts: *left, right, both* hands, motor imitation

Source   Wood, L. 1971. *February Holidays: Rhythms to Reading.* Glendale, CA: Bowmar Publishing Company (book and record set). Use "Three Cheers for the Red, White, and Blue," "Yankee Doodle," "Stars and Stripes Forever," and "Jimmy Cracked Corn and I Don't Care" from Side I.

Materials   recordings of American marching songs appropriate for children to sing
record or tape player
American flags the children have made (from the Arts and Crafts lesson above)
pictures of Washington, Lincoln, marching bands, drummers, flags, etc.

Preparation
1. Set up the record or tape cassette player.
2. Lay out pictures randomly on the floor.
3. Have the flags the children made in the above Arts and Crafts activity ready for them to wave while they march.

Procedure
1. *Today we will march and wave our American flags.*
2. Have children sing each song through at least once, so they are somewhat familiar with the words (although this is not the goal of this activity).
3. Show the pictures to the children and briefly discuss what is in each picture and its relevance to patriotic folklore or history. Lay the pictures randomly in a large open space in the classroom or hallway.
4. As the song is played, have an adult lead the group as the children wave their flags and march around the pictures in various patterns.
5. For "Jimmy Cracked Corn," the middle verses indicate "right hand up, left hand up, both hands up, and clap your hands." Have children imitate these motions as they march.

March
Green Day (St. Patrick's Day)
Making Green Playdough
(Arts and Crafts lesson)

Language targets
- WH questions: What are we going to make today?
- Negatives/positives: It *isn't* something to eat. It is something to play with.
- Yes/No questions: Is it _____? Do we eat playdough? Why not? (It isn't food.)
- Vocabulary: Can you tell me what the ingredients are? (Ingredients are what we use to make the playdough.) Have the children name the ingredients. What does *measure* mean?
- Narrative/instructional sequences: Have children who arrived earlier explain to latecomers what the group is doing and how to do it.

- See also Arts and Crafts general language targets:
  Verbs: I'm mixing/measuring ____; I measured/mixed/made ____.

Materials
1 C flour
½ C salt
1 tsp cream of tartar
1 Tbsp oil
1 C water
green food color or tempera paint powder
mixing bowl
measuring cups
mixing spoon
stove
pot
airtight container

Preparation
1. Place ingredients (bag of flour, cream of tartar, box of salt, bottle of oil, water, food color or tempera powder) and utensils on a tray.

2. Draw a picture recipe chart to illustrate each step.

Procedure
Have the children refer to the recipe chart and take turns measuring the ingredients into the mixing bowl. Allow the children to mix the ingredients, assisting if necessary when the mixture becomes too thick to handle easily. An adult should be in charge of cooking the dough, heating it until it becomes stiff. Distribute small portions to the children for them to knead when it becomes cool enough to handle.

Experiment with Green Water (Science lesson)

Language targets
- Comparative adjectives:
  green, greener, greenest
  dark, darker, darkest green
  more drops, the most drops

- Future tense: *will*

- WH questions: Which one will be a darker shade of green? Why?

Materials
clear plastic or glass cups
water
green food coloring
droppers

Preparation
1. This activity can be done at the snack tables after cleanup.

2. Prepare trays with a cup of water on each (one tray for each group of three children).

Procedure
1. *Today we will show you how we can make water turn green. We will make light green water, regular or medium green water, and dark green water. We will use this green food coloring.*

2. *We will put one drop of green food coloring into this cup of water.* (Child may assist in adding the drops.) *We will put two drops of food coloring into this cup, and three drops of food coloring into this cup.* Before you add the drops, ask the children: *Now which cup will be a darker green color? Which will be the darkest green? Why?*

Note: You can empty the cups and repeat the experiment several times, if desired. You can also let one or more of the children conduct the entire experiment and do all the talking.

Teddy Bear Week

Designate a specific week as Teddy Bear Week. Communicate with the parents, indicating that children may bring up to three teddy bears to school, and send home tags to label the bears. If children don't have bears, they could bring other stuffed animals.

Set up a Teddy Bear House in the theme area, with plenty of spaces for the bears to "spend the night" if the children want to leave them at school. (If not, the bears can "commute" with the children.) Children can formally introduce their teddy bears during show-and-tell time on the first day of Teddy Bear Week.

Provide teddy bear songs, arts and crafts experiences with soft, squishy materials, and teddy bear favorites for snacks. Let the children take their teddy bears to various play areas during the day to play with them.

Culminate Teddy Bear Week with a contest, awarding each child a blue ribbon for the "best," "most," "cutest," "biggest," "smallest," "oldest" bears, etc. (See Contest outline below for specific categories.)

Decorate the room with pictures, posters, and books about bears—toy bears, grizzly bears, polar bears, panda bears, koala bears, The Three Bears, etc.

A list of books for Teddy Bear Week is given in the Story Time unit; see also the Structured Language Therapy section for four special 10-minute Teddy Bear Week language lessons.

Fuzzy Teddy Bears
(Arts and Crafts lesson)

Language targets
- Sequential instructions: Comprehension and retention of three steps: (1) color the bear brown; (2) color eyes and nose black (or glue on buttons); (3) glue on cotton.

- Ability to retell instructions to latecomers

- Vocabulary and concepts:
  inside, on, part of body (ears, feet, tummy)
  the color brown
  soft, furry, cotton, fur, name of materials
  hard, smooth, buttons

- Verb forms:
  Use contracted copulas and auxiliaries to model them: She's making, gluing.
  Have children tell someone else what they are doing: I'm coloring, gluing.

- Future tense for telling latecomers what to do: We will _____.

- Regular and irregular past tense: You may ask early finishers to describe their activities to a teacher or another person who isn't familiar with the project: I glued, I colored, I made.

Materials a pattern for tracing teddy bear onto 8½" x 11" construction paper
white sheets of construction paper (one sheet per child)
colored cotton or fuzzy material
glue
flat black buttons (or black markers)
brown crayons

Preparation Trace the bear pattern onto the construction paper (make one copy per child).

Procedure 1. Have the children color the bear brown. They can either glue buttons on for the eyes and nose or use a black marker to draw them in.

2. Glue cotton balls inside the ears, on the soles of the feet, and on the tummy.

The Bear Went Over the Mountain (Music lesson)

Language targets
- Irregular past tense verbs: went, saw
- WH question/complex sentence: What do you think he saw?
- Creative word findings

Materials Song, "The Bear Went Over the Mountain" (suggested source: Warren, J. 1984. Story Time: Early Learning Activities. Palo Alto, CA: Monday Morning Books, p. 27)

The Bear Went Over the Mountain

The bear went over the mountain,
The bear went over the mountain,
The bear went over the mountain,
And what do you think he saw?

He saw a ____ ____,
He saw a ____ ____,
He saw a ____ ____,
And what do you think he did?

The bear went over the mountain,
The bear went over the mountain,
The bear went over the mountain,
And what do you think he saw?

etc.

Procedure — Sing "The Bear Went Over the Mountain" with your children. Let them take turns filling in whatever they want the bear to see. (Examples: purple dragon, flying saucer, big circus, candy store.)

Teddy Bear Contest

Language targets
- Comparative adjectives: superlative form *-est*
- Vocabulary: contest, judge, prize

Materials — blue ribbons (one per child)
gold shiny paper for the center of each ribbon

Preparation
1. Have the children arrange their teddy bears in groups (each group consists of a single child's bears).
2. Select adults to be the contest "judges" and to judge the teddy bears according to the categories listed below. Each child will receive a first prize.

    Categories for first prize (add more as necessary so that each child can win a blue ribbon):
    biggest
    smallest
    cutest eyes
    cutest nose
    chubbiest
    funniest
    biggest ears
    cutest tail
    happiest
    darkest color
    lightest color
    best dressed
    softest
    most cuddly
    sweetest

3. On each blue ribbon, write the child's name and the teddy bear quality that won the prize.
4. Seat the children in front of the theme area where their bears are arranged.

Procedure
1. Today we will have a contest. What is a contest? Ask older children to define "contest," "judge," and "prize."
2. *First prizes are blue ribbons. That means the best. The judges will be [names].*
3. Award the ribbons to the children.

Language curriculums for your young clients from Lynn Plourde, M.A., CCC-SLP . . .

CLAS PRESCHOOL

Here's a complete 10-month program of listening and speaking activities to use in a day-care center or preschool setting. Weekly activities develop oral language skills such as auditory memory and question-asking abilities. Get parents involved too, with home activities based on classroom lesson plans. The program is organized so completely that substitute teachers can use it easily! **Catalog No. 7570-YCS $55**

CLAS Kindergarten

CLAS has never been easier to use. Now you can develop students' language skills within the structure of the regular classroom curriculum. This book includes many new oral language activities—plus some old favorites—all arranged in a classroom-friendly format. You'll no longer need to plan extra time to teach language skills. Use *CLAS Kindergarten* to develop those skills during your regular routine. **Catalog No. 3047-YCS $55**

CLAS 1-2

Develop students' language skills within the structure of the regular classroom curriculum. In contrast to previous *CLAS* products, this resource coordinates skills activities with actual class sections. Skills targeted for improvement include vocabulary, listening, grammar, auditory memory, rhyming, role-playing, storytelling, giving and following directions, and many more! Plus, this product includes three target concepts new to the *CLAS* family: oral presentation, similarities/ differences, and group cooperation.
Catalog No. 3046-YCS $55

CLAS BY THEMES

Mix and match 20 learning themes with 20 classroom activities to create 400 stimulating activities! Based on the materials in the *CLAS* series, these activities are organized into themes for a wide range of children. You'll have themes and vocabulary words divided into three levels—preschool, kindergarten through 2nd grade, and 3rd through 4th grade.
Catalog No. 7673-YCS $29.95

Everything you need in language curriculum materials . . .

DIRECTING SCHOOL DISCOURSE
Language Training Kit
by Marion Blank, Ph.D., M. Ann Marquis, M.S., CCC-SLP, and Michele O. Klimovitch, M.S., CCC-SLP
Foreword by Katharine G. Butler, Ph.D

Help your students, 7 through 12 years old, comprehend instructional texts and achieve academic success. Learn how to address language learning disabilities by applying the best of current research to discourse and texts. Promote a holistic approach while teaching oral and written language. You'll have everything you'll need for 40 complete lessons that fit into any school curriculum. Enhance each lesson with games, storybooks, and newspapers. Create your own lessons using the same technique. **Catalog No. 7184-YCS $149**

TOTAL™
Teacher Organized Training for the Acquisition of Language
by Beth Witt, M.A., and Jeanne Boose Morgan, M.A., CCC-SLP

If you already own the original best-selling *TOTAL*™ program, you know how functional and indispensable it is! If you're one of the few who hasn't adapted this time-saving resource, you're missing out on a practical approach to teaching language to your preschool and language-delayed children. Rest assured you'll have the latest research and theory in this revised kit! *TOTAL*™ (Revised) reflects state-of-the-art language intervention and the best practices in the field of early childhood special needs. You'll have a more pragmatically and culturally sound base on which to implement your therapy. Expanded, detailed lessons save you valuable planning time for every day of the year! **Catalog No. 7733-YCS $425**

GREAT BEGINNINGS FOR EARLY LANGUAGE LEARNING
Nouns 1, Nouns 2, Concepts, Associations, Verbs, and Prepositions
with Language Activity Booklets by Linda Levine, M.Ed.

Great Beginnings is ideal for speech-language clinicians and teachers who need specialized materials for language and speech delayed and developmentally delayed children who are acquiring basic language skills. The complete kit includes a manual featuring a complete description of all the materials in each set, instructional objectives, and important information about early language development for paraprofessionals or offering a quick review for speech-language professionals.

Select from all of these *Great Beginnings* kits for your early learners. Color photographs, pictures, and manipulatives help you use play therapy as well as traditional drill activities to stimulate language acquisition.

Nouns 1 and **Nouns 2** each include 40 color photographs that are sure to appeal to youngsters. *Nouns 1* features food and animals, *Nouns 2* includes toys and body parts. Each set includes 40 full-color photo cards and activity booklet.

Concepts features 57 color photographs plus more than 35 manipulatives to introduce and reinforce concepts such as colors, singular and plural, big and little, same and different, categorization, prepositions, and associations.

Associations shows 20 nouns in color photographs, two color illustrations, and two black-and-white drawings. Each picture depicts the noun in a slightly different way.

Verbs includes 15 actions presented two times—once by a boy and once by a girl. Thirty color photographs introduce pronoun use and teach early verb vocabulary.

Prepositions introduces eight early-developing prepositions—in, out, on, off, under, in front of, in back of (behind), and next to (beside)—with 24 color photographs.

Order the entire *Great Beginnings for Early Language Learning* kit and save! You'll get the set of manipulatives, plus a special instructional manual and storage box.

Nouns 1, Catalog No. 2221-YCS	$29
Nouns 2, Catalog No. 2222-YCS	$29
Concepts, Catalog No. 2223-YCS	$89
Associations, Catalog No. 2225-YCS	$45
Verbs, Catalog No. 2226-YCS	$35
Prepositions, Catalog No. 2227-YCS	$29
Great Beginnings Complete Kit, Catalog No. 2220-YCS	$225

ORDER FORM

Ship to:
INSTITUTION: _____
NAME: _____
OCCUPATION/DEPT: _____
ADDRESS: _____
CITY: _____ STATE: _____ ZIP: _____

☐ Please check here if this is a permanent address change.
Telephone No. _____ ☐ work ☐ home

Payment Options:
☐ My check is enclosed.
☐ My purchase order is enclosed. P.O.# _____
☐ Charge to my credit card.   (Net 30 days)
  ☐ VISA ☐ MasterCard ☐ American Express

Card No. ☐☐☐☐ ☐☐☐☐ ☐☐☐☐ ☐☐☐☐

Expiration Date: Month _____ Year _____

Signature _____

QTY.	CAT. #	TITLE	AMOUNT

Please add 10% for postage and assured delivery. 8% for orders over $500.
Arizona residents add sales tax.
Canada: Add 22% to subtotal for shipping, handling, and G.S.T.
Payment in U.S. funds only.   **TOTAL**

MONEY-BACK GUARANTEE
You'll have up to 90 days of risk-free evaluation of the products you ordered. If you're not completely satisfied with any product, we'll pick it up within the 90 days and refund the full purchase price!
No questions asked!

We occasionally backorder items temporarily out of stock. If you do not accept backorders, please tell us on your purchase order or on this form.

FOR PHONE ORDERS
Call 1-800-866-4446. Please have your credit card and/or institutional purchase order information ready.
9 AM–6 PM Central Time
Voice or TDD / FAX (602) 325-0306

Send your order to:
Communication Skill Builders
a division of The Psychological Corporation
3830 E. Bellevue / P.O. Box 42050-YCS / Tucson, AZ 85733